Importing Poverty?

Importing Poverty?

Immigration and the Changing Face of Rural America

Philip Martin

Yale University Press

New Haven & London

Set in Adobe Garamond type by Westchester Book Group
Printed in the United States of America by

Library of Congress Cataloging-in Publication Data

Martin, Philip L., 1949–
    Importing poverty? : immigration and the changing face of rural America /
Philip Martin.
        p. cm.
    Includes bibliographical references and index.
    ISBN 978-0-300-13917-4 (hardcover : alk. paper)   1. United States—Emigration
and immigration.   2. Immigrants—United States—Economic conditions.
3. Alien labor—United States.   4. Alien labor—Government policy.   I. Title.

JV6456.M36 2009
331.5′440973—dc22

                                                                        2008045622

A catalogue record for this book is available from the British Library.

This paper meets the requirements of ANSI/NISO Z39.48-1992 (Permanence of
Paper). It contains 30 percent postconsumer waste (PCW) and is certified by the
Forest Stewardship Council (FSC).

10 9 8 7 6 5 4 3 2 1

"Migrants are children of misfortune . . . We depend on misfortune to build up our force of migratory workers and, when the supply is low because there is not enough misfortune at home, we rely on misfortune abroad to replenish the supply."
—President's Commission on Migratory Labor, *Migratory Labor in American Agriculture* (1951), p3.

Contents

Foreword

In *Importing Poverty?* Philip Martin shows how the American farmers' demand for a perpetual supply of low-cost labor transfers poverty from rural Mexico to rural America. He also demonstrates that, as it is currently organized, farmwork is sufficiently undesirable that not even desperate immigrants will continue to do it once they have nonfarm options. This reality causes farmers and their political allies to oppose simply legalizing unauthorized workers, which would enable them to get nonfarm jobs. Instead, farmers agree to legalization only in exchange for large guest-worker programs that give employers considerable control of foreign workers. Farmers and their allies likewise often oppose funding for the public services needed to help integrate immigrants and their children into the mainstream of American life, and have succeeded in weakening legal measures to protect the working conditions of foreign and domestic workers.

Martin covers U.S. immigration patterns and farm labor history, as well as the impacts of migrant flows in California, Florida, and the Midwest (meatpacking). The California chapter shows how agriculture expanded by assuming that a ready supply of workers would be available, and the ways in which the cities that house many of the farmworkers have developed unique economies where ex-farmworkers serve newcomers. The Florida chapter shows that the availability of guest workers slowed sugar harvest mechanization, and that farm wages and trade policy are likely to determine how rapidly the orange harvest is mechanized. The meatpacking chapter emphasizes the wage and other incentives that have encouraged production to shift to rural areas and explores the government's failure to prevent the employment of unauthorized workers.

The two chapters on farmworkers deal with the flows in and out of the farm labor market, emphasizing that a person who is a farmworker one year may not be the next. The chapter on federal assistance programs shows that in most cases, the best way to assist farmworkers is to help them find nonfarm jobs. The book concludes with chapters that deal with mechanizing labor-intensive farm tasks, the struggle for U.S. immigration reform, and a proposal to regularize farmwork and rationalize the farm labor market. Martin's proposal to begin collecting payroll taxes on guest-worker wages to fund labor-saving research and provide incentives for a dwindling number of guest workers to return to their home countries could help keep agriculture competitive and promote the development of the migrants' areas of origin.

The U.S. farmers who receive taxpayer subsidies are richer than the average American, while the farmworkers who labor in the fields are among the poorest. Easy access to immigrant farmworkers has the same subsidy effects in agriculture as price supports, increasing land prices and explaining why farmers have a keen interest in ensuring that the government provide them with "the workers they need" to harvest crops. Giving in to such demands risks putting a special interest ahead of the national interest.

Although *Importing Poverty* focuses on rural America, its lessons are relevant for other areas that rely heavily on immigrant workers. The most basic of these is the importance of understanding the strong self-reinforcing relationships between desperate foreign immigrants and employers seeking low-cost, easily controlled labor. This relationship explains why many employers prefer guest workers to fully empowered legal immigrants, as well as why it is so difficult to test the market to determine the availability of domestic workers for the jobs filled by foreign workers. It is clear, moreover, that employers' preference for foreign workers is not restricted to low-wage farmworkers—it also applies to professional and technical workers brought in under the H-1B and L-1 visa programs.

Unlike many economists who ignore the dynamic institutional impacts of foreign worker programs, Martin understands the broader social and economic aspects of employing easily exploited foreign workers. He shows, for example, that low wages do not strengthen the kind of economic competition we should encourage. While wage competition might be in the short-run interest of employers, a high productivity strategy would be better for workers, communities, and countries.

The kind of dynamic analyses employed by Martin teaches scholars and policy makers to question myths and superficial conclusions produced by static analyses. For example, high-tech industry employers assert the need for guest workers to fill labor shortages created by low enrollments of American students in science and engineering classes. They fail to explore, however, the extent to which a ready supply of foreign students depresses earnings and opportunities for natives in these fields relative to business and law, which are much harder for foreigners to enter. Nor do employers explain why it would be better for the country to admit larger numbers of guest workers instead of immigrants with full legal rights. Dynamic analyses likewise teach the importance of basing immigrant worker allotments on objective labor market tests instead of employer-dominated political processes.

Another important lesson from Martin's book, often overlooked by static analyses, is the availability of alternatives to low-wage foreign worker treadmills, including the mechanization and rationalization of work to increase productivity and create better jobs, the promotion of high-productivity economic development in Mexico and other sending countries, the admission of market-tested immigrants with full legal rights, measures to more fully assimilate immigrants into American communities, and more effective protections for the wages and working conditions of foreign and domestic workers. Contrary to common arguments against labor market rationalization, *Importing Poverty?* shows that measures to improve conditions for workers do not lead to much higher prices for consumers.

As one who was actively involved in the debates leading to the Immigration and Reform Control Act (IRCA) of 1986, I recognize the difficulty of achieving consensus on immigration reforms that reflect the national rather than special interests. I also know that immigration reform done badly can make matters worse, as the IRCA experience demonstrates (Marshall, 2007). Recognizing the key role of the labor market generally, and the farm labor market in particular, and designing policies to ensure that the United States has legal workers with competitive productivity and working conditions would be a powerful step toward developing a durable immigration policy for the twenty-first century.

There are no easy answers to the migration that has transferred 10 percent of the 120 million persons born in Mexico to the United States. Most arrived in the past quarter century and many had their first U.S. job in agriculture. The ultimate solution to such migration is the development of more attractive jobs in Mexico. Until Mexico develops, the U.S. government's responsibility is to ensure that U.S. policies protect foreign and domestic workers and do not make unauthorized migration worse. For that reason, it is essential to wean American employers from their growing dependence on unauthorized migrants.

Philip Martin is a leading economist with knowledge of immigration that is both broad and deep, as is his understanding of how labor markets work. His book is valuable for policy makers, scholars, and all who are interested in this important subject.

Ray Marshall

Preface and Acknowledgments

This is a book about the employment of immigrant workers on U.S. farms. During the nineteenth century, European immigrants arrived to become farmers but, with the exception of some Chinese and Japanese migrant and seasonal farmworkers in the western states, relatively few newcomers began their American journeys as hired workers in the fields. This changed in the twentieth century, especially after the U.S. government allowed farmers to recruit Mexican workers or tolerated their presence.

Mexico looms large in the debate over immigrant farmworkers. Mexico is the number one source of legal immigrants to the United States, accounting for a third of foreign-born U.S. residents, almost 60 percent of unauthorized foreigners, and three-quarters of hired farmworkers. Mexican-born farmworkers in the United States are mostly from rural Mexico, where education levels lag and poverty is widespread.

This book outlines the risks posed by the transfer of Mexico's rural poor to rural America. I was drawn into farm labor issues by accident, arriving in California when Cesar Chavez and the United Farm

Workers were front-page news, and their protests and bargaining enabled many California farmworkers to earn twice the minimum wage and receive some of the same benefits enjoyed by factory workers. My colleagues with more experience in farm labor issues envisioned a future in which unions would help those who harvested fruits and vegetables to be akin to construction workers, earning high wages when they filled seasonal jobs and relying on unemployment insurance benefits during the off-season.

Most farm labor contracts disappeared in the 1980s, as labor contractors and unauthorized workers replaced union hiring halls deploying Mexican Americans to the fields. Farm wages stagnated, benefits disappeared, and fruit and vegetable agriculture expanded. Immigration reform in 1986 was expected to reverse these trends, but instead accelerated them and added several new twists, including the diffusion of Mexican-born farmworkers throughout the United States, the spread of rural Mexican immigrants from the fields to food-related factories such as meatpacking, and the settlement of Mexican immigrants in towns and cities throughout rural America.

The changing face of rural America raises many questions. How long will newcomer immigrants remain farmworkers? Will the U.S. government continue to tolerate an influx of unauthorized workers to fill jobs in areas with few people? What will happen to ex-farmworkers and their children in areas with pyramid job distributions that offer few rungs to middle-class jobs? With the support of the Farm, Giannini, and Rosenberg Foundations, we held seminars in agricultural areas being transformed by immigration from rural Mexico. We followed the logic of migration—visiting employers whose demand for labor encouraged migration, meeting community leaders who acted as bridges between newcomers, and then hearing from settled residents and migrants and their children.

This book, supported by the Smith-Richardson Foundation, summarizes what we learned in rural and agricultural America. I am indebted to the many employers, community leaders, and migrants who shared their insights; to the foundations that supported the work; and to colleagues from around the United States whose studies of particular commodities and communities are reflected in this book. I am especially indebted to Elizabeth Midgley, with whom I discussed immigration reform proposals.

Prologue: Coming to America

As spring approached, 19-year-old José Gonzalez borrowed $2,000 from relatives and left his home in Oaxaca for the United States, promising his mother that he would soon send her enough money to fix up the family house. Although he had never been far from his village before, he did not feel out of place as he joined others traveling by bus to the Mexico-U.S. border, where smugglers waited to guide him across the border and on to California's Central Valley. José's group eluded the Border Patrol, and traveled by van to Fresno.

José bought a driver's license and green card for $50 at a swap meet, presented his documents to a labor contractor, and went to work hoeing weeds and thinning peaches so that the fewer buds remaining would yield larger fruit. It was hard to save money, since work was intermittent and the labor contractor charged José for everything from rides to work to gloves and work tools. However, José stayed with the contractor, who promised more work when the raisin harvest began. The contractor assured José that a good worker could earn $100 a day, six or seven days a week, harvesting the grapes that dry into raisins.

In mid-August, José joined 40,000 other workers for the most labor-intensive harvest in North America. He reached under vines in dusty vineyards to cut bunches of green grapes, dropped them into 25-pound plastic tubs, then dumped them from the tubs onto paper trays, so that the green grapes could dry into raisins in the 100-degree heat. José earned a cent a pound, amounting to $10 an hour, $100 for a 10-hour day and $4,000 during the six-week harvest. By working in other crops as well, José found 1,000 hours of work and earned $8,500 in his first year, the average for seasonal farmworkers in California.

José wanted to visit his family in Mexico at Christmas, but feared he could not afford to pay smugglers another $2,000 to return to the United States. Instead, he stayed in Parlier, a city of 11,000 in Fresno, the nation's leading farm county.[1] José felt at home in Parlier, where two-thirds of the adults told the Census in 2000 that they did not have a high school diploma and more than 80 percent reported speaking Spanish at home. Parlier's per capita income was $5,300 in 2000, about the same as the per capita income of Mexico. However, as a rural resident of Oaxaca in southern Mexico, José would have earned less than the Mexican average if he had stayed at home.

José lived in a "back house" in Parlier, a storage shed he shared with three other men for which he paid $10 a night. He paid $5 a day for rides to the fields and spent $10 a day on meals, so that almost a third of his earnings went for food, lodging, and rides to work. The *raiteros*[2] who drove José to work, the labor contractors who hired him, and the stores where he cashed paychecks and sent money to Mexico were owned by Mexican-born U.S. residents who had settled. The cash-based farmworker service economy was a major source of nonfarm jobs in Parlier; the absence of these jobs in official statistics helps to explain why less than the U.S. average of 64 percent of residents 16 years and older were in the labor force in Parlier.

José had a fiancée at home, and after another year in Parlier without her, he sent money so that she could pay a smuggler and join him. When she arrived, the family moved into a two-bedroom house they shared with two other families. Soon there were U.S.-born children who went to the local schools. Most ninth graders do not graduate from high school in Parlier, but these U.S.-educated children of farmworkers rarely follow their parents into the fields. Many leave school without the English, skills, and connections necessary to get one of the few jobs in Parlier that can support a middle-class lifestyle, such as working at the post office or for the city government.

The future of José and his family, the raisin industry, and Parlier are uncertain. After a decade as a seasonal harvester, José will be too old to keep up with the younger migrants who continue to arrive. If he can learn English, he may be able to find an easier farm job such as an equipment operator or a nonfarm job in a warehouse; otherwise, his piece rate earnings are likely to decline. José's children are likely to be propelled toward one of two extremes: they could join the handful of Parlier students who complete high school and leave the area for college or the military, or be among the many who do not graduate and remain in the area seeking alternatives to seasonal harvesting jobs, including providing housing and rides to newcomers.

The United States produces a third of the world's raisins and typically exports a third of its production. The 3,500 raisin farmers in the Fresno area worry that, with more than half of the harvest workers such as José illegally in the United States, immigration reform could deny them the seasonal harvesters on whom they have depended for more than a century. Grapes are literally sugar balls, with twice as much sugar as sugarcane or sugar beets. Every August, farmers measure the rising level of sugar in their grapes and when they contain 22–23 percent sugar, they call "their" labor contractor for harvesters.

Farmers know that the longer they wait to harvest their grapes, the more sugar and the better the raisins, but waiting also increases the risk that rain will spoil the raisins as they dry on the ground. Many farmers buy crop insurance so they will have some income even if their drying raisins are damaged by rain, but insurance payments are made only if raisins are harvested by mid-September. The longer farmers wait to begin the harvest, the more workers are needed to harvest the 2 million tons of green grapes that dry into 400,000 tons of raisins.[3] If the harvest begins 15 days before the "rain date," twice as many workers are needed than if the harvest begins 30 days before the rain date.

There is always a "labor shortage" in this race between sugar and rain. There is no government or economic definition of labor shortage, which means that a farmer may complain of a labor shortage if he requests two 40-worker harvesting crews and gets only two 25-worker crews, increasing the risk that rain will damage the drying raisins. Farm organizations have reported in recent years that farmers were "short" 10 to 20 percent of the workers needed to harvest raisins.[4]

There is an alternative to scanning the skies for rain clouds and complaining of labor shortages. Some grape varieties reach optimal sugar levels earlier, at the beginning rather than the end of August. A machine can cut the canes holding bunches of green grapes so they begin to dry into raisins while still on the vine—the so-called dried-on-the-vine (DOV) method of harvesting. Another machine with rotating fingers knocks the raisins from the vine onto a conveyor belt for transport to a bin traveling alongside the harvester, eliminating 90 percent of the harvesting jobs and worries about rain-damaged raisins.

Mechanization is spreading, and at least a third of California's raisins are harvested with some type of mechanical assistance. The reason that more farmers do not mechanize is monetary. To use machines, vineyards must be retrofitted with stronger stakes and trellising at a cost of at least $2,000 an acre. Growers in their 60s and 70s with 40 acres of raisins are reluctant to invest $80,000 in their vineyards and buy or lease $150,000 harvesting machines, especially since Turkey, Iran, and China can produce cheaper raisins. Faced with uncertainty about the future demand for their raisins, California raisin growers find it more advantageous to lobby the federal government to allow migrants like José to harvest raisins than to borrow money and mechanize.

The immigration of raisin harvesters and other farmworkers is transferring the rural poor of Mexico and other countries to rural and agricultural America. Rural poverty has been the subject of some of America's best-known literature, including John Steinbeck's *The Grapes of Wrath*, which told of the reception of Dust Bowl migrants in California's fields and orchards in the 1930s. Reports of "the people left behind" in rural America, portrayed in Michael Harrington's *The Other America*, helped to inspire the War on Poverty in the 1960s by warning that rural poverty today can become urban poverty tomorrow.

This book outlines the dimensions of the new rural poverty that is developing in rural and agricultural America as a result of immigration. José and other immigrants arriving to fill jobs on U.S. farms are forming or unifying families in the agricultural areas where they work. Seasonal work such as harvesting raisins attracts newcomers, most of whom are unauthorized immigrants, but does not provide careers for them or their children who are born and educated in the United States. The result is an immigration treadmill in rural America, with farmers demanding that the government keep border gates ajar so that newcomers can fill seasonal jobs, but with most newcomers filling seasonal farm jobs for only a decade. As it is currently structured, fruit and vegetable agriculture requires a constant inflow of workers from abroad who are willing to accept seasonal farm jobs.

An immigration treadmill is not optimal for U.S. agriculture or for society. If the status quo continues, agriculture will rely on newcomers with no other U.S. job options to keep labor costs low in an ultimately fruitless attempt to compete with even lower-cost fruits and vegetables produced in other countries. The strategy of importing workers to fill seasonal farm jobs discourages the labor-saving innovations necessary to increase productivity in U.S. agriculture so that farmers can compete effectively with ever more nimble producers abroad.

The status quo could also leave rural America with a new type of rural poverty. Immigrants with little education who are arriving to fill farm jobs that require brawn rather than brains are settling in areas that have pyramid-shaped job structures, meaning there are large numbers of jobs at the bottom of the ladder and few rungs offering a path up to the middle class. Trapped at the bottom of the pyramid, immigrant farmworkers and their children may form a new rural underclass analogous to the sharecroppers and tenant farmers of a century ago. Frustrated by an inability to move up in rural America, this twenty-first-century rural underclass could unleash another Great Migration off the land like that of the 1950s and 1960s, when a million Americans a year moved from the rural South to midwestern cities, with side effects that included massive public housing projects and, eventually, urban riots.

The picture is not altogether bleak. Some of the migrants and their children are climbing the U.S. job ladder, moving from seasonal to year-round farm and nonfarm jobs and buying homes.[5] However, when the shortest route to upward mobility is moving out of seasonal farmwork, the vacuum created by the success of some migrants often draws in even needier newcomers to replace them. It is in this sense that the status quo is more likely to create a new rural poverty than a globally competitive agricultural system that offers hired farmworkers incomes above the poverty level.

Most farmers would agree that unauthorized newcomers with little education dominate among newly hired farmworkers and that their U.S.-educated children shun field jobs. But many farmers say the answer to the farm labor problem is a guest-worker program that rotates seasonal farmworkers in and out of the United States. In other words, farmers acknowledge that today's seasonal farm labor market resembles a half-open door that admits a constant stream of newcomers from abroad, but they want the federal government to legalize the status quo, and to enact rules that would rotate seasonal farmworkers in and out of the country. The United States had such a program, a series of agreements to recruit Mexican farmworkers or braceros to harvest crops, and their legacy includes the largest flow of unauthorized migrants between any two countries in the world.

If importing guest workers is a hollow promise at one end of the spectrum, tolerating the status quo and eventually legalizing unauthorized workers and their children lies at the other extreme. Legalization advocates acknowledge that regularizing the status of farmworkers will likely speed their exit from the farm workforce, and that helping ex-farmworkers and their children to achieve upward mobility in the United States will require significant new public spending to help them learn English and acquire the skills needed to succeed in the United States.

Most Americans oppose simply legalizing the status quo with a new guest-worker program, but they are also reluctant to pay higher taxes to improve the odds of successfully integrating immigrants and their children who arrive with little education and poverty-level incomes. But the United States does not have to choose between a new guest-worker program and new integration programs for farmworkers and their children. Many of the farm jobs filled by newcomer immigrants could be mechanized, restructured to make them more attractive to workers already in the United States, or eliminated by freer trade in farm commodities.

It will not be easy to change the trajectory of a U.S. agricultural system that has become increasingly reliant on immigrant farmworkers over the past several decades. Change is disruptive and costly, and the change to a more mechanized agriculture will be more disruptive in some commodities than in others. Employers are reluctant to make expensive and risky labor-saving changes, and in the past, farmworker advocates opposed government-subsidized labor-saving mechanization. However, resisting labor-saving changes will ultimately reduce the competitiveness of U.S. agriculture in an increasingly globalized economy.

This book outlines a "regularize and rationalize" strategy that can bring about fundamental changes in the farm labor market. As proposed by both farm employers and farmworker advocates, we would allow some currently unauthorized farmworkers who have developed U.S. roots to become legal immigrants, which we expect to hasten exits from the farm workforce and increase the demand for guest workers. To avoid having guest workers maintain the status quo, the Social Security and Unemployment Insurance taxes that are not currently collected on guest-worker wages should be paid, and these payroll taxes should be used to subsidize mechanization and job restructuring and to provide bonuses to encourage guest workers to return to their countries of origin.

This plan to regularize and rationalize includes the two key elements contained in the AgJOBS proposal pending in Congress: legalization of some unauthorized farmworkers and easy access to legal guest workers.[6] It differs from AgJOBS in using the economic mechanisms of taxes and subsidies to wean agriculture from its dependence on low-skilled immigrant workers and to encourage guest workers to return home at the end of their contracts. Unlike the rule-based Bracero Program, which showed how hard it was to enforce rules that ran counter to the incentives of employers and migrants, our proposed incentive-based plan is far more likely to achieve the goals of keeping U.S. agriculture competitive and reducing dependence on imported guest workers over time.

There are no magic-bullet solutions to the seasonal farm labor issue. However, one thing is clear: the government will have little power to change the trajectory of the farm labor market as long as illegal migration continues. If farm employers can hire unauthorized workers, they have little incentive to mechanize and restructure farm jobs to keep current farmworkers longer or to hire legal guest workers. If unauthorized migrants can arrive in the United States and find jobs, there is little incentive for them to utilize a guest-worker program to enter and leave the country.

Part One Immigration and Agriculture

Chapter 1 Immigration to the United States

Almost 100,000 foreigners arrive in the United States every day. There are three major groups: About 3,000 are legal immigrants, invited to the country to settle and, usually after five years, to become naturalized U.S. citizens. Another 94,000 are temporary visitors, mostly tourists and businesspeople, but also foreign students and guest workers who are expected to return to their countries of origin. Finally, about 1,500 unauthorized foreigners settle in the United States; even more are apprehended just inside the U.S. border.[1]

Should the arrival of so many foreigners be welcomed or feared? There is no single answer, which helps to explain American ambivalence about immigration. The United States has always celebrated its immigrant heritage, and American leaders often recount the story of renewal and rebirth brought about by newcomers from abroad. At the same time, Americans have worried since the days of the Founding Fathers about the economic, political, and cultural changes associated with immigration.

For its first 100 years, the United States facilitated immigration, welcoming foreigners to settle a vast country. In the 1880s, the country began to bar certain types of foreigners, including prostitutes, indentured servants (workers who arrived with contracts that tied them for several years to the employer who paid for their transportation), and Chinese, beginning the era of qualitative restrictions on immigration. In the 1920s, the United States added quantitative restrictions or quotas on the number of immigrants accepted each year.

In 1965, the United States changed the priority for legal immigrants from northwestern Europeans to foreigners whose relatives already in the country asked the government to admit their spouses, children, parents, and brothers and sisters. At the time, no one expected the origins of immigrants to change. Speaking during the debate in Congress, Senator Edward Kennedy (D-MA) said, "The ethnic mix of this country will not be upset. Contrary to the charges in some quarters, [switching from national origins to family unification] will not inundate America with immigrants from any one country or area, or the most populated and deprived nations of Africa and Asia."[2]

It is often hard to predict the effects of changes in immigration policy, and Kennedy was wrong about the effects of the 1965 changes. The number of immigrants has averaged more than a million a year since the 1990s, and their origins have changed. During the 1950s, more than two-thirds of U.S. immigrants were from Europe and Canada. By the 1990s, more than 75 percent were from Latin America and Asia.[3]

Immigration and integration are much-debated issues, often framed by extreme proponents of "no immigrants" and "no borders." The Federation for American Immigration Reform (FAIR), for example, charges that large-scale immigration contributes to population growth and environmental degradation, displaces low-skilled American workers and depresses their wages, and threatens the cultural bonds that hold Americans together. Consequently, FAIR calls for a sharp reduction in immigration—from more than a million a year to perhaps 300,000.[4] FAIR argues that an "immigration time out" would have the added benefit of allowing recent arrivals and Americans time to adjust to one another.

At the other extreme, the *Wall Street Journal* (*WSJ*) has several times advocated a five-word constitutional amendment: "There shall be open borders."[5] The *WSJ*'s major argument for open borders is economic: more people mean more workers, more consumers, and an expanding economy, and the editorial writers believe that these benefits offset any costs, including lower wages for workers who compete with newcomers. Others argue that immigrants add "fresh blood" by injecting new entrepreneurial spirit in the U.S. economy (Millman, 1997). The Catholic Church and some other religious organizations

oppose immigration controls because they believe that national borders artifi-
cially divide humanity.[6] Finally, groups such as the Organization of Chinese
Americans and the Irish Lobby for Immigration Reform favor more immigration from particular countries or regions.

The United States is a nation of immigrants. U.S. presidents frequently re-
mind Americans that, except for Native Americans, they or their forebears left
another country to begin anew in the "land of opportunity," suggesting that
immigration permits individuals to better their lives and at the same time
strengthens the country. Yet immigration also brings many changes that raise
fundamental questions for Americans. What does it mean to be American?
What kind of society have we created, and who shall be welcomed to join it?
What should be done about foreigners who arrive uninvited?

IMMIGRATION PATTERNS AND POLICIES

Between 1990 and 2005, some 14 million immigrants were admitted to the
United States, an average of almost a million a year. The number of legal immigrants has been increasing. Immigration averaged 250,000 a year in the
1950s, 330,000 a year in the 1960s, 450,000 a year in the 1970s, and 735,000 a
year in the 1980s. Until the 1960s, most immigrants were from Europe, but
immigrants from Latin America and Asia have accounted for three-fourths of
U.S. immigrants since the 1970s (see figure 1).

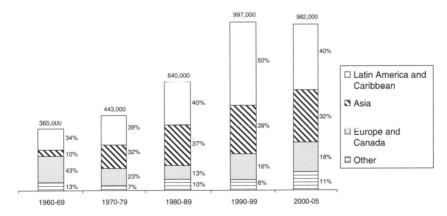

Figure 1 Immigration by Region of Birth
Average Annual Legal U.S. Immigrants by Region of Origin, 1960 to 2005
Note: Percentages may not add to 100 because of rounding.

Immigration is often imagined as a process in which anxious foreigners have interviews at U.S. consulates abroad to prove that they would be good Americans. Some immigrants do line up at U.S. consulates to be interviewed for immigrant visas, but they are the exception. Two-thirds of the immigrants "admitted" each year are already in the United States. When they receive immigrant visas, they adjust their status from student, temporary worker, or unauthorized foreigner to legal immigrant. The annual number of immigrants reflects when foreigners get immigrant visas, not necessarily when they entered the United States.

There are three major streams or flows of foreigners into the United States, sometimes described as front, side, and back doors. Legal front-door immigrants are eligible to settle and naturalize after five years. Legal temporary visitors enter via a side door, suggesting they are expected to depart after a period of tourism, work, or study. Unauthorized foreigners enter via a back door, or do not depart after being a temporary visitor, and they can be removed if apprehended.

There are subflows at each door. For example, there are four major types of front-door immigrants. Two-thirds are family-sponsored, which means that family members in the United States petitioned the U.S. government to allow the admission of their relatives. Family-sponsored immigrants are further divided into two subcategories: those who are the immediate relatives of U.S. citizens and other relatives of U.S. residents.

Immigration policy is most generous to immediate relatives of U.S. citizens, allowing an unlimited number of their spouses, parents, and children to enter. However, there are caps on the number of visas available to relatives of legal immigrants settled in the United States and on the number of more distant relatives of U.S. citizens, which lead to long waits for visas. Mexican spouses of U.S. immigrants, for example, may have to wait seven years for immigrant visas, and adult brothers and sisters of U.S. citizens up to 20 years.[7] Many foreigners do not wait, instead arriving as temporary visitors and overstaying or crossing the border illegally. This means that part of the unauthorized foreign population consists of U.S. residents' relatives who are expected to eventually become immigrants.

About a sixth of front-door immigrants are foreigners (and their family members) who are admitted because U.S. employers find them uniquely qualified to fill vacant jobs.[8] The U.S. Department of Labor must generally certify that U.S. workers are not available to fill the job for which the employer is seeking a visa for a particular immigrant, and usually accepts employer assertions that U.S.

workers did not respond to recruitment ads that offered prevailing wages.[9] In fact, the immigrant is generally filling the job when the employer advertises for U.S. workers, which helps to explain why more than 90 percent of the immigrant visas issued for employment reasons go to foreigners already in the United States.[10]

The third group of front-door immigrants consists of refugees and asylum applicants. Refugees are granted immigrant visas to begin anew in the United States because they have a well-founded fear of persecution in their home country due to their race, religion, nationality, membership in a particular social group, or political opinion. Asylum applicants are foreigners who arrive in the United States and request permission to stay because they fear persecution at home for the same reasons. Most refugees are resettled in the United States after they have fled their country and waited in a third country, as with Iraqis living in Jordan and Syria. Most asylum applicants are found not to be refugees, but those recognized as in need of protection are allowed to stay in the United States as immigrants.

The fourth front-door group includes diversity immigrants, a category created in 1990 to bring in new blood. Changes in the 1965 immigration policy favored the admission of foreigners who had close relatives in the United States. This restricted the flow of Irish immigrants because few Irish had close relatives living in the United States. Instead, network or chain migration from Latin America and Asia dominated immigration, as recent immigrants sponsored their relatives.

Diversity visas thus offer an opportunity for foreigners to emigrate from countries that have not recently sent large numbers of immigrants to the United States. Between 2004 and 2006, more than 10 million foreigners applied for a diversity immigrant visa, 50,000 of which are available each year (see table 1).[11]

Once they reach the United States, immigrants normally stay, although during the 1930s Depression, more people moved out of America than moved in. Between 1901 and 1990, the number of people emigrating from the United States was equivalent to about 31 percent of the number immigrating. In making population projections, the U.S. Census Bureau assumed that about 300,000 U.S. residents a year would emigrate, equivalent to 30 percent of projected net immigration (Hollman, Mulder, and Kallan, 2000).

The United States is eager to attract most types of temporary visitors (also known as nonimmigrants), as evidenced by airline and hotel ads for foreign tourists, and there are no limits on most categories. Citizens of most countries

Table 1 Foreigners Coming to or in the United States, 2004–2006

Category	2004	2005	2006
Immigrants	957,883	1,122,373	1,266,264
Immediate Relatives of U.S. Citizens	417,815	436,231	580,483
Other Family-Sponsored Immigrants	214,355	212,970	222,229
Employment-Based	155,330	246,878	159,081
Refugees and Asylees	369,685	459,848	381,310
Diversity and Other Immigrants	99,153	83,332	88,017
Estimated Emigration	308,000	312,000	316,000
Temporary Visitors	30,781,330	32,003,435	33,667,328
Pleasure/Business	27,395,921	28,510,374	29,928,567
Foreign Students	613,221	621,178	693,805
Temporary Foreign Workers	676,218	726,535	821,006
Illegal Immigration: Apprehensions	1,264,232	1,291,142	1,206,457
Removals or Deportations	189,368	202,842	
Stock: Unauthorized Foreigners	10,100,000	10,950,000	11,800,000

Sources: 2006 Yearbook of Immigration Statistics, Tables 6, 26, and 35; Emigration from Census. Unauthorized estimate from Passel, 2005, p. 2.
Foreign students and workers excludes their spouses and children.

must obtain visas that admit them to the United States for a specific purpose, such as visiting, working, or studying, but nationals of 27 countries can visit the United States without visas.[12] Arrivals of temporary visitors increased in the 1990s, reached 34 million in 2000, and then fell after the September 11, 2001, terrorist attacks, when the U.S. government made it more difficult to obtain temporary visitor visas.[13] Most of the post-9/11 decline was in tourist and business visitors, but there were also changes in two visitor categories of special interest: foreign students and foreign workers.

Foreign student admissions doubled between 1990 and 2000, as the number of students seeking degrees from U.S. institutions rose with economic growth abroad, especially in Asia, and as some American universities sought foreign fee-paying students. After 9/11, foreign student admissions from the Middle East and in some scientific fields declined, and foreign students were required to pay $100 to support a database that tracks them while they are in the United States. U.S. universities must provide information about the foreign students they enroll to the Student and Exchange Visitor Information System (SEVIS), which reported 750,000 foreign students and exchange visitors in the United States in 2006.

Some educators blame SEVIS and other post-9/11 policies for the decline in the number of foreigners applying to U.S. graduate programs in science and engineering—in many U.S. universities, more than half of the graduate students in these fields are foreigners. The National Science Board, among others, has warned that the United States risks losing its competitive edge in the global economy unless it persuades more Americans to study science and engineering or allows foreigners who have graduated from U.S. universities in these fields to stay and work.[14] Others argue that there is no shortage of U.S. science and engineering students, noting that U.S. students rationally avoid fields of study marked by six or more years of graduate study followed by five to ten years of low-paid postdoctoral research, the pattern in many basic sciences (Teitelbaum, 2003).

Many foreign students stay in the United States after graduation, often as temporary foreign workers. Most guest workers leave the United States after several weeks, months, or years, but some—including those with H-1B visas (given to foreigners with college degrees who fill U.S. jobs that require college degrees)—are permitted to stay if they can find a U.S. employer to sponsor them for an immigrant visa during the six years they may be in the country.

The H-1B Program was created in 1990, when it was assumed that the United States had enough workers, but that there were mismatches in the labor market, with the result that there were not enough workers to fill jobs in some fast-growing sectors, including high-tech and health care. The compromise in the H-1B Program gave employers easy access to foreign college graduates, but capped the number of visas at 65,000 a year, which was about twice the number of professionals being admitted each year at the time. The combination of the high-tech boom in the late 1990s and the emergence of labor recruiters who brought Indian computer workers and others to the United States and farmed them out to employers exhausted the supply of H-1B visas, prompting employers to successfully petition Congress to raise the cap, eventually to a peak 195,000 a year, and to allow nonprofit organizations such as universities to secure as many H-1B visas as they wanted outside the cap.

Foreign workers and high technology seem to inspire extreme assertions. Bill Gates of Microsoft said: "The terrible shortfall in the visa supply for highly skilled scientists and engineers stems from visa policies that have not been updated in more than 15 years. We live in a different economy now, and it makes no sense to tell well-trained, highly skilled individuals—many of whom are educated at our top universities—that they are not welcome here."[15] Critics counter that there is no shortage of Americans interested in science and engineering careers, only a shortage of U.S. workers willing to work long hours for low wages and short careers in the fast-changing high-tech industries. They note that most students earning BA degrees in science and engineering are U.S. citizens; few pursue advanced degrees because they do not find the extra earnings and opportunities sufficient to warrant the time and expense. Instead of making it easier for foreign students to stay and work, critics say that the U.S. government should encourage employers to restructure salaries and incentives so that Americans find it worthwhile to earn advanced degrees in science and engineering.

Unauthorized foreigners, also known as undocumented or illegal migrants, are persons in the United States in violation of U.S. immigration laws. The best estimate is that there are about 12 million, with the number increasing by 500,000 a year. There were 37 million foreign-born U.S. residents in 2005, including 31 percent naturalized U.S. citizens, 39 percent legal immigrants and nonimmigrants such as foreign students and legal temporary workers, and 30 percent unauthorized foreigners. More than half of the unauthorized foreigners entered the United States without inspection, meaning they evaded border controls, while up to 45 percent entered legally but did not leave as required. An estimated 6 million of the unauthorized are Mexicans (see table 2).[16]

The Department of Homeland Security (DHS) is responsible for preventing unauthorized foreigners from entering the United States and finding and removing those already there. DHS's Customs and Border Protection agency includes the Border Patrol, which had 14,000 agents in 2007 to discourage foreigners from attempting to enter the United States between designated ports of entry. Border Patrol agents apprehend more than a million foreigners a year, 90 percent of whom are Mexicans caught just inside the Mexico-U.S. border.

Almost all Mexicans who are apprehended volunteer to return to Mexico unless they have been caught so many times that they appear to be smugglers,

Table 2 Status of Foreign-Born U.S. Residents, March 2005

	Percent	Millions
Naturalized U.S. Citizens	31	11.5
Legal Immigrants and Nonimmigrantss	39	14.4
Unauthorized	30	11.1
Total	100	37

Source: Passel, 2005, p. 3.

in which case they can be prosecuted by U.S. authorities.[17] Apprehended foreigners who are "other than Mexicans" (OTMs) have the right to go before an immigration judge and explain why they should not be formally deported or removed from the United States; deportation usually prevents legal admission in the future.

Another DHS agency, Immigration and Customs Enforcement (ICE), enforces immigration laws inside the United States, including locating and removing foreigners whose deportation has been ordered and enforcing laws that prohibit U.S. employers from knowingly hiring unauthorized workers. In 2007, more than 275,000 foreigners were deported, including half who had been convicted of U.S. crimes. However, ICE has made locating and removing foreign criminals a much higher priority than enforcing employer sanctions. There were 65 ICE agents focused on work site enforcement in 2004, when they cited just 3 of the 8 million U.S. employers for violating laws against employing unauthorized foreigners (Government Accountability Office, 2005). Workplace enforcement has since increased, and ICE is targeting U.S. employers whose "business model" depends on "making an illegal workforce part of the structure of their business." As we see in Chapter 5, many of the firms targeted by ICE are in meatpacking.

PUBLIC OPINION

Americans have long worried about the changes associated with immigration. In opinion polls, a majority of respondents agree that legal and illegal immigration should be reduced, while fewer than 10 percent want immigration increased.[18] Opinion polls find a sharp difference between elite and mass opinion; support for immigration rises with income and education. For example, in one poll, 55 percent of the public said legal immigration should be reduced, compared to 18 percent of opinion leaders.[19]

Public opinion toward immigration often changes with economic circumstances. During the late 1990s, when unemployment rates were low, public opinion became less restrictionist. A 1997 poll, for example, found that fewer than 50 percent of Americans wanted immigration reduced, but 63 percent of those polled were concerned about immigrants taking jobs from Americans or causing racial conflict, and 79 percent were concerned that immigrants were overburdening the welfare system and pushing up taxes.[20]

Fears of terrorism and a weakening economy made Americans more restrictionist in the early years of the twenty-first century. An opinion poll taken just after 9/11 reported that 65 percent of Americans favored stopping all immigration during the war on terror.[21] However, a *Los Angeles Times* article noted that "the most significant development in the national immigration debate is what hasn't happened [after 9/11]: No lawmaker of influence has moved to reverse the country's generous immigration policy, which for more than three decades has facilitated the largest sustained wave of immigration in U.S. history."[22] The reason is that most Americans agreed with then Immigration and Naturalization Service (INS) commissioner James W. Ziglar, who repeated: "These weren't immigrants. They were terrorists."[23]

Congress began to debate measures to reduce illegal migration, prompting a new round of polls that found strong majorities urging that the federal government do more to prevent unauthorized foreigners from entering or remaining in the United States. A December 2005 *Washington Post*-ABC News poll, for example, reported that 80 percent of Americans think the federal government should do more to reduce illegal immigration, and 56 percent believe unauthorized migrants hurt the United States more than they help it.[24] A March 2006 Pew Research Center poll found that 53 percent of Americans want illegal foreigners removed, while 40 percent agreed that at least some unauthorized foreigners should be allowed to legalize their status.[25] An April 2006 *Los Angeles Times* poll found that 63 percent of Americans favored stepped-up enforcement as well as a new guest-worker program to deal with illegal migration, while 30 percent favored stepped-up enforcement only.[26]

Many politicians and researchers dismiss public concerns about immigration by pointing out that past fears of "unassimilable foreigners" proved to be unfounded. Benjamin Franklin worried about integrating German immigrants in the 1700s. Why, he asked, should "Pennsylvania, founded by the English, become a colony of aliens, who will shortly be so numerous as to Germanize us, instead of our Anglifying them?"[27] Less than two centuries later, a descendant of these immigrants, Dwight Eisenhower, was elected president of the United States. Many immigrants have been entrusted with high public office, from Henry Kissinger to Arnold Schwarzenegger.

The United States celebrates its immigrant heritage with mass naturalization ceremonies on the Fourth of July that associate immigration with the founding of the country. Most Americans share an immigrant legacy, which can make those who want to restrict immigration appear "un-American." Public attitudes toward immigration and questions about the social and economic impacts of immigrants are closely linked. The fortunes of immigrants and their effects on the economy, the political system, and society shape public opinion toward additional immigration, especially from Mexico.

MEXICO–U.S. MIGRATION AND THE NORTH
AMERICAN FREE TRADE AGREEMENT (NAFTA)

Since the United States began to record arriving immigrants in 1820, more than 70 million immigrants have arrived. About 55 percent are from Europe, including 10 percent from the leading country of immigration, Germany. In a sign of the shift in migrant origins over the past four decades, Mexico surpassed Germany as the leading source of U.S. immigrants in 2008.

How did Mexico wind up as the major source of U.S. immigrants? In 1800, Mexico and the United States had populations of roughly equal size, 6 million, and Mexico's gross domestic product (GDP) per capita was about half that of the United States. Northern Mexico was transferred to the United States by the Treaty of Guadalupe Hidalgo in 1848, ending a war that began when American settlers moved into Mexican territory and rebelled against Mexican authority. The relatively few Mexican residents of what is now the southwestern United States became Americans, and there was little migration across the Mexico-U.S. border until World War I (Weintraub, 1990).

Mexico was in the midst of a civil war when U.S. farmers asked for permission in 1917 to recruit Mexican farmworkers to harvest their crops. This first Bracero Program ended in 1921, but there was no Border Patrol until 1924, making it easy for Mexicans who had learned about U.S. jobs to travel north. During World War II, U.S. farmers again recruited Mexican workers, and this time the program continued for almost two decades after the war ended.[28] Both Bracero Programs got larger and lasted longer than expected. The fact that seasonal workers were readily available encouraged farmers to plant additional crops, enabling California to replace New Jersey as the nation's Garden State in the 1950s. During the War on Poverty in the 1960s, Congress was convinced that the braceros held down the wages of U.S. farmworkers and ended the program despite the protests of farmers.

The late 1960s were a time of farm labor protest, rising farm wages, and labor-saving mechanization. The readjustment of the farm labor market after several decades of bracero workers was not easy, nor was it easy for ex-braceros to adjust to the loss of U.S. jobs and wages. Dealing with bracero legacies laid the groundwork for subsequent Mexico–U.S. migration.

For example, U.S. farmers had to pay for the transportation of the braceros from the place where they were recruited to the farms. This rule this prompted some Mexicans to move to the border to lower the transportation bill and increase their chances of being selected. When the Bracero Program ended, ex-braceros in Mexican border cities had no job prospects, so the Mexican and U.S. governments modified their trade laws to allow the creation of maquiladoras—factories in Mexico that import components, hire Mexican workers to assemble them into goods such as TVs, and reexport the finished products. The maquiladoras never provided many jobs for ex-braceros, who were mostly young men, at a time when they preferred to hire young women. Maquiladoras expanded and drew more Mexicans to border cities, with the women staying to work in the factories and many of the men continuing to cross the border.

However, there was relatively little illegal Mexico–U.S. migration until the early 1980s. Mexico had extremely high population growth when oil was discovered in the late 1970s, and the Mexican government went on a spending spree, taking out loans to accelerate development for its expanding population and assuming that oil revenues would repay them. After oil prices fell in the early 1980s, the Mexican government could not repay its debts, leading to a devaluation of the peso, a recession, and increased Mexico–U.S. migration. Networks soon linked a growing number of Mexican villages to U.S. farms and, with no penalties on U.S. employers who knowingly hired illegal migrants, unauthorized Mexican workers began to spread from agriculture to construction, manufacturing, and services jobs.

Congress responded to rising unauthorized migration with the Immigration Reform and Control Act (IRCA) of 1986, which imposed federal penalties on U.S. employers who knowingly hired unauthorized workers. The theory was that "closing the labor market door" would discourage Mexicans from attempting illegal entry, since a migrant would not risk an illegal border crossing only to discover that employers would hire unauthorized workers. However, there was a fatal flaw in the IRCA's employer sanctions. The IRCA required newly hired workers to show their employers documents to prove that they were legally authorized to work in the United States. However, the employers did not have to verify the authenticity of the documents, so they could lawfully hire workers with forged work authorization documents. Proposals for fraud-proof documentation—either an improved Social Security card or a new worker identification card—were rejected by those who feared the creation of a "Big Brother" government.

The IRCA's employer sanctions provision did not close the door to the U.S. labor market, while the other half of the act's grand bargain—legalization—turned 2.7 million unauthorized foreigners into immigrants. More than 85 percent of those legalized were Mexican, creating new networks between legal immigrants and Mexican villages. Within a few years, a combination of false documents, relatively few Border Patrol agents, and ineffective workplace enforcement turned pathways into freeways for migrants from Mexico to the United States (Commission on Agricultural Workers, 1993).

In the early 1990s, Mexico's economy was about 5 percent as large as the U.S. economy, roughly equivalent to the economy of Los Angeles County. Beginning in the mid-1980s, the Mexican government changed its economic policies, shifting from no-trade and inward-oriented policies to free-trade and outward-oriented policies. As with the Asian Tiger economies, the Mexican government hoped to attract foreign investors who would build factories and hire Mexicans to produce goods for export.

Reflecting a historical aversion often summarized as "poor Mexico, so far from god, so close to the United States," the Mexican government looked for non-U.S. investors. However, with the fall of Communism in Europe and the continued economic boom in Asia, it soon became clear that Americans were most likely to invest in Mexico. However, many Americans who remembered the expropriations of U.S. assets in Mexico in the 1930s, and aware of numerous restrictions on foreign investment in Mexico, were reluctant to invest in Mexico. In part to overcome this resistance, the Mexican government in 1990 proposed the North American Free Trade Agreement (NAFTA), which aimed to extend the existing Canada-United States FTA investment and markets.

Negotiated in 1992 and presented to Congress for approval in 1993,[29] NAFTA aimed to lower barriers to trade and investment, which economic theory predicts will increase employment and incomes in participating countries because comparative advantage allows each to specialize, with trade providing goods that other countries can produce relatively cheaply (Hufbauer and Schott, 1992).[30] The faster employment and income growth due to freer trade was expected to reduce unauthorized migration or, in the words of Mexican President Salinas: "More jobs will mean higher wages in Mexico, and this in turn will mean fewer migrants to the United States and Canada. We want to export goods, not people."[31]

Most of NAFTA's benefits, as well as most of the adjustments in its wake, were expected to be in Mexico—few expected much American interest in freer trade with the much smaller Mexican economy. However, both the

American Federation of Labor and Congress of Industrial Organizations (AFL-CIO) and 1992 presidential candidate Ross Perot made defeating NAFTA among their top priorities. Perot predicted there would be a "giant sucking sound" as good U.S. jobs moved to Mexico, while the AFL-CIO warned that U.S. employers would use the threat of moving jobs to Mexico to win wage and benefit concessions from U.S. workers.

The U.S. controversy over NAFTA prompted both supporters and critics to make extreme predictions. Supporters predicted that free trade would quickly solve the poverty problem in Mexico, reducing unauthorized Mexico–U.S. migration. Critics of NAFTA predicted a race to the bottom as U.S. employers moved jobs to take advantage of lower wages. Both supporters and critics were proven wrong (Weintraub, 2004b). The United States lost some jobs to Mexico, but the late 1990s proved to be a period of record high U.S. job growth and record low unemployment despite NAFTA. There was foreign investment in Mexico that created jobs, but not enough to reduce Mexico–U.S. migration (Hufbauer and Schott, 2005).

NAFTA got off to a very rocky start in Mexico. On January 1, 2004, the so-called Zapatista uprising in Chiapas unsettled some foreign investors. However, the major problem during the summer and fall of 1994 was that the Mexican peso was overvalued, encouraging Mexicans to import goods and to convert their pesos into dollars. The Mexican government ran out of reserves to continue an exchange rate of three pesos for one dollar, and in December 1994, the peso was devalued sharply. The result was a severe economic recession in which a tenth of Mexican workers with formal sector jobs lost them, real wages fell, and inflation topped 50 percent. The U.S. government provided emergency aid, but many Mexicans lost faith in Mexico's future and emigrated.

The Mexican economy recovered, probably faster than it would have without NAFTA, but Mexico–U.S. migration accelerated for three major reasons. First, freer trade displaced Mexican workers in previously protected industries, while the much larger U.S. economy was able to quickly produce additional goods for Mexican consumers. Foreign investors were creating jobs in Mexico, but this took time, and many Mexican workers who were displaced migrated rather than waiting for new jobs.

Second, NAFTA accelerated change in rural Mexico that encouraged out-migration. About a quarter of Mexicans live in rural areas, and NAFTA was expected to encourage many of them to switch from being corn farmers to growing fruits and vegetables, some of which could be exported to the United

States. The United States has a comparative advantage in corn production—the state of Iowa produced twice as much corn as Mexico in the early 1990s at half the Mexican price—while Mexico has a comparative advantage in producing labor-intensive commodities such as strawberries. It proved easy to ship U.S. corn to Mexico, but much harder to ship Mexican fruits and vegetables to the United States. Instead of becoming fruit and vegetable farmers, many rural Mexicans migrated to the United States.[32]

The third reason for more Mexico–U.S. migration was the U.S. economic boom, which reduced unemployment rates below 4 percent in the late 1990s. The word spread quickly in Mexico that the false documents needed to get American jobs were readily available, and Mexicans already settled in the United States often provided the funds for friends and relatives to be smuggled across the border. Once in the United States, these settled Mexicans could provide shelter, contact with employers seeking workers, and often training on the job. Meanwhile, Mexicans who waited for jobs in Mexico soon realized that countries with lower wages such as China were drawing more of the foreign investment that had been expected to create jobs in Mexico.

Elections in 2000 gave both Mexico and the United States new presidents and hope for a comprehensive Mexico–U.S. migration agreement. Mexican President Vincente Fox took the initiative, asking President George W. Bush to endorse the "whole enchilada" in summer 2001, a four-part plan to legalize unauthorized Mexicans in the United States, create a new guest-worker program, cooperate to reduce deaths and violence on the Mexico-U.S. border, and grant Mexico an exemption from the usual limit of 20,000 immigrant visas a year for each country.[33]

However, no migration agreement was imminent when the September 11, 2001, terrorist attacks stopped the discussions. Legal and illegal Mexico–U.S. migration continued, so that by 2006 an estimated 12 million Mexican-born people resided in the United States, and most were unauthorized (Passel, 2005). The Mexican-origin population of the United States (Mexican-born and their U.S.-born children) is at least 25 million, explaining why Fox said he was president of 125 million Mexicans—100 million in Mexico and 25 million in the United States.

Mexico and the United States have shared a 2,000 mile border for the past 150 years, but most Mexican-born U.S. residents arrived since 1985. The surge in Mexico–U.S. migration has its roots in earlier Bracero Programs, a flawed enforcement and legalization program in the mid-1980s, and a Mexican crisis in the mid-1990s, when the United States enjoyed an economic boom.

For the past several years, the U.S. Congress has been debating what to do about Mexico–U.S. migration, the scale of which is remarkable. In 1970, when Mexico had about 50 million residents, there were fewer than 800,000 Mexican-born U.S. residents. By 2000, when Mexico's population had doubled to about 100 million, there were more than 8 million Mexican-born U.S. residents. Mexico's population is expected to stabilize at about 130 million in 2030, raising the question of how many more Mexican-born persons will move to the United States. The answer depends in large part on what happens in the U.S. farm labor market.

Chapter 2 Agriculture and Migrants

Agriculture is a sector of the economy riddled by paradoxes. Farmers are often praised as the independent yeomen who provide a living link to the nation's Founding Fathers, yet agriculture may be more dependent on federal subsidies than any other U.S. industry. There were too many farmers during the 1950s, prompting a million Americans a year to move to cities, while alleged shortages of farmworkers were the rationale for importing almost 500,000 Mexicans a year to work in the fields in the mid-1950s.

During the Depression, the U.S. government developed policies to support the incomes of farmers but excluded farm workers from the protective labor laws that established minimum wages and provided social security benefits. One reason for the government's embrace of farmers and its neglect of farmworkers comes from Thomas Jefferson and other agrarian fundamentalists. Jefferson, the third U.S. president, believed that family farmers were the backbone of American democracy, as exemplified by a phrase engraved on the wall of a reading room in the Library of Congress: "Those who labor in the earth are the chosen people of God."[1] Jefferson believed that rural life was superior to urban life and that a nation of self-sufficient family farmers who owned the land they farmed would guarantee respect for private property and preserve American democracy.

Family farms were the ideal as well as a widespread reality in 1790, when the first Census of Population found that 90 percent of the 4 million U.S. residents lived in rural areas. The model farm included a farmer, a large family, and perhaps a hired hand, usually a young man who lived with the farmer's family and, in that egalitarian world, perhaps married the farmer's daughter before becoming a farmer in his own right. Everyone on family farms worked to meet peak seasonal labor needs, which explains why school schedules were adjusted so that children were available when needed on the farm.

The fact that crops needed more workers during some seasons than others encouraged diversification to spread out the work and to ensure self-sufficiency. Most family farms in the early nineteenth century raised crops and tended livestock, and most did not generate a surplus to sell. As technology increased the productivity of farmers, family farms got larger, producing a surplus to sell to urban residents in expanding cities. Land was gradually consolidated into fewer and larger farms, but the supply of food and fiber generally increased faster than demand, putting downward pressure on farm prices and incomes. The economic fact that farm productivity rose faster than the demand for food was the raison d'etre for government support programs to prop up farm prices and thus farmers' incomes (Cochrane, 1993).

There were two other U.S. farming systems that dealt very differently with the need for seasonal farmworkers. In the southeastern states, plantations produced cotton and tobacco that was exported to northern Europe and other areas that could not grow these long-season crops. Slaves were bound to their plantations, ensuring that seasonal workers were available when needed, and eventually supplanted by sharecroppers who lived and worked on small plots of plantation land.[2]

The western states had large landholdings often assembled by entrepreneurs who grazed cattle or raised wheat. The transcontinental railroad, irrigation, and other innovations made it profitable to switch to labor-intensive commodities in the second half of the nineteenth century. Land holdings were concentrated, and large landowners expected to sell small plots to family farmers who, it was assumed, would provide most of the labor necessary to produce fruits and vegetables. However, a seasonal workforce was available in the Chinese workers who were imported to build the railroad and, when discrimination drove the Chinese out of cities, farmers hired them. Unlike

plantation owners, western farmers were not responsible for "their" farmworkers when seasonal work ended.[3]

WAVES OF MIGRANTS

Large farms that specialized in a few crops and relied on migrant and seasonal
workers to harvest them developed in the western states as the frontier was
closing in the 1880s and 1890s. The key to the emergence of commercial farms
in California and other western states was the transcontinental railroad, which
integrated these distant places into the U.S. economy. The result was lower
transportation costs, which opened new markets for California commodities,
and lower interest rates, which encouraged the planting of fruit trees that required a several-year wait between planting and harvesting (Fuller, 1942).

California agriculture began with the establishment of the 21 Spanish mis-
sions along El Camino Real (today's Highway 101) between 1769 and 1833.
Mission agriculture relied on local Indian workers, and was replaced between
the 1830s and 1860s by "ranchos" established with large land grants made by
the Spanish and Mexican governments, often tracts of 5,000 to 50,000 acres.
When the golden spike was driven to mark the completion of the transcontinental railroad on May 10, 1869, California agriculture was dominated by
large cattle and sheep grazing operations and "bonanza" wheat farms. Many
of these bonanza farms were operated by hired managers for their absentee
owners. Wheat seed was planted in the fall and, if winter rains produced a
crop, the crop was harvested in the spring (Steven Street, 2004, chap. 9).

The switch from grazing and grains to fruits required investments in infrastructure, including irrigation systems and packing plants. However, California could not become a fruit bowl without seasonal workers, which most observers expected to be provided by farm families. Large wheat farms were
expected to be broken up into family-sized units and sold to the farmers arriving on the railroad, allowing an Iowa-style family farming system to be re-
created in California and other western states.

The flaw in this thinking involved low wages and high land prices. Irrigated
land used to produce fruit was worth far more than nonirrigated land that
grew wheat. Owners of large farms who hired Chinese migrants and paid
them only when they were needed could earn nice profits from fruit farming,
and land prices soon reflected these profits. Family farmers who paid going
prices for land and did their own farmwork complained of "being paid like
Chinamen," since the value of their work was equivalent to what farmers of

large properties paid the Chinese. Most aspiring farmers abandoned plans to become family farmers in the West, and relatively few eastern and southern Europeans who were pouring into the United States traveled to California and other western states because they could find year-round nonfarm jobs in the East and Midwest.

Owners of large farms worried about who would replace aging Chinese farmworkers after the Chinese Exclusion Act of 1882 blocked the entry of additional Chinese. An editorial in the *Pacific Rural Press* in 1883 expressed their concern: "The [fruit] crop of the present year, although deemed a short one, taxed the labor capacity of the State to the utmost . . . If such was the situation this year, what will it be when the numerous young orchards now just coming into bearing will be producing full crops? The labor is not now in the country to handle such an increase in production. Will the demand for labor to meet and handle this increase of production be responded to when made? If so, where from?" (quoted in Fuller, 1942).

There were alternatives to finding another source of seasonal farmworkers abroad. Western farmers could have diversified their crops in order to offer at least some farmworkers year-round employment. Alternatively, seasonal factories in the field could have raised wages and benefits in order to attract U.S. workers, especially since most of the fruit crops produced generated high profits. California official John Enos blamed farmers for ignoring "unskilled white labor" because they were accustomed to having "China men in sufficient numbers" who were paid only when needed "during the busiest seasons of the year" (quoted in Fuller, 1967, 433–434). Farmers countered that they could not afford to raise the wages they paid seasonal workers, and paying workers only when they were needed was "a condition of things entirely unsuited to the demands of the European [immigrant] laborer" (quoted in Fuller, 1942, 1981c).

The economic imperative to find another source of "nonwhite" seasonal workers was significant. In 1888, California orchard land was worth $200 to $300 per acre, reflecting in part the low wages paid to Chinese workers, $1.00 to $1.25 per day. Land used to produce grain, by contrast, was worth only $25 to $50 an acre, and the white workers on grain farms were paid $2 to $3 a day (Fuller, 1942, 1981b). Without a replacement for the aging Chinese, farm wages were expected to rise and land prices to stabilize or fall.

A new seasonal farm workforce was found in Japan, which legalized emigration in 1885 to relieve population pressures. Some 130,000 Japanese arrived in the United States between 1901 and 1907, half became farmworkers, and the Japanese were half of California's seasonal farmworkers by 1905 (Fuller 1942, 19829). The Japanese were unique among the waves of newcomers who filled seasonal farm jobs—they were the only group from which a significant number of seasonal workers climbed the agricultural ladder to become farmers. The keys to the Japanese workers' success included a willingness to mount so-called quickie harvesttime strikes in support of demands for higher wages and offering to work for a share of the crop rather than for wages, a sharecropping that enabled some Japanese workers to gain experience selling produce to consumers and allowed some to buy marginal farmland and produce fruits and vegetables in competition with their ex-employers. California farmers soon became disenchanted with the Japanese, and did not actively oppose a "gentlemen's agreement" that stopped Japanese immigration in 1907.[4]

California attracted only 100,000 of the 12 million European immigrants who arrived between 1900 and 1914, in part because of the presence of Chinese and Japanese workers who held down wages.[5] Owners of large farms who were worried about labor turned to what is now the Punjab region of India and Pakistan, reasoning that, as British subjects, "Hindu" farmworkers could be admitted to the United Sates despite the general ban on Asian immigrants.[6] Perhaps 10,000 "Hindus" arrived in California, but most abandoned farmwork after two or three years (Fuller, 1991, 34). Just before World War I, farmers recruited blacks in the southeastern states and American Indians on reservations to be seasonal farmworkers.

During World War I, the military draft and wartime industries absorbed many of the men who could have supplemented the seasonal farm workforce. Farmers warned of a labor supply "crisis" and asked the U.S. Department of Labor (DOL), which included the Bureau of Immigration, "to admit temporarily otherwise inadmissible aliens" to do seasonal farmwork.[7]

The Immigration Act of 1917 imposed a literacy test on foreigners 16 years of age and older and doubled the head tax to $8, which blocked the entry of most Mexicans. To get around these bars to the immigration of Mexican farmworkers, who would be arriving with contracts that tied them to a particular farm employer,[8] the DOL waived the literacy test and head tax on May 23, 1917, to allow the admission of Mexicans primarily for "employment in the sugar beet fields of California, Colorado, Utah, and Idaho, and in the cotton fields of Texas, Arizona, and California" (Scruggs, 1960, 322).[9] The Bureau of Immigration reported that, assured of ample numbers of workers in 1917, "large acreages were planted and record crops harvested throughout the Southwest" (quoted in Congressional Research Service, 1980, 7).

Scruggs, the leading authority on the use of Mexican labor in southwestern agriculture, emphasized that "by the early 1920s" Mexicans were "the principle work force in many southwestern farming areas" (1960, 319). The Mexican government, initially lukewarm toward the first Bracero (strong-arm) Program, became more enthusiastic as it realized that U.S. jobs could support many of the peasants displaced by Mexico's civil war. By July 1918, the Mexican government was providing trains to transport workers to the U.S. border (Kiser, 1979, 128).

The World War I Bracero Program included guarantees and protections for Mexican farmworkers. U.S. farm employers were to make written offers of "wages, housing conditions, and duration of employment," and the wages paid to Mexicans were supposed to be the same as those "for similar labor in the community in which the admitted aliens are to be employed."[10] Housing had to satisfy state laws or standards set by the DOL if there were no state laws governing farmworker housing. Farm employers were to report absconding workers, and some of the wages earned by braceros were withheld by employers and deposited with the U.S. Postal Savings Bank, to be repaid to workers when they returned to Mexico.

These rules were not always followed. In 1921 the Bureau of Immigration reported that 72,862 aliens had been admitted under the DOL's exceptions to immigration law between 1917 and 1921, some 21,400 absconded, and "15,632 are still in the employ of their original importers" (quoted in Congressional Research Service, 1980, 11). Only 34,922 or 48 percent were returned by farm employers to Mexico, which the El Paso immigration supervisor attributed to farmers having no incentive to cover the cost of return transportation, and the immigration service having too few inspectors to police the program. Scruggs agreed with the El Paso inspector that the "basic weakness of the program was the lack of adequate enforcement machinery" to require either workers or employers to live up to the contracts they signed (Scruggs, 1960, 324).[11]

During the 1920s, the U.S. imposed quotas on immigration from southern and eastern Europe. Farmers feared that Mexican migration might also be limited, and they successfully opposed efforts in Congress to extend immigration quotas to Western Hemisphere nations. Farmers acknowledged contemporary sentiments that Mexicans were not desirable Americans, but argued that they required a foreign source of seasonal workers. One California farm representative testified in 1926: "We, gentlemen, are just as anxious as you are not to build the civilization of California or any other western district upon a Mexican foundation. We take him because there is nothing else available. We have gone east, west, north, and south and he is the only manpower available to us" (quoted in Fuller 1942, 19859).

Farm labor reformers highlighted the link between an ample supply of foreign workers and low farm wages. They argued that if farmers paid higher wages and offered year-round jobs, they could find U.S. workers to fill farm jobs. Farmers countered that because they sold their crops in competitive markets, they could not afford to raise wages, and neither could they pay workers year-round if jobs were seasonal. Congress agreed with the farmers, and Mexico and other Western Hemisphere countries were exempted from the 1920s immigration quota. There was no U.S. Border Patrol until 1924, allowing Mexicans who had gained experience during the first Bracero Program to enter the United States with few obstacles.

Reformers came closest to achieving fundamental change in the migrant farm labor system near the end of the 1930s. California had 5.7 million residents in 1930, and Dust Bowl migration brought 1.3 million farmers known as Okies and Arkies to the state, swelling the population by 25 percent. Steeped in the Jeffersonian family farm ideal, many drove up to farmhouses and asked for work, expecting to be treated as hired hands who would live and work alongside their employers before becoming farmers themselves.

However, Dust Bowl migrants soon learned that California's commercial farms hired crews of seasonal workers when needed, not year-round hired hands. Many wound up in tent camps known as Hoovervilles, where unions and "agitators" highlighted the inequities of large landowners who benefited from government irrigation projects but who paid seasonal workers only when they were needed. Dust Bowl migrants were citizens who could vote, and there was concern that Hoovervilles could become a fertile breeding ground for Communists and others who wanted to make major changes in the socioeconomic system.[12]

Two congressional committees examined farm labor conditions in California and other western states during the late 1930s. They agreed that there were serious problems, but disagreed on the appropriate federal response. The House Committee on Un-American Activities warned that worker dissatisfaction was allowing Communist-led unions to attract adherents, and urged enforcement against Communist agitators. Many cities and counties in agricultural areas enacted ordinances, later declared unconstitutional, that prohibited "labor agitation," rallies, and picketing.

The Senate Education and Labor Committee, on the other hand, concluded that the solution to farmworker poverty was to extend collective bargaining rights to farmworkers. The National Labor Relations Act (NLRA) of 1935 gave nonfarmworkers the right to form unions and bargain collectively with their employers, in part to reverse the cuts in wages that were thought to be prolonging the Depression. However, farmworkers were excluded from the NLRA's protections under the theory that most were hired hands with the same interests as farmers; the assumption was that hired hands were more interested in government programs that raised farm prices than in legal protection to form unions.[13]

The Senate Committee, chaired by Robert LaFollette (R-WI), saw large farms as factories in the fields, and emphasized that the workers employed on them had more in common with factory workers than farmers. The committee used strong language to urge fundamental reforms:

> The economic and social plight of California's agricultural labor is miserable beyond belief. . . . The California agricultural laborer is under-employed . . . has no control over wage rates and no voice in fixing them. He must be housed for the most part in private labor camps dominated by the employer. He lacks adequate medical attention. His children are unable to secure satisfactory continuous education. He has no adequate protection from industrial accidents and no workmen's compensation. State minimum-wage and maximum-hour laws do not give him any protection. Residence requirements often bar him from relief. Organized protests on his part have been met with the blacklist, the denial of free speech and assemblage through the application of illegal ordinances of various kinds and through acts of outright vigilantism. His right to organize and bargain collectively is unprotected. (U.S. Senate Education and Labor Committee, 1942, 37–38)

The fact that the House and Senate Committees agreed there was a farm labor problem, but disagreed on what to do about it, contributed to a policy stalemate. Farm labor reformers were also divided. Some embraced the LaFollette Committee view that western farms were like factories, and that farmworkers should be covered by factory labor laws. Others clung to the Jeffersonian ideal of family farms and urged the federal government to launch programs that would help farmworkers to become farmers.

BRACEROS, DISTORTION, AND DEPENDENCE

Congressional disagreements and conflicts among farm labor reformers prevented quick action, and the outbreak of World War II shifted government attention elsewhere. The tenor of the farm labor debate quickly changed, from surpluses of workers during the 1930s to complaints of shortages.

Although the conventional wisdom is that World War II drew men who could have been farmworkers into the military and wartime industries, contemporary observers stressed that the farm labor surpluses of the 1930s persisted. For example, the secretary of agriculture testified before a Senate subcommittee in 1940 that the number of farmworkers far exceeded the number who could expect to make a decent living from agriculture (Rasmussen, 1951, 14). California farmers nonetheless requested supplemental foreign workers in 1941, but their request was rejected by the DOL at the behest of the California governor (200).[14]

The United States declared war on Germany and Japan in December 1941. During the spring of 1942, a federal interagency committee concluded that supplemental foreign farmworkers would be needed for the fall harvest. Despite protests from unions and Mexican American groups,[15] the interagency committee drafted a new bracero agreement and sent it to Mexico, where it was modified slightly before being approved.[16] As a result, the first of what became a series of bracero agreements was signed on July 23, 1942, via an exchange of diplomatic notes.[17]

The first World War II Mexican braceros entered the United States at El Paso, Texas, on September 27, 1942, and headed to work in the sugar beet fields near Stockton, California. Only 4,189 Mexican braceros were admitted in 1942 (Congressional Research Service, 1980, 16), in part because the bracero agreement called for a minimum wage of $0.30 an hour, the federal minimum wage at the time.[18] The federal minimum wage did not cover U.S. farmworkers, and many farmers initially refused to hire braceros, fearing that they would have to pay their U.S. workers at least $0.30 a hour as well (22).[19]

The Bracero Program expanded slightly during World War II, and some 310,000 foreign workers were admitted by 1947—71 percent from Mexico and 29 percent from Canada and the Caribbean (workers returning each year are counted multiple times in these admission data). Foreign farmworkers were about 2 percent of U.S. farmworkers during World War II and, although they were employed in 24 states, half were in California. The major crops in which braceros worked were cotton, sugar beets, fruits, and vegetables (Scuggs, 1961, 163).

As with most guest-worker programs, the Bracero Program grew larger and lasted longer than anticipated. Wartime admissions peaked at 62,000 in 1944, and a decade later reached 450,000. Illegal immigration increased as well, especially in the late 1940s and early 1950s. Braceros often had to pay bribes in Mexico to get on recruitment lists, and they soon learned that U.S. employers preferred to hire illegal workers to avoid paying transportation costs and the minimum wage. In 1954, there were 3.5 Mexicans apprehended for every bracero admitted (both tallies record events, not individuals, since the same individual is counted each time he is admitted as a bracero or apprehended; see table 3).

It is sometimes said that opening side doors for guest workers takes the pressure off the backdoor for unauthorized foreigners. However, between 1942 and 1964, more Mexicans were apprehended than were admitted legally as workers. Some 2 million Mexicans gained legal work experience as braceros, as did a similar number of unauthorized Mexicans, blurring the lines between

Table 3 Bracero Admissions, Apprehensions, and Immigrants, 1942–1964

Year	Bracero Admissions	Apprehensions	Mexican Immigrants
1942	4,203	11,784	2,378
1943	52,098	11,175	4,172
1944	62,170	31,174	6,598
1945	49,454	69,164	6,702
1946	32,043	99,591	7,146
1947	19,632	193,657	7,558
1948	35,345	192,779	8,384
1949	107,000	288,253	8,803
1950	67,500	468,339	6,744
1951	192,000	509,040	6,153
1952	197,100	528,815	9,079
1953	201,380	885,587	17,183
1954	309,033	1,089,583	30,645
1955	398,650	254,096	43,702
1956	445,197	87,696	61,320
1957	436,049	59,918	49,321
1958	432,857	53,474	26,721
1959	437,643	45,336	22,909
1960	315,846	70,684	32,708
1961	291,420	88,823	41,476
1962	194,978	92,758	55,805
1963	186,865	88,712	55,986
1964	177,736	86,597	34,448
TOTAL	4,646,199	5,307,035	545,941

Source: Congressional Research Service, 1980.

Note: Bracero admissions and apprehensions record events, not unique individuals, so a person admitted or apprehended multiple times is counted each time in these data.

legal and illegal. For example, when illegal Mexican workers were apprehended, they were often taken to the border, issued work authorization, and
returned to the farm on which they were found, a process that official U.S.
government publications called "drying out the wetbacks" (President's Commission on Migratory Labor, 1951).

The Bracero Program was controversial. A President's Commission on Migratory Labor was asked whether bracero admissions should be increased to
reduce illegal migration and head off farm labor shortages due to the Korean
War. It concluded with a resounding no, arguing instead that the presence of
braceros and illegal workers held down farm wages and discouraged both innovation and U.S. workers. Instead, the President's Commission urged the
federal government to extend the minimum wage and union protections to
farmworkers and to impose sanctions on farmers who hired illegal workers
(President's Commission on Migratory Labor, 1951, 178).

U.S. President Truman and Mexican President Miguel Aleman agreed with
the commission. The Mexican government asked the U.S. government to approve sanctions on U.S. employers who hired illegal Mexican workers, issuing
a statement that concluded: "The wetback exodus could be stopped only
when [U.S.] employers were penalized for hiring them" (Craig, 1971, 75).
However, farmers had the upper hand in Congress, which extended the
Bracero Program in 1951 without employer sanctions. The Immigration and
Nationality Act of 1952 formalized no employer sanctions with the so-called
Texas proviso, which made "harboring" illegal aliens a felony, but exempted
employing unauthorized workers from the definition of harboring.

Bracero admissions and illegal Mexico–U.S. migration rose together in the
early 1950s. U.S. Attorney General Herbert Brownell toured the border, pro-
nounced that he was "shocked" by migrants massing in Mexico waiting to enter the United States under the cover of darkness, and appointed ex-general
Joseph Swing to be the Immigration and Naturalization Service (INS) commissioner. Swing launched "Operation Wetback" in June 1954, a "direct attack" on the "hordes of aliens facing us across the border." Federal agents and
state and local police quickly removed 1.1 million Mexicans, including some
U.S.-born (citizen) children of unauthorized Mexicans. Simultaneously, the
DOL relaxed housing and other Bracero Program regulations, and the result
was more bracero admissions—445,197 in 1956 and fewer apprehensions,
87,696 (Craig, 1971).

The availability of braceros held down farm wages during the 1950s, allowing labor-intensive agriculture to expand in California and other states.[20] In

the words of Ernesto Galarza (1977, 265), hiring braceros was "like the sprinkling systems of mechanized irrigation, Braceros could be turned on and off" and paid only when there was work for them to do.

Numerous commissions and reports criticized farmers for mistreating and underpaying braceros and U.S. farmworkers. The Columbia Broadcasting System (CBS) documentary *Harvest of Shame,* which aired on Thanksgiving Day in November 1960, featured Edward R. Murrow challenging the U.S. government to improve conditions for farmworkers. The DOL reversed its policy and began to enforce bracero regulations, raising the cost of braceros and prompting labor-saving mechanization in some of the field crops that had been reliant on braceros, including cotton harvesting and sugar beet thinning.

President Kennedy approved even more aggressive enforcement of farm labor laws in the early 1960s. Farmers fought back by unsuccessfully trying to have the Bracero Program transferred from the "union-friendly" DOL to the "farmer-friendly" USDA (California Senate, 1961). As Congress debated the future of the Bracero Program, Kennedy issued a statement asserting that braceros were "adversely affecting the wages, working conditions, and employment opportunities of our own agricultural workers" and announced plans to end the program unilaterally in 1961. U.S. farmers and the Mexican government protested. Kennedy, citing the "serious impact in Mexico if thousands of workers employed in this country were summarily deprived of this much-needed employment" agreed to a two-year extension, until the end of 1963 (Craig, 1971, 172–173).

With the end of the Bracero Program looming in December 1963, congressional hearings during the summer of 1963 featured studies that concluded braceros were needed to keep fruits and vegetables affordable for American families. Farmers seemed to have the upper hand during these hearings, and may have won another extension of the Bracero Program if there had not been a tragedy in the Salinas Valley (Galarza, 1977). A modified bus used to transport braceros was hit by a train in the small town of Chualar in September 1963, leaving 32 braceros dead. Their bodies were not claimed immediately, as farmers and labor contractors disagreed about who was responsible for them, strengthening the hand of those who argued that the Bracero Program was out of control. Nonetheless, farm employers demonstrated their clout in Congress by winning a final one-year extension of the program, until December 31, 1964.

In 1965, many California farmers expected to employ Mexican workers under a guest-worker program that had been used to import Caribbean workers to hand cut sugarcane in Florida and to harvest apples along the eastern seaboard, the H-2 (changed to H-2A in 1986) Program. However, the DOL issued regulations that required farmers seeking H-2 workers to pay the highest of three wages: the federal or state minimum wage, the prevailing wage, or the DOL-calculated Adverse Effect Wage Rate (AEWR), and limited the employment of H-2 workers to a maximum 120 days.[21] This time limit was not a problem in the eastern states that had shorter growing seasons, but California farmers wanted to employ Mexican workers 11 months a year, and at lower wages. Growers tried to transfer the authority to certify the need for H-2 workers from the DOL to the USDA, but the effort failed in the Senate when Vice President Hubert Humphrey cast the deciding vote against the growers (Congressional Research Service, 1980, 42).

AFTER BRACEROS: HUMAN RESOURCES, MECHANIZATION, AND UNIONS

The end of the Bracero Program and the failure to win easy approval to hire H-2 workers was expected to usher in a new era for farmworkers. There were many changes in how seasonal farmworkers were hired and deployed, and three stand out: (1) professional management of seasonal farmworkers, so that the fewest number of workers necessary to get farmwork done were hired; (2) labor-saving mechanization, which often required government to act as a neutral coordinator between growers and processors; and (3) unionization, as the absence of braceros emboldened U.S. workers in long-season crops such as table grapes and lettuce to seek wage and benefit increases.

Many California farmers joined or formed associations that acted as "super labor contractors" and used modern human resource methods to recruit crews of U.S. workers. The associations increased labor market efficiency, since they relied on professionals to determine the demand for seasonal workers, implemented systems to select and retain the best workers, and used the minimum number of workers needed to get the work done in particular commodities and regions.

The Coastal Growers Association (CGA) provides an example of these win-win efficiencies for growers and workers. The CGA was founded in 1961 to harvest lemons in Ventura County, north of Los Angeles, and relied on professional managers to ensure that its members picked their lemons in a timely fashion. By raising wages and identifying and retaining the best pickers, the CGA reduced the number of pickers from 8,517 in 1965 to 1,292 in 1978 (see figure 2).

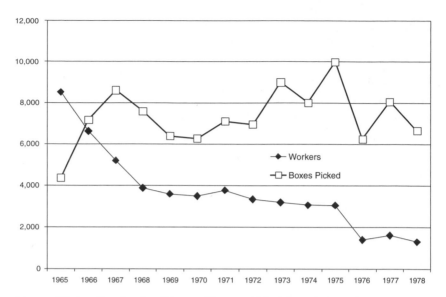

Figure 2 Workers Employed and Boxes of Lemons Picked (1000s), Coastal Growers Association, 1965–1978
Source: Mamer and Rosedale, 1980, table 3, 10.

Lemons are harvested by workers who climb ladders, clip ripe lemons with small scissors, and drop them into a canvas bag worn over the shoulder that weighs up to 70 pounds when full. The average hourly earnings of CGA pickers rose from $1.77 to $5.63 an hour between 1965 and 1978 (the minimum wage in 1978 was $2.65), and the number of hours worked per year rose from 151 to 609. Grower costs did not rise as much as worker earnings because of rising productivity: workers picked an average 3.4 boxes an hour in 1965 and 8.4 boxes an hour in 1978, so the wage costs of picking lemons rose from $0.53 a box in 1965 to $0.67 a box, far less than the rate of inflation (Mamer and Rosedale, 1980).

These efficiencies allowed the CGA to offer workers benefits that were rare in agriculture, including health insurance, paid vacations, and subsidized housing. Workers earned piece-rate wages, so their earnings reflected how fast they picked. However, worker productivity varied with factors beyond their control, including the height of the trees, the average size of the lemons being picked, and the yield. In a move rare in agriculture, consultants were hired to develop a "rate sheet" that adjusted the piece rates according to these factors.

The win-win benefits of applying modern human resource policies to seasonal farmworkers spread quickly, and most agribusinesses had a personnel manager and employee handbook by the early 1980s. Like the CGA, many were unionized in the late 1970s under California's unique Agricultural Labor Relations Act, in part because personel managers coming to agriculture from nonfarm firms were familiar with unions.[22] Cesar Chavez and the United Farm Workers Union (UFW) won significant wage and benefit increases for farmworkers, but in 1979 and 1982 called strikes that accelerated the demise of unions.

Many farm employers were unhappy with their experience under UFW contracts. The UFW was sometimes slow to deal with grievances that could slow farmwork, and often wanted to negotiate about issues that employers thought should be left to government, such as rules on pesticides. When the UFW asked for significant wage increases in the late 1970s and early 1980s, farm employers, aware that peso devaluations were increasing the availability of unauthorized workers, used labor contractors to break union-called strikes, including a strike at the CGA in 1982. Many of the contractors remained in business after the strikes ended, and some growers switched from associations such as the CGA to contractors. The associations went into a death spiral, since they could no longer spread their extra costs over a large number of boxes, and the CGA went out of business in 1986 (Lloyd, Martin, and Mamer, 1988).

The CGA experience demonstrated that modern personnel policies could be mutually beneficial for employers and seasonal workers, but only if there were no labor contractors hiring unauthorized workers and providing a cheaper alternative. Machines were also a threat to high-wage jobs done by hand on farms, especially during the 1960s, when the United States celebrated the accomplishments of the engineers who met the Sputnik challenge and put an American on the moon in 1969. In agriculture, engineers cooperated with biologists in a systems approach to mechanizing the harvesting of fruits and vegetables.

The systems approach to labor-saving farm mechanization had one of its most spectacular successes in processing tomatoes, which are turned into catsup, tomato paste, and other products. In the early 1960s, most of the workers who picked processing tomatoes were braceros.[23] Growers warned Congress that ending the Bracero Program would force the processing tomato industry to shrink or move to Mexico to find harvest workers.[24] However, plant scientists developed tomatoes that ripened uniformly, engineers developed machines to cut tomato vines and shake tomatoes from them, and processors added sorters to remove debris from mechanically harvested tomatoes. The processing tomato harvest was mechanized within five years, the industry expanded, and the prices of tomato products fell (see figure 3; Martin and Olmstead, 1985).[25]

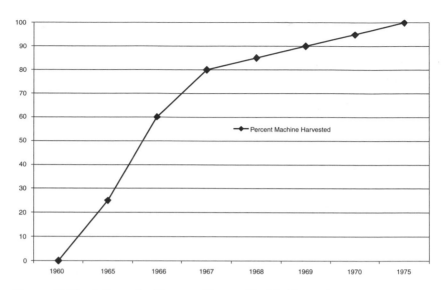

Figure 3 California Processing Tomatoes Harvested by Machine, 1960–1975
Source: Schmitz and Seckler, 1970; CGTA.

There was labor-saving mechanization in many other commodities during the late 1960s and 1970s, as farm wages rose faster than nonfarm wages. Forklifts and bulk bins became routine in fields and orchards, eliminating thousands of jobs that involved lifting 50- to 60-pound boxes of fruit and vegetables. Machines that grasped tree trunks and shook fruits and nuts into catching frames or onto the ground for pickup were developed, eliminating more jobs. Finally, improved seeds and chemicals eliminated the need for workers to thin growing plants and hoe weeds. Economists studying this wave of farm mechanization in 1970 predicted that within a decade only mechanically harvested fruits and vegetables would be grown in the United States (Cargill and Rossmiller, 1970).

The third response to the end of the Bracero Program was unionization. There had been efforts to organize farmworkers in the 1950s and early 1960s, but farmers were usually able to break strikes and get their crops picked by borrowing braceros from their neighbors. Unions complained that braceros were used illegally to break strikes, and the DOL generally agreed, but by the time the DOL made its decision, the harvest was over and farmers had avoided "labor troubles" for another year.

The union picture changed in 1965, when the National Farm Workers Association (NFWA) headed by Cesar Chavez joined a strike called by the Filipino-dominated Agricultural Workers Organizing Committee (AWOC), an affiliate of the American Federation of Labor-Congress of Industrial Organizations (AFL-CIO). Filipino grape pickers went on strike over the decision by California table grape growers to offer them lower wages than the growers were required to pay braceros. The growers used labor contractors to get their grapes picked, but Chavez quickly took control and tried a new tactic—a boycott of the wine and liquor sold by a conglomerate, Schenley Industries, that also grew table grapes. Sympathetic students and clergy picketed liquor stores during the Christmas season, and many Americans avoided Schenley products.

Chavez was a master publicist, attracting high-profile visitors to Delano, California, to call attention to the dispute over the grape workers' wages. For example, in March 1996, the U.S. Senate Subcommittee on Migratory Labor held a hearing in Delano, and Senator Robert Kennedy (D-NY) had a televised argument with the Kern County sheriff over the constitutional rights of Americans. The sheriff arrested UFW picketers because, he said, they were about to break the law. Kennedy countered that Chavez and the farmworkers had the right to picket and not be arrested until they actually broke laws. The publicity elicited sympathy for poor farmworkers confronting agribusiness that clearly had the support of local law enforcement.

In March 1966, the merged AWOC–NFWA, which soon became the United Farm Workers Union, marched 300 miles from Delano to Sacramento to publicize the grape dispute. During the march, Schenley recognized the UFW as bargaining agent for its workers and signed an agreement that raised wages 40 percent, from $1.25 to $1.75 an hour, well above the federal minimum wage of $1.25 in 1966.

The UFW then turned to DiGiorgio Fruit Corporation,[26] a longtime target of unions, which responded that its farmworkers were represented by the Teamsters. Chavez protested that there had not been an election to determine the preferences of the farmworkers; an election was not required since farmworkers were not covered by federal or state labor laws.[27] Eventually, the American Arbitration Association supervised an election at DiGiorgio, and the UFW and DiGiorgio signed an agreement in 1967.

The UFW organizing activities and conflicts with the Teamsters kept farmworkers and their disputes in the news during the late 1960s and 1970s. Churches, unions, students, and politicians boycotted table grapes, lettuce, and wine in support of the UFW, while growers complained that they were forced to sign contracts opposed by most of their workers. Most California growers were not affected directly by union activities, but many raised wages to discourage unionization.

This pattern of union avoidance by growers, competition between the UFW and the Teamsters to represent workers, and the extension of minimum wage and unemployment insurance protections to California farmworkers combined to raise farm wages sharply in the 1970s. Many farm labor reformers thought that the seasonal farm labor market would soon resemble the unionized construction labor market, offering higher than average wages to compensate for seasonality (Martin, 2003b, 70).

UNAUTHORIZED MIGRATION AND THE DEMISE OF UNIONS

The years between the end of the Bracero Program in 1964 and the Mexican economic crisis of 1982 were a golden era for farmworkers. During this period, farm wages rose faster than nonfarm wages, benefits for even seasonal workers were common, and unionized farmworkers often earned twice the minimum wage.

Unauthorized immigration brought this golden era to an end. During the late 1960s, farmers could obtain immigrant visas for Mexicans by issuing letters that offered seasonal jobs. Many growers asked ex-braceros to become immigrants, and many did, receiving immigration visas printed on green paper. There were at least 65,000 "green-card commuters" employed in U.S. agriculture in 1967 (London and Anderson, 1970, 10), and green cards were easy to forge or lend from one person to another.

Most U.S. farmworkers during the golden era were U.S. citizens, but there was also illegal immigration, and it increased after 1976, when the Mexican peso was devalued. Since there were no sanctions on U.S. employers who knowingly hired unauthorized workers, more farmers turned to labor contractors. Some green-card commuters became contractors and foremen who found it easy to recruit relatives and friends from their villages of origin to work in U.S. fields.

By the early 1980s, unauthorized workers were a quarter of California farmworkers, and they were deployed across commodities as would be predicted by the risk of losing perishable crops in the event of enforcement (Mines and Martin, 1986). Enforcement of immigration laws at the workplace usually involved the Border Patrol driving vans into fields and orchards and attempting to apprehend workers who tried to run away, which meant that farmers risked losing unauthorized workers and perhaps losing crops if they could not hire replacements immediately. Such people-chase enforcement produced a higher share of unauthorized workers in less-perishable oranges and lemons, up to 50 percent, than in more-perishable lettuce and strawberries, less than 20 percent (Mines and Martin, 1983).

The UFW, knowing that unauthorized workers were often used to break strikes, urged Congress to enact and enforce immigration laws. Stephanie Bower, UFW legislative director, testified in 1981: "We therefore concur with the AFL-CIO's position that imposing sanctions on employers who hire illegal aliens would be a good vehicle for controlling the hiring of illegal aliens, if the proposed legislation could be effectively enforced." Bower recommended a fine on employers of $1,500 per illegal worker hired per day, and added "we strongly urge that a large budget for staff and operations be allocated toward the enforcement" of sanctions.[28] The UFW also considered labor-saving mechanization a threat, and joined California Rural Legal Assistance to sue the University of California for using tax funds to develop labor-saving machines.[29]

The UFW was aware of the threats posed by rising illegal migration and mechanization, but ignored structural changes in agriculture that were reducing its bargaining power. Inflation and prices for farm commodities fell in the 1980s, prompting many of the conglomerates most vulnerable to union-led boycotts to sell their farming operations. As a result, the UFW lost contracts with drink maker Seven Up and oil companies such as Shell and Tenneco, and the farmers who took over this land often turned to labor contractors to obtain workers.

Most UFW efforts to help farmworkers during the 1980s urged consumers to boycott particular stores or commodities. In 1984, the UFW sent millions of letters to consumers in zip codes believed to include large numbers of UFW sympathizers, warning that the pesticides used on table grapes caused illnesses among farmworkers and their families and left residues that posed threats to consumers.[30] With grocery stores operating on thin profit margins, the UFW reasoned that if 5 to 10 percent of shoppers switched stores, they would drop grapes or stop promoting them, pressuring grape growers to recognize the UFW as a bargaining agent for their workers.

Chavez fasted to call attention to the boycott and was arrested several times while picketing stores in the Los Angeles area, but the UFW's "wrath of grapes" campaign did not result in new members or in contracts with growers. The campaign did contribute to the closure of a chain of stores targeting Hispanics,[31] but did not slow rising table grape consumption: per capita consumption of table grapes increased from 5.6 pounds per person in 1983–1984 to 8.2 pounds in 1999–2000 (the grape boycott officially ended on November 21, 2000).

When Cesar Chavez died in 1993, the UFW was a mere remnant of its former self, operating with a largely volunteer staff from a former sanitarium far from fields with most of the state's farmworkers. Chavez was nonetheless widely praised, hailed as the "Hispanic Martin Luther King," and awarded a posthumous Medal of Freedom in 1994, when President Clinton said: "All Americans have lost a great leader. . . . An inspiring fighter for the cause to which he dedicated his life. Cesar Chavez was an authentic hero to millions of people throughout the world. We can be proud of his enormous accomplishments and in the dignity and comfort he brought to the lives of so many of our country's least powerful and most dispossessed workers. He had a profound impact upon the people of the United States." Schools, streets, libraries, and parks around the United States have been named in honor of Chavez.

Arturo Rodriguez, Chavez's son-in-law, became UFW president in 1994 and vowed to revive the union's organizing efforts. The average seasonal worker remains in the U.S. farm labor force only 10 years, and many newcomers in the 1990s confused UFW leader Chavez with Mexican boxers who had the same name.[32] With Rodriguez at the helm, the UFW focused on the expanding strawberry industry, launching a "Five Cents for Fairness" campaign that asked growers to raise the piece rates they paid to pickers by $0.05 a pint. The result, according to the UFW, would be a doubling of worker wages but only a $0.05 increase in the price of strawberries at the supermarket.[33]

The UFW targeted the largest employer of strawberry pickers, Garguilo, a subsidiary of the agrichemical firm Monsanto. Under pressure from the UFW and its political allies, Monsanto sold Garguilo to pro-union investors who renamed it Coastal Berry and pledged to remain neutral during the UFW's efforts to organize its pickers. Many Coastal Berry pickers opposed the UFW and, in an election supervised by the state's Agricultural Labor Relations Board (ALRB) in July 1998, the rival Coastal Berry Farmworkers Committee (CBFWC) defeated the UFW in a 523–410 vote.

The UFW complained that irregularities marred the vote and demanded a second election, which the CBFWC won in May 1999. There was a third vote in June 1999, again won by the CBFWC. However, Coastal Berry had operations in both Northern and Southern California, and the votes were tallied separately. The UFW won a majority vote in Coastal Berry's Southern California operations, and the ALRB allowed the creation of two bargaining units, with Coastal Berry workers represented by the CBFWC in northern California and by the UFW in Southern California.

The Coastal Berry experience showed that despite several years and millions of dollars, it was very hard to organize farmworkers, many of whom were unauthorized and hoping to get nonfarm jobs as soon as possible. There was a slightly different lesson at Gallo of Sonoma, a subsidiary of the E.&J. Gallo Winery that employed about 300 workers.[34] The UFW won an election at Gallo of Sonoma in 1994, but Gallo resisted signing a first contract until 2000. This contract was not very favorable to the union, providing only a 2 percent wage increase, exactly the amount of union dues, and allowed Gallo to continue to obtain two-thirds of its farmworkers via labor contractors. The resulting worker dissatisfaction led to the UFW being decertified at Gallo of Sonoma in June 2007.[35]

The strawberry and Gallo campaigns demonstrate the difficulty of organizing and winning benefits for workers in the face of large-scale unauthorized migration. Many newcomer farmworkers are reluctant to risk voting for a union, especially when ex-farmworkers acting as labor consultants explain that unions take 2 percent of their earnings as dues, that unions can only ask growers for wage and benefit increases, and that employers do not have to agree to union demands. Newcomers who see farmwork as a first rung on the U.S. job ladder are often unwilling to make the sacrifices to support union demands.

The UFW may have more clout in the California legislature than in the fields. In 2002, the UFW called for mandatory mediation to reach first contracts with growers to avoid the Gallo of Sonoma problem, which was a six-year lag between the union winning an election and the first contract. The UFW had been reluctant to propose amendments to the Agricultural Labor Relations Act of 1975 (ALRA), fearing that opening the door to amending what is arguably the nation's most pro-union private-sector labor law could allow growers to offer amendments as well. However, frustration with late-1990s campaigns led the UFW to win enactment of a mandatory mediation amendment to the ALRA, ensuring that most newly organized farmworkers would have a first contract within eight months (Martin and Mason, 2003).[36]

During the 1960s and 1970s, the UFW often accused the Teamsters Union, which represented truck drivers and packinghouse workers, of signing "sweetheart agreements" with growers to keep the UFW from representing field-workers. This experience prompted Cesar Chavez to demand that the state's ALRA require secret ballot elections to determine if farmworkers wanted a union to represent them.

However, the UFW lost an election at table grape grower VBZ Grapes in September 2006, by a 425–793 vote despite getting about 70 percent of VBZ workers to sign union authorization cards. This election loss prompted the UFW to persuade the legislature to approve another amendment to the ALRA, SB 180, which would have allowed a union to be recognized as bargaining agent for workers without a secret-ballot election.[37] SB 180, approved by the legislature but vetoed by the governor, would have allowed farmworker unions to be recognized as the bargaining representative of a farm's workers without an election if a majority signed union authorization cards.[38]

The UFW has been reporting 5,000 to 6,000 members to the U.S. Department of Labor for the past decade.[39] In a bid to boost its membership, the UFW in 2006 signed a three-year agreement with Los Angeles-based Global Horizons, a labor contractor that was importing Thai and Vietnamese workers under the H-2A guest-worker program. Under the UFW-Global agreement, farmworkers brought into the United States by Global became UFW members. Global agreed to pay its H-2A workers 2 percent more than the required minimum wage to cover UFW dues.

Global proved to be a troublesome partner. Its farm labor contractor's license was revoked by the state of Washington for violations that included deducting state income tax from worker pay (Washington has no state income tax). Global went out of its way to avoid hiring U.S. workers in order to open up jobs for the Thais, in part because they paid up to $8,000 each for their U.S. jobs. By 2007, Global was the only U.S. employer barred by the Department of Labor from importing more H-2A workers because of repeated violations of program rules.

The UFW has been active in immigration reform, endorsing the Agricultural Job Opportunity, Benefits, and Security Act (AgJOBS) and cooperating with growers to persuade Congress to approve AgJOBS. Since the UFW can do little to organize and win wage and benefit increases when half of U.S. farmworkers are unauthorized, helping farmworkers to become legal immigrants is seen as the best way to empower them and to win their loyalty. The provisions of AgJOBS and its likely effects on farmers, workers, and rural communities are discussed in Chapter 10.

Part Two The Changing Face
of Rural America

In 1900, when the U.S. population was 76 million, most Americans were farmers. Many of the millions of immigrants pouring into the United States via Ellis Island from eastern and southern Europe had been farmers, but most found factory and service jobs in U.S. cities. As U.S. farms became fewer and larger during the 1920s, farm families joined these immigrants in the cities, and shared with them an interest in higher factory wages and better schools for their children.

Today, fewer than 2 percent of Americans live on farms. Most farmers are older white men born in the United States, while most hired farmworkers are young men born in Mexico. This difference in the origins of farm employers and their employees is just one of many between immigration patterns at the beginning of the twentieth and twenty-first centuries. A century ago, immigrants were more similar to the native-born population in the sense that both had little education, while immigrants today are at the extremes of the education ladder—they are either more likely than U.S.-born adults to have an advanced degree or more likely to have less than a ninth-grade education. Urban areas receive both well-educated and poorly educated immigrants, while rural areas receive primarily those with little education.

The following three chapters examine the role of immigrant workers in harvesting California's labor-intensive fruit and vegetable crops; in the Florida sugarcane, citrus, and tomato industries; and in meatpacking and poultry processing, the largest manufacturing industry in rural America. Each chapter tells an important story of how agriculture encourages a type of revolving-door migration: newcomers arrive to fill seasonal farm jobs, but eventually abandon those jobs for year-round farm or nonfarm jobs, thus creating a vacuum that draws even needier migrants into the United States to replace them.

In California, many farmers stopped offering housing to seasonal workers to eliminate the cost and a source of conflict with unions and regulators. As a result, many seasonal workers settled with their families in towns and cities in agricultural areas, giving some areas boomtown population growth rates despite double-digit unemployment rates and widespread poverty. Some cities in agricultural areas became "overgrown labor camps" with per capita incomes equal to the per capita income of Mexico. The combination of poverty (represented by poor residents) amid the prosperity (represented by rising farm sales) highlights the central question of this book—does the United States risk creating a rural underclass in order to get a seasonal farm workforce?

Chapter 4 explores the employment of Caribbean guest workers in the Florida sugarcane industry. For a half century between the 1940s and 1990s, Florida cane growers insisted that they could not find U.S. workers to cut cane and could not mechanize the cane harvest because the soil would not support the weight of harvesting machines. Every year, more than 10,000 workers from Jamaica and other Caribbean islands came to Florida to hand cut sugarcane. Lawsuits alleging that the cane cutters were underpaid led to rapid harvest mechanization in the early 1990s, casting doubt on grower assertions "that there is no alternative to migrants."

Meatpacking underwent significant changes in the 1980s. Unions that won wages for workers in urban slaughterhouses equivalent to those paid to autoworkers encouraged some slaughterhouses to move to rural areas. Better transportation and refrigeration technologies allowed the "disassembly lines" to move closer to the animals they processed, and lower wages in these rural plants prompted more of the preparation of meat to shift from retail stores to slaughterhouses. Rural plants soon ran out of local workers, and many began to recruit refugees who had resettled in the United States and workers in areas with high unemployment, especially in Mexico-U.S. border areas. These newcomers soon changed the face of small towns with meat and poultry processing plants, putting them on the road to an uncertain future.

Chapter 3 California
Fruits and Vegetables

California has been the nation's leading farm state since 1950, primarily because its farms produce high-value fruit and nut, vegetable and melon, and horticultural specialty (FVH) crops such as flowers and mushrooms. California's farm sales were $32 billion in 2005, double those of Texas, the number two farm state.[1] California produces more than 350 crops, including half of the FVH commodities grown in the United States. Many are labor intensive, meaning that wages and benefits account for a third or more of farm production costs.

Over the past half century, FVH commodities have almost doubled as a share of California farm sales. The sharpest increase was in sales of horticultural specialties such as nursery products, flowers, and mushrooms—they were 3 percent of the state's farm sales in 1955 and 11 percent in 2005. Fruits and nuts were second among expanding commodities, almost doubling from 17 percent of farm sales in 1955 to 33 percent in 2005. Vegetables and melons remained at about 20 percent of farm sales over this period, but field crops such as cotton, wheat, and sugar beets saw their share of farm sales fall sharply, from 28 to 10 percent. The share of livestock commodities such as cattle, dairy, and poultry also dipped, from 33 to 27 percent.

The expansion of FVH production stabilized the employment of hired workers despite significant labor-saving mechanization. Jobs eliminated in cotton and sugar beet fields by precision planters, herbicides to control weeds, and harvesting machines were replaced by additional jobs picking strawberries, tree fruits, and broccoli. However, instead of living in barracks on the farms where they work, as in the 1950s and 1960s, most seasonal workers today live in cities and towns in agricultural areas and commute to farm jobs. Most farmworkers were born in Mexico, so the face of agricultural California is literally changing with immigration (see figure 4).

Several groups have a keen interest in the farmworkers in California's agricultural heartland: farmers whose demand for seasonal workers stimulates

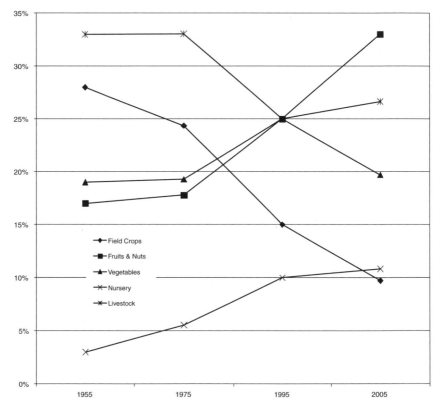

Figure 4 California Farm Sales by Commodity, 1955–2005
Source: Johnston, 2003, 41; and CDFA.

immigration; mayors, teachers, and police who act as bridges between new-comers and established residents; and migrants and their children who seek upward mobility in the United States. The profiles in this chapter explore immigration and integration in three agricultural valleys named for the rivers that run through them—San Joaquin, Salinas, and Napa—and then examine the changing face of agricultural California in the Imperial Valley in the southeastern corner of the state.

We begin with an analysis of the interrelationships between immigration and seasonal farm jobs, which shows that adding farm jobs can increase both immigration and poverty. The reason for this counterintuitive result is simple: most seasonal farmworkers have incomes below the poverty level. Thus, adding more seasonal farm jobs adds to the number of poor people because the average seasonal farmworker's earnings are under the poverty line, which was $10,210 for an individual and $20,650 for a family of four in 2007.

FARM JOBS, IMMIGRATION, AND POVERTY

During the 1960s, the end of the Bracero Program put upward pressure on farm wages, enabling workers such as those employed at Coastal Growers to achieve a lower-middle-class lifestyle by earning more than twice the minimum wage harvesting lemons. Thus, having more farm jobs such as those offered by Coastal Growers was associated with less poverty, fulfilling the age-old American promise of opportunity, as people worked their way out of poverty.

Today, an increase in the number of seasonal farm jobs is associated with more rather than fewer poor residents, primarily because the average earnings of seasonal farmworkers are consistently below the poverty line. This means that planting more strawberries and depending on newcomers from abroad to harvest them increases the number of poor people in agricultural areas.

Farmers do not plant oranges and strawberries unless they believe there will be workers available to harvest them, creating a circular relationship between farm jobs, immigration, and poverty. Farmers create farm jobs, the workers who fill these jobs are immigrants with low earnings, and the result can be poverty amid prosperity: rising farm sales, more immigrant farmworkers, and more poor people.

We examined the linkages between farm jobs, immigration, and poverty with census data and found that an additional 100 farm jobs were associated with an average 34-person increase in the foreign-born population across census tracts in agricultural areas (Martin and Taylor, 2003). An increase in the foreign-born population, in turn, increased farm employment slightly.[2] During the 1980s, a 100-person increase in the farm workforce was associated with a 57-person *decrease* in the number of people living in impoverished households in California's agricultural towns, suggesting that immigrant farmworkers could work themselves out of poverty. By the 1990s, however, a 100-person increase in farm employment was associated with an 85-person *increase* in the number of poor people, reflecting falling real farm wages and fewer hours of work.

These findings, based on the relationships between farm jobs, immigration, and poverty in 66 California cities in 1990 and 2000, enable us to answer the question: Given immigration, farm employment, and poverty levels in these cities in 1990, what explains the poverty observed in these towns in 2000? The key dependent variables are farm labor demand, the farm share of employment in each community in 2000, the foreign-born population, the share of foreign-born persons in the town, and poverty—the share of people in households with incomes below the poverty level.[3] We assumed that farm employment depends on the availability of foreign-born workers.[4] The foreign-born share of the population is a proxy or indicator of the supply of immigrant labor available to farms, and we expect to find that the number of farm jobs is a key variable explaining the foreign-born share of a city's population. We hypothesized that more farm jobs are associated with more poor residents, since most offer earnings below the poverty level. Since immigration in response to employment can influence poverty independently because most immigrants in agricultural areas are poor, we included the foreign-born share of the population as an explanatory variable in the poverty equation.

Each of the equations in the model includes, as an explanatory variable, the level of the dependent variable in the previous census.[5] These lagged variables are largely exogenous, determined at least 10 years earlier, and the unobserved factors shaping them are likely to be similar in 1990 and 2000. However, these lagged explanatory variables turn out to be highly significant, suggesting a path dependency that may make it hard for an area to change its economy and labor market.

The average population of the 66 farmworker cities was 7,784 in 2000, including a third of residents who were born abroad. The 2000 census reported that 27 percent of residents in these 66 cities lived in poor households and 24 percent were employed in agriculture. Between 1990 and 2000, the foreign-born share of residents in these California cities rose between 30 percent and 36 percent (California's population rose 14 percent in the 1990s), and the share of workers employed in agriculture decreased from 28 percent to 24 percent.[6]

Poverty fell slightly, from 28 to 27 percent of the cities' residents between 1990 and 2000.

We found a circular relationship between farm employment, immigration, and poverty. A one-percentage-point increase in the share of a city's workforce employed in agriculture was associated with a 0.51 percent increase in the share of foreign-born residents, while a 1 percent increase in the share of residents who were foreign-born was associated with a 0.85 percent increase in the share of workforce employed in agriculture. Meanwhile, a 1 percent increase in the share of the workforce in farm jobs, other things equal, increased the share of the population in poverty by 0.39 percent.[7]

Most of the cities in our sample were in the San Joaquin Valley, the nation's Fruit Bowl. It appears that these cities suffer from a vicious circle between farm employment, immigration, and poverty. As FVH production expands, more jobs are created for seasonal farmworkers, most of whom have incomes below poverty level. The optimistic scenario is that this vicious circle can be converted into a virtuous circle in which agricultural expansion is associated with less poverty by raising worker productivity and thus wages and incomes. The pessimistic scenario is that, as labor-intensive agriculture continues to expand, rural poverty will be transferred from Mexico and Central America as farmers seek seasonal workers, setting the stage for socioeconomic problems in the future.

SAN JOAQUIN: THE FRUIT BOWL

The eight-county San Joaquin Valley (SJV), anchored by the city of Fresno and drained by the San Joaquin River, has 3.5 million residents, almost a tenth of California's people. If the San Joaquin Valley were a state, it would rank first in farm sales and 48th in per capita income, which means that per capita income in the San Joaquin Valley is lower than in the 68-county Central Appalachia region (Cowan, 2005).[8] Agriculture provides about 20 percent of the San Joaquin Valley's jobs, and the valley's unemployment rate is typically twice the statewide rate, reflecting the seasonality of farming.

The San Joaquin Valley is an agricultural powerhouse, producing milk and cotton and most U.S. wine, raisin, and table grapes; most fresh oranges and melons; most tree fruits such as plums, peaches, and nectarines; and most tree nuts such as almonds, pistachios, and walnuts. At least a quarter of this agricultural bounty is exported to destinations outside the United States.

Fresno is the nation's leading farm county, reporting farm sales of almost $5 billion in 2006, more than all but a handful of states.[9] Almost half of Fresno

County's farm sales are fruits and nuts, including grapes, almonds, peaches, and nectarines. There has long been poverty in America's Fruit Bowl, and the census reported that 20 percent of Fresno County's residents had incomes below the poverty line in 1999. Poverty persisted even as agriculture and the nonfarm economy expanded, as needier newcomers replaced those who moved out of seasonal farmwork.

Poverty in the San Joaquin Valley Fruit Bowl is most severe among the newcomers arriving from rural Mexico and Central America, most of whom have very little education. The census reported that 30 percent of San Joaquin Valley adults (those 25 and older) did not have a high school diploma in 2000, compared to 20 percent of all California residents. Half of the K–12 students in the San Joaquin Valley are Hispanic, and two-thirds of the K–12 students in key farming counties such as Fresno, Tulare, and Kern receive free or reduced-priced school meals.

Six of the 10 poorest cities in the state are in Fresno County, and most are places that house farmworkers. An average 46,000 of the 278,000 private-sector workers employed in Fresno County worked for wages on area farms in 2007, 17 percent, but farmers paid only 10 percent of the county's $8.3 billion in private-sector workers' wages.[10] About 40 percent of average farm employment was with labor contractors, who paid workers an average $260 a week in 2005, well below the $350 average in Fresno County agriculture and the $575 for all Fresno County private-sector workers.[11]

Unemployment mirrors farm employment. When farm employment is highest in the summer months, Fresno County's unemployment rate is lowest; it dipped below 7 percent in August–September 2006, for example. And, when farm employment reaches its low for the year in the winter months, Fresno County's unemployment rate approaches 10 percent, such as between January and March 2006 (see figure 5).

Parlier is one of 15 cities in Fresno County, and its large farmworker population helps to explain its extreme employment and unemployment patterns. When seasonal employment peaks during the summer months, Parlier's unemployment rate dips below 20 percent, but the rate tops 25 percent during the winter months. The census reported that Parlier had 11,000 residents in 2000, and that 52 percent of adults did not finish ninth grade, 66 percent did not finish high school, and only 3 percent had college degrees. Most of Parlier's residents speak Spanish: 82 percent of those older than 5 years spoke Spanish at home, explaining why a visit to Parlier can seem like a trip to a Mexican city.

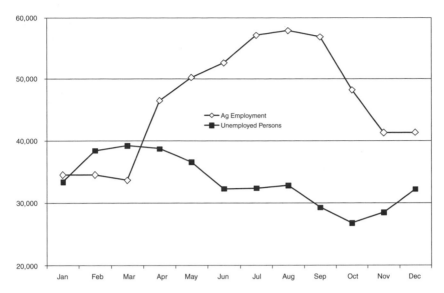

Figure 5 Fresno County: Agricultural Employment 2005, Unemployed Persons 2006
Source: LMID.

Parlier's per capita income was $7,100 in 1999, a third of the U.S. and state average but more than the per capita gross national income of Mexico, which was $4,400.[12] Parlier's job pyramid is very steep, offering many seasonal jobs in the fields and packinghouses, but few ladders to jobs that would support a middle-class lifestyle.

Farmworkers are often associated with hard work, but a lower than average share of Parlier residents age 16 and older were in the labor force. Parlier's labor force participation rate was 62 percent in April 2000, about the same as the California rate but below the U.S. rate of 64 percent. However, of the 4,900 Parlier residents who worked in 1999, a third worked less than 26 weeks. Most Parlier residents are poor, but the receipt of welfare benefits is uneven, since many immigrant residents are not eligible for benefits.[13]

It is sometimes argued that immigrants who obtain political power will make the changes necessary to ensure that immigrants and their children succeed. Hispanics were first elected to Parlier city government offices in 1972, and made expanding the supply of affordable housing their top priority. They were very successful in obtaining government housing assistance, and a sixth of Parlier's residents received some form of housing subsidy in 1989–1990, making it one of the largest per capita users of U.S. Department of Agriculture (USDA) subsidies for rural housing and infrastructure (Kissam, 1998). Parlier welcomed developers, some of whom offered new homes for less than $100,000 and "executive homes" that started at $180,000 in 2004.[14] The availability of affordable housing allowed farmworkers to pool their savings to buy homes, and allowed their children who found nonfarm jobs to live in Parlier and commute to the nearby cities of Fresno and Visalia, each about 20 miles away.

Some settled residents provided services such as housing and transportation to newly arrived farmworkers. Parlier has flexible housing regulations, permitting garage conversions to house family members but not unrelated renters, a rule enforced loosely by the local government (Kissam, 1998).[15] So-called backhouses range from converted garages to storage sheds, and they may house half of the 4,000 to 5,000 migrants who arrive each summer to harvest tree fruits such as peaches and raisin grapes. In the late 1990s, these migrants, often unauthorized, paid $30 to $40 a week to live in informal housing with six to eight others. They also paid for food and rides to work, creating a farmworker service economy that operated on a cash basis and was equivalent to 10 to 20 percent of the city's economic output.

Parlier has one of the largest publicly funded migrant farmworker housing centers in the United States. Residents of the 130 two- and three-bedroom units must be legal U.S. residents with a usual residence at least 50 miles from the center and earn most of their income from farmwork or food processing.[16] More than 80 percent of the center's residents are migrants from south Texas, and some are associated with the farmworker service economy, acting as foremen or *raiteros* (those who drive workers to the fields in their vans for $4 to $5 a day); others are employed as cannery and packinghouse workers. As with other migrant housing centers, the Parlier center is filled soon after it opens in April, as returning residents receive priority to move in and take advantage of no-cost child care provided by Migrant Head Start and low-cost health-care services at a nearby clinic.

Parlier's political leadership has changed several times, and new leaders often try a different path to economic development. The affordable housing leaders were voted out in 2000, after newly elected leaders accused the incumbents of pursuing an affordable housing policy in order to maximize patients for the federally funded United Health Center clinic that several were involved with. The newly elected leaders created an industrial park on the edge of the city, had it designated an enterprise zone so that new businesses could receive tax credits for each local resident hired, and hired consultants who issued a $7 million bond to develop the infrastructure for new firms. It is not yet certain that this new development policy will transform Parlier, but it is clear that the change of direction was made by the relatively few voters. There were 2,800 registered voters in Parlier in 2001, a quarter of its residents, and fewer than half typically vote in elections.

Parlier's largest single employer is the local school system, employing one in eight local workers. Student performance lags; more than 40 percent of teens do not finish high school and those who stay in school have some of the lowest test scores in the state.[17] Virtually all students qualify for free meals, and two-thirds are classified as English learners. Even though spending per pupil is above the state average, many teachers say resources are insufficient to prepare students who do not speak English for good U.S. jobs.

Local youth know what they do not want to do—work in the fields—but they are vague about their interests. There is little interaction between Parlier schools and a nearby agricultural research station that employs several hundred professionals and technicians to develop improved crops.[18] Instead, a teacher takes some of the best students on an annual college recruitment trip that usually leads to several going to Ivy League schools, while other high school graduates often attend local community colleges. Whether they graduate or not, most of those who pass through the local high school reject careers in agriculture, associating the dominant local industry with the hard work and low wages of their parents and relatives.

Parlier raises a host of questions about immigration and integration. What happens to immigrant farmworkers when they leave seasonal jobs in the fields? What does the future hold for their children who attend low-performance schools and shun their parents' jobs? Will ex-farmworkers wind up in the farmworker service economy, dependent like farmers on a continued influx of newcomers, or will they find upward mobility in the local construction industry or the city's new industrial park? Most of Parlier's children who leave for continuing education do not return, but will the children who remain be forced to move to larger cities to find nonfarm jobs that offer higher incomes?

Parlier is not the only place in which the interactions of farm jobs, immigration, and poverty are visible. Nearby farmworker cities also have growing populations despite double-digit unemployment rates, few jobs that offer wages sufficient to support middle-class lifestyles, and economic development plans that depend on tax breaks or prisons. One such city is Huron, described as "knife-fight city" because of the evening activities of some of the migrants who descend every spring and fall to cut heads of lettuce for six weeks. Many residents rent out bedrooms and garages to lettuce harvesters, creating a seasonal farmworker service economy. [19]

Huron's 5,800 residents are served by six bars, reportedly five gangs and a fa-
mous drug alley (Street, 2000). Unemployment averages more than 15 percent,
and is likely to rise as irrigated farmland is taken out of production because of
insufficient water and problems draining excess irrigation water from nearby
property.[20] Huron's economic development strategy is based on attracting prisons, and the city received a $3.4 million grant in 1999 to upgrade its water
treatment plant to bolster its bid for federal, state, and private prisons.[21]

Orange Cove is another farmworker city in Fresno County, with 10,000
residents nestled against the western side the Sierra Mountains in the state's
Orange Belt. Unemployment averages 30 percent, and more than 40 percent
of residents have incomes below poverty level. The city has no traffic signals,
movie theaters, or major retailers, but the long-time mayor was extraordinar-
ily successful in obtaining federal and state aid to spur economic development, taking credit for attracting $63 million in federal and state grants be-
tween 2001 and 2005 (the city has a budget of $16 million a year). A handful
of voters determine the outcome of city elections. Orange Cove had 1,700
registered voters in November 2006, and only 851 cast ballots.

The economic development challenges in Parlier, Huron, Orange Cove, and
other farmworker cities echo throughout Fresno County, which had more
than 900,000 residents in 2006. The county's population is young, with a median age of 30 (the U.S. median age is 36), and is almost half Hispanic. At least
30 percent of adults did not graduate from high school, and less than 20 percent have college degrees. More than 20 percent of Fresno County residents
have incomes below the poverty line, including a third of the children under
age five. A quarter of Fresno County residents receive benefits from at least one
of the three major social programs—CalWORKS (the California version of
Temporary Assistance to Needy Families), Food Stamps, and Medi-Cal (California's version of Medicaid)[22]—explaining why almost half of the $962 mil-
lion in county government expenditures in 2003 went for public assistance.[23]

Fresno County leaders want to foster economic development that protects
agriculture while creating nonfarm jobs with wages high enough to support
middle-class lifestyles. Governor Arnold Schwarzenegger summarized the
plan: "The San Joaquin Valley already is the number-one agricultural area in
the world, but we can diversify the economy and make it even stronger."[24]
The county's so-called 30-30 Initiative, unveiled in September 2003, aimed to
add 30,000 jobs paying at least $30,000 a year in construction, distribution,
health care, back office information processing, manufacturing, tourism, and
water technology over five years.[25]

The 30-30 Initiative missed its goal, in part because so few San Joaquin Valley adults have high school diplomas. There are plenty of seasonal farmworkers, but few workers attractive to employers offering jobs paying $30,000 a year.[26] Farmworkers generated about 35 percent of the 90,000 unemployment insurance claims in Fresno County in 2002, and Hispanics, who dominate the farm workforce, accounted for 70 percent of the unemployment insurance (UI) claims; 60 percent of those applying for UI benefits do not have high school diplomas.

Attracting new businesses that offer high wages is challenging because of the characteristics of the workforce and because of the region's poor air quality. The five U.S. cities with the worst air quality, as measured by one-hour peak pollution levels, are Los Angeles, Fresno, Bakersfield, Visalia-Tulare, and Houston. However, if air pollution is measured over eight-hour periods, the San Joaquin Valley has the nation's worst air quality, with September the worst month. One consequence is that a sixth of Fresno County children suffer from asthma, the highest rate in California.

During the 1930s, Dust Bowl farmers moved from the Midwest to California to begin anew. In an ironic reversal, several San Joaquin Valley governments now offer payments to poor people receiving welfare assistance who leave, often for the Midwest. The More Opportunity for Viable Employment (MOVE) program paid more than 1,000 families receiving welfare assistance to move to areas with jobs by 2004 (Johnson and Hayes, 2004, 76). In exchange for payments of $1,000 to $3,000, these recipients agree not to apply for aid for at least 180 days.

In 2003 Fresno County spent about the same amount to move people out of the county as it spent on economic development—$600,000. The head of Fresno County's Economic Development Corporation suggested that outmigration was more promising than economic development: "Unemployment gets resolved by people moving out of the area. . . . We'll push them out."[27] However, if newcomers continue to arrive to fill seasonal farm jobs for a decade or less, and their children educated in the United States seek welfare assistance rather than following their parents into the fields, the nation's Fruit Bowl may become a port of entry for immigrants today and domestic migrants tomorrow.

SALINAS: THE SALAD BOWL

The Salinas Valley in Monterey County is the nation's Salad Bowl, producing most of lettuce and other leafy green vegetables consumed in the United States. John Steinbeck, the only person to win both the Nobel and Pulitzer

Prizes for literature, worked in Salinas Valley sugar beet fields as a teenager before moving to the coastal city of Carmel. Some of his writings reflect his youthful experience as a farmworker, as in *East of Eden* (1952), when he described the Salinas Valley as "a long narrow swale between two ranges of mountains and the Salinas River twists up the center until it falls at last into the Monterey Bay."

Most Salinas Valley vegetable growers are agribusinesses with farm and nonfarm divisions that grow, harvest, pack, and market fresh vegetables. These firms have a history of innovation, including developing systems to cool lettuce in vacuum tubes,[28] package fresh salads in bags that are refrigerated,[29] and transplant seedlings to speed up production and enable two or three harvests a year. Salinas Valley growers move production around the state and to nearby Arizona to supply fresh vegetables year-round.

As some of the largest and most profitable agribusinesses, Salinas Valley farms were leaders in introducing modern personnel management. By the 1970s, most developed company handbooks that laid out work rules and trained supervisors to treat workers fairly. Many Salinas Valley farms screened new hires to ensure that they were authorized to work in the United States before being required to do so by the Immigration Reform and Control Act of 1986, and some offered unemployment insurance benefits to their workers before the state required UI coverage in 1978. Under pressure from both the United Farm Workers (UFW) and Teamsters unions, Salinas Valley farmworker wages reached twice the minimum wage by 1980, and most seasonal farmworkers received employer-paid health insurance and other benefits.

However, a combination of illegal migration and declining union influence soon changed the Salinas Valley farm labor market. Wages fell toward the minimum in the 1980s, and fringe benefits disappeared as the conglomerates with brand names that made them vulnerable to consumer boycotts went out of business. Remaining farms with brand names sometimes bought vegetables from independent growers that were grown to their specifications, meaning that the brand name firm hired no farmworkers. Today, most seasonal farmwork in the Salinas Valley is done by workers brought to farms by a variety of middlemen such as labor contractors and custom harvesters.[30]

According to the census, 47 percent of Monterey County's 402,000 residents were Latino in 2000.[31] Since many were recent immigrants from Mexico, 40 percent of county residents spoke Spanish at home. However, Monterey County adults, when arrayed by their level of schooling, have the hourglass- or barbell-shaped characteristic of U.S. immigrants elsewhere—large and growing groups of residents at the extremes of the education ladder, with a college degree and without a high school diploma.[32] This educational distribution results from Monterey County being adjacent to Silicon Valley, so its residents include professionals seeking lower-cost housing and immigrant farmworkers seeking jobs.

Almost 40 percent of Monterey County residents—151,000 people—lived in the city of Salinas in 2000. The importance of farmworkers is reflected in the fact that Salinas had the highest ratio of males to females among major U.S. cities—114 to 100, respectively, in the 2000 census. Housing in Salinas is relatively expensive, which leads to severe overcrowding, especially in the eastern part of the city, where the census counted seven or more persons in a third of the typical one- and two-bedroom housing units. Salinas was ranked the least affordable U.S. city in 2006, as measured by the percentage of median income needed to finance the purchase of a median-priced home,[33] helping to explain why the average number of persons per household rose from 3.4 in 1990 to 3.6 in 2000.[34]

Farming has maintained its share of county employment, averaging 22 percent of the county's employment since 1985, and farm services (farmworkers employed by custom harvesters and labor contractors) accounting for 56 percent of Monterey County's farm employment.[35] These data, from reports that employers file with the California Employment Development Department when they pay unemployment insurance taxes on the earnings of their workers, show that farm employment rose in step with nonfarm employment in the county (see table 4).

What would happen if farmworker wages once again rose to twice the minimum wage, as they did in the early 1980s? California's minimum wage was $8 an hour in 2008, and a doubling of farm wages would likely spur mechanization. There are machines that would likely replace many hand harvesters if wages rose sharply, such as a machine that cuts heads of lettuce and eliminates the wrapper leaves as it travels a mile an hour. The machine (with nine workers) can harvest 15,000 heads or 30,000 pounds of lettuce an hour that is destined to be chopped and bagged at that rate, about the same as a crew of 35 workers harvesting by hand.[36] As more uniformly ripening lettuce varieties are developed, and if wages rise significantly, the harvesting machine would likely be adopted quickly. Lettuce imports are rising, but were less than two percent of U.S. consumption in 2006.

It may be harder to develop a labor-saving machine to harvest strawberries, one of the fastest-growing crops in the area. The United States is the world's

Table 4 Average Annual Employment, California and Monterey County, 1985–2000

Monterey	1985	1990	1995	2000	1985–2000	1995–2000
Employment All Industries	122,800	138,900	141,200	166,400	36%	18%
Farm Employment	24,200	28,500	31,900	36,900	52%	16%
Farm Share	20%	21%	23%	22%		
Farm Production			13,700	16,400	20%	
Farm Services			18,200	20,500	13%	
California						
Employment All Industries	11,105,200	12,863,400	12,795,700	14,896,600	34%	16%
Farm Employment	335,400	363,600	373,500	408,500	22%	9%
Farm Share	3%	3%	3%	3%		
Farm Production	232,700	218,200	228,400	228,600	−2%	0%
Farm Services	102,700	123,800	145,100	179,900	75%	24%

Source: LMID.

Notes: Monterey County had farm sales of $3.5 billion in 2006, including $2.4 billion or two-thirds from the sale of vegetables. Fruit and nut sales were $700 million and nursery crops $340 million, making the value of labor-intensive crops 98 percent of the county's farm sales. The most valuable crops were leaf lettuce worth $630 million, head lettuce worth $450 million, and strawberries worth $440 million. Monterey County agricultural commissioner reports are available at: www.co.monterey.ca.us/ag/archived_reports.htm.

leading producer of strawberries (China is number two, but consumes most of the strawberries it producers, while number three Spain is the leading exporter of fresh strawberries). California produces 85 percent of U.S. strawberries, and the value of California strawberries doubled from less than $600 million in 1995 to $1.2 billion in 2006.

Each of the state's 36,000 acres (an acre is about the size of a football field) produces 30 tons of berries a year; the fields are picked up to 10 times a season by workers who wheel 12-pint trays with plastic containers between two raised rows, picking from both. A rule of thumb is that one harvester is needed for each acre of strawberries.

Strawberries are typically grown by independent growers under contract to cooling and marketing companies such as Driscoll Strawberry Associates, Naturipe Farms, and Well-Pict. These firms usually provide growers, more than half of whom are Hispanic, with plants and boxes; the growers are responsible for growing and harvesting the berries and delivering them to the firm with which they have a contract. The marketer receives the berries and deducts fees for everything from plants and fertilizer to cooling and marketing costs. The growers are technically independent businesses, responsible for finding employees to harvest their berries, although some have alleged that the marketers with whom they sign contracts exercise enough control over how the berries are grown and harvested to make the growers in effect employees of the marketers (Wells, 2000; Manion, 2001).[37]

As with most other farm commodities, farmers receive a small fraction of the retail price of strawberries, even though the berries are picked directly into the plastic clamshells in which they are sold. In the mid-1990s, farmers received about $0.50 per pound or $0.37 per 12-ounce pint of strawberries, while consumers paid about $1.13 per pint, making the farm share of the average retail price 33 percent. With labor a third of farmers' costs, the price of each pint includes about $0.12 of farmworker wages and benefits, 11 percent of the retail price.

The fact that strawberry production expanded rapidly in an area that had once been a UFW stronghold was undoubtedly a factor in the UFW's Five Cents for Fairness campaign. Charging that strawberries were *La Fruta del Diablo* (the fruit of the devil) because workers had to bend most of the day, the UFW demanded that growers pay workers $0.05 more per pint box, doubling their wages but adding only $0.05 to the retail price.[38] Despite extensive support from the American Federation of Labor and Congress of Industrial Organizations (AFL-CIO), the UFW wound up representing only the workers employed by two of the 600-plus growers in the state, Coastal Berry (bought by Dole Food Company in 2004) and Swanton Berry.[39]

The Salinas Valley, which stretches 60 miles from north to south, produces a cornucopia of fresh vegetables, from artichokes and broccoli to lettuce and zucchini. During the 1970s, the Salinas Valley farm labor market was transformed in ways that seemed to encourage farmworkers to view seasonal farm jobs as careers—workers earned some of the highest farm wages when they worked, and they received maximum unemployment insurance benefits during the off-season. In addition, most seasonal workers were eligible for health insurance, paid vacations, and other benefits, prompting many Salinas Valley farmworkers to say they would continue doing farmwork as long as they could.

However, most of these aspiring career farmworkers did not remain in the farm labor market. A combination of rising illegal migration and declining union clout meant that the construction-style farm labor market, high wages when work was available and unemployment insurance when it was not, soon disappeared. Instead, labor contractors began to match more farmworkers with jobs, and the Salinas Valley wage and benefit premium disappeared. Today, the children of Salinas's farmworkers avoid following their parents into the fields, meaning that the Salad Bowl, like the Fruit Bowl, depends on a continued influx of newcomers to harvest its crops.

NAPA: THE WINE VALLEY

The Napa Valley, America's Eden, is 5 miles wide and 30 miles long, but the wine from its 40,000 acres of wine grapes make it perhaps the best known of California's 58 counties. The Napa Valley attracts 5 million visitors a year to sample its wine, making it a leader in agri-tourism. Most of Napa's 400 wineries sell much of their wine to visitors and via wine clubs.

There has been commercial production of wine grapes in California since the 1830s, before California became a state. Charles Krug is credited with establishing Napa Valley's first commercial winery in 1861, but phylloxera, aphidlike insects that feed on the roots of grapevines, almost wiped out Napa's wine industry in the 1870s. Prohibition between 1920 and 1933 limited wine production to the handful of wineries that produced sacramental wines. California was known for producing low-quality wine until Robert Mondavi broke away from his family's Charles Krug winery to launch Napa's first new large-scale winery since Prohibition in the mid-1960s.

Napa Valley wines drew international attention on May 24, 1976, when French experts in a blind tasting in Paris ranked Napa's Stag's Leap Cabernet and Napa's Chateau Montelena Chardonnay as the world's best red and white wines. Americans interested in food and wine began to drink more California wines, and consumption of especially red wine rose after the November 1991 CBS News program *60 Minutes* explored the French paradox that there is less heart disease in France than in the United States despite the high-fat French diet.

Napa County produces only 5 percent of the state's wine, and uses a relatively large number of farmworkers to produce this premium wine. Many Napa farmworkers are employed almost year-round—pruning vines in the winter, thinning the growing clusters of grapes in the spring, and removing leaves so that the sun can reach ripening bunches of grapes in the summer. Napa grapes command premium prices, an average $3,000 a ton in 2006, which made the value of the 2.7 pounds of Napa grapes crushed to make a typical 750 ml bottle $4, four times the statewide average.[40]

Grapevines growing out of tubes are trained to grow on cordon wires; most varieties begin producing bunches of grapes by the second year.[41] Pruning is done between December and February to remove last season's cane growth, followed by cordon shoot removal, suckering, thinning, moving wires, and leaf removal. Hand harvesting begins in late August, when crews of 10 to 20 workers cut bunches of grapes, drop them into plastic tubs that weigh 50 to 60 pounds when full, and dump the tubs into gondolas that hold two tons of grapes.

Hand harvesting costs $150 to $200 a ton or $525 an acre in vineyards with 3-ton yields. Mechanical harvesting is cheaper, costing $200 an acre regardless of yield.[42] However, 75 percent of Napa County's wine grapes are handpicked, reflecting the general rule that the more expensive the grapes, the more likely they are to be hand harvested.

Less than 10 percent of Napa County's employment is in agriculture, compared with 20 percent in Fresno County.[43] Napa's wineries employed another 10 percent of the county's workers, but most of county's jobs and job growth are in the service sector. Leisure and hospitality industries, for example, employ more workers than vineyards or wineries despite tasting rooms that can have more employees than vineyards. Employment in vineyards peaks in summer for the thinning and leaf removal aimed at producing high-quality wines, and again in September–October for the harvest (see figure 6).

Farmworkers may be hired directly by grape growers or obtained through labor contractors. A growing share of Napa Valley farmworkers are hired by

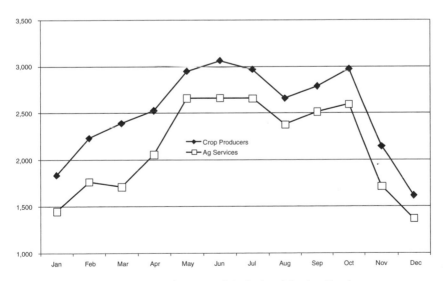

Figure 6 Napa County: Crop Production and Agricultural Services Employment, 2005
Source: LMID. ES-202 Data.

farm management companies and labor contractors, many from other counties. There is seasonality in farm employment, with two workers employed in
October for every worker employed in January.

This seasonality has led to visible homelessness, especially during the harvest, when workers sleep on church porches in St. Helena and along the Napa
River. Homelessness offends Napa's image and poses a threat to agri-tourism,
prompting several innovative responses. Napa County supports three farmworker centers open to solo male farmworkers who are legally in the United
States.[44] Each center has 30 rooms with two beds each, and in 2005 residents
paid $11.50 a day or about $350 a month for room and board. Napa grape
growers who do not provide housing for their workers pay $10 an acre to keep
the cost to workers well below the actual $27 a day cost in a unique housing
assistance program.

Napa's public labor camps are not full, and subsidized centers with empty
beds amid homelessness and overcrowded apartments has led to hand-
wringing in the image-conscious Napa Valley. There is a well-established Hispanic community, and during the peak thinning and harvesting seasons,
many workers join friends and relatives, which explains the overcrowding.
Many of the migrants who come to Napa to harvest grapes prefer living in
cities to be closer to day-labor markets and employers who often pay cash
wages for construction and gardening jobs, as well as for setting up tents for
weddings and parties. Residents of the farmworker centers, by contrast, must
provide proof of legal U.S. residence, abide by rules that prohibit alcohol, and
live far from nonfarm job opportunities.

The Napa Valley may be "as good as it gets" for most farmworkers, offering
hourly earnings that are among the highest in the state. A significant number
of Napa's year-round workers are legal immigrants, some of whom return to
the houses they built in Mexico for the Christmas holidays.[45] Some established
farmworkers have also pooled their savings to invest in job-creating ventures in
their villages of origin. Both the housing and job-creating investments often
turn out to be white elephants, as children educated in Napa rarely return to
their parents' village, even to live in the most elaborate of houses.

Napa Valley leaders wrestling with the challenge of housing the migrants
who arrive each year for the harvest have several options, including encouraging mechanical harvesting of grapes to reduce the need for migrant workers.
Napa could also subsidize commuting from lower-cost areas, which would
expand a practice already common for many nonfarmworkers employed in

service jobs. Land-use policies aimed at preserving farmland make it hard to build housing for low-wage workers, including farmworkers, and may have to be revisited if Napa continues to attract millions of visitors. Napa growers and wineries have played a laudable role in seeking solutions to the area's lack of affordable housing, but the wine industry has also been a strong proponent of efforts to limit population growth and to keep much of the county's land zoned for agricultural use, making housing expensive for the workers on which the industry relies.[46]

IMPERIAL VALLEY: WINTER VEGETABLES

California's other agricultural valleys face similar challenges with the newcomers who arrive to fill seasonal farm jobs. The Imperial Valley in the southeastern corner of the state is among the most farm-dependent, with 30 percent of its average employment in agriculture. The main harvest season is in winter and spring, as vegetables and melons are harvested and shipped throughout the United States. Imperial County's unemployment rate typically approaches 30 percent in the summer months, when there are fewer farm jobs, and reaches a low of 15 percent in the winter months.

There are two distinct hired farmwork forces in the Imperial Valley. Most equipment operators, irrigators, and other regular or year-round workers live in the United States, and many earn more than the minimum wage and own homes in the area that has the lowest house prices in California. Most of the 15,000 to 18,000 seasonal farmworkers employed during the peak January–March harvest season live in Mexicali, the capital of Mexico's Baja California state, and commute daily to Imperial Valley farm jobs. Farm labor contractors recruit these workers at the port of entry early each morning, and their buses depart for the fields at 6 a.m. each day during the harvest season.

Imperial Valley agriculture depends on water from the Colorado River, which lies 50 miles to the east. Because the Imperial Valley is lower, water flows west from the Colorado River by gravity. The California Land Company constructed a canal from the Colorado River, and a flood in 1905 diverted the entire lower Colorado River into the Imperial Valley, creating California's largest lake, the Salton Sea.[47] The main canal that flooded, today called the New River, begins in Mexico and flows about 60 miles north through Imperial County to the Salton Sea.

There is a long tradition of protest among Imperial farmworkers, including the first significant strike called by Mexican farmworkers in the United States, a 1928 protest organized by the Confederation of Mexican Labor Unions that demanded an end to the requirement that workers be hired via labor contractors. Although no contract was signed between the growers and the union, Imperial Valley growers agreed to stop withholding 25 percent of each worker's wages until the harvest was complete, and growers rather than contractors assumed responsibility for assuring that workers received their full wages (Jamieson, 1945, 77).

There was labor conflict again in 1934–1935, when some 8,000 farmworkers went on strike to support demands for higher wages and toilets in the fields. The strikes were led by the Cannery and Agricultural Workers Industrial Union (CAWIU), a Communist-dominated union that led a wave of farm labor strikes across the state in 1933. With the support of the Associated Farmers, a group of growers who provided supplemental funds to rural law enforcement during the 1930s, the Imperial County district attorney prosecuted CAWIU leaders who were jailed for criminal syndicalism, ending that era's "labor troubles."

The Imperial Valley loomed large in the history of the UFW, since it was where the UFW used the traditional union weapon of strikes in an effort to win wage increases in the late 1970s. The strikes backfired, increasing rather than decreasing grower revenue, and the unauthorized workers who helped to break UFW strikes accelerated the union's demise in the 1980s.

The story of the UFW's battle with Imperial Valley vegetable growers began in 1975–1976, when the first contracts negotiated under California's historic Agricultural Labor Relations Act were signed. Most of these agreements raised wages substantially for the workers employed by lettuce and other vegetable companies. As these contracts expired near the end of 1978, the UFW demanded another round of significant increases, including a 42 percent wage increase for field-workers to raise the entry wage on most farms from $3.70 to $5.25 an hour. The UFW also wanted five more paid holidays, cost-of-living wage increases, and standby and reporting pay.[48]

Early 1979 was a period of very high inflation. President Carter asked that unions restrict their wage demands to 7 percent, which is what a coalition of 26 vegetable growers offered in January 1979. The growers also wanted changes in the standard UFW agreement, including an end to the requirement that they use a UFW hiring hall to obtain seasonal workers. The UFW called a strike to put pressure on the growers, and stationed pickets at the port of entry from Mexicali to discourage strikebreakers from entering the United States.

The UFW reported that more than 4,000 workers were on strike in February 1979, and there was violence as strikers attempted to discourage replacement workers from going to work. Growers hired replacement workers as well as security guards, and a UFW striker was killed February 10, 1979, by a foreman. Reflecting the tensions of the time, then governor Edmund G. (Jerry) Brown Jr. marched in the funeral procession, while the Imperial County district attorney ruled there was insufficient evidence to prosecute the foreman.

The growers raised their wage offer to 21 percent over three years and, after the UFW failed to lower its demands in February 1979, the growers declared that bargaining was at an impasse and began to change their wages and benefits unilaterally, suggesting an initial defeat for the UFW.[49] There was no further bargaining until September 1979, when the Sun Harvest Company (a subsidiary of Chiquita), which was most vulnerable to boycotts, agreed to raise wages by 42 percent as the UFW demanded. Another 14 growers followed and reached new agreements with the UFW that raised farmworker wages by about 40 percent.

The UFW's strike strategy seemed to be vindicated by the victory at Sun Harvest and the other growers vulnerable to consumer boycotts. The union used a provision of the Agricultural Labor Relations Act to charge that the growers who refused to sign new agreements violated the law by bargaining in bad faith, that is, the UFW alleged that there was no impasse as the employers alleged before they began making unilateral changes in wages and benefits. The agency that supervises collective bargaining in California agriculture, the Agricultural Labor Relations Board (ALRB), agreed with the UFW, and ordered the growers who refused to sign new contracts to pay the striking workers the same wages and benefits that the UFW negotiated with Sun Harvest. The ALRB presumed that if these growers had bargained in good faith, similar agreements would have been negotiated, making the amount growers owed over $100 million.[50]

The UFW celebrated its victories at the ALRB, but they proved to be short-lived. The growers appealed the ALRB decision to the courts, and a state court of appeals in 1984 sided with them, concluding in a 2–1 decision that "neither party can be said to be solely responsible for the impasse" because of the large gap between the union's wage demand, which the court put at 123 to 190 percent, and the employers' 21 percent offer. By ruling that the employers had bargained hard but lawfully, the court eliminated the ALRB's back-wage award to striking workers.[51] The apparent victory with

Sun Harvest also proved short-lived, as Sun Harvest went out of business before the end of the three-year contract it signed in 1979.[52]

The UFW's troubles were not yet over. The strike, combined with bad weather and disease, reduced the supply of winter lettuce by a third. The demand for lettuce is inelastic, meaning that consumers buy about the same amount whether prices are high or low. The reduced supply of lettuce in February 1979 led to a tripling of lettuce prices and a doubling of grower revenues, meaning that the strike helped growers as a group rather than hurting them, although growers who could not ship lettuce could not benefit from the higher prices.

The lettuce strike highlighted the inadequacy of traditional union weapons in fruit and vegetable agriculture. In a normal February, Imperial Valley growers sent 10.4 million 24-head cartons of lettuce to market at an average price of $3.75 a carton, generating $39 million in revenues. In February 1979, only 6.6 million cartons went to market, but the average price rose to $10.50 a carton, generating $69 million in revenues (Carter et al., 1981).

The fact that consumers buy about the same amount of lettuce at high and low prices meant that the UFW's partially successful strike *increased* grower revenues, albeit unevenly. The major beneficiaries of the strike included Bud (now Dole), which had a Teamster's contract and thus was not affected by the UFW-called strike, as well as lettuce producers in neighboring Arizona. In response to the strike, some lettuce growers established a strike insurance fund to redistribute the extra revenues that arise during strikes,[53] but it has not been needed because there have been no significant farmworker strikes since 1979.

The Imperial Valley today is an important winter vegetable garden for the United States, producing farm commodities worth $1.4 billion in 2006. Vegetables and melons account for a third of the county's farm sales, and lettuce is a third of the vegetable sales. There have been complaints of farm labor shortages because Border Patrol agents sometimes stop buses headed from the border to the fields,[54] but fears of too few workers have not discouraged growers from planting crops for which they believe there is a market.

Most border-area harvest workers are green card commuters, Mexican citizens with U.S. immigrant visas who live in Mexico and commute daily or weekly to U.S. farm jobs. These green card commuters are aging, and the younger workers who sometimes join the crews are often unauthorized, using false documents to get across the border and find jobs. When Border Patrol agents began checking buses leaving ports of entry for the fields, unauthorized workers lost any incentive to return to Mexico after a day of harvesting vegetables and risk being apprehended again. Instead, once inside the United States, younger unauthorized workers tend to keep going north to get away from the border, where wages are higher and there is less enforcement.

However, fears of labor shortages have not deterred Imperial farmers from planting more vegetables. The most valuable vegetable in Imperial County is lettuce, typically accounting for a quarter of the value of the county's vegetables. The acreage, value, and production of head and leaf lettuces rose between 2003 and 2006, and farmers complaining of labor shortages had higher sales in 2005 than in the year before or after. Farmers plant fruit and vegetable crops for which they have a market, and assume that workers will be available when needed to harvest their crops.

Water is the other threat to Imperial Valley farm production. Under pressure from both the federal and state governments, the Imperial Irrigation District (IID) in 2003 agreed to transfer up to 200,000 acre-feet of water to the San Diego County Water Authority, with San Diego compensating the IID for the water it takes. In addition, San Diego agreed to pay for any negative third-party effects of the water transfer, as when fewer farmworkers are employed and there is less spending at local businesses because of reduced farm production.

The first years of water sales produced a curious economic outcome. The reduced availability of water meant that farmers stopped producing lower-value commodities such as hay, and used available water to grow high-value vegetables. Studies of the economic impacts of reduced farming found that payments for idling farmland generated more economic activity than farming, suggesting that it was economically beneficial to reduce farming, transfer water to cities, and spend the resulting monies to generate nonfarm jobs.[55]

Chapter 4 Florida Sugar, Oranges, and Tomatoes

About 60 percent of Americans live in the eastern time zone that includes Florida, but more than 60 percent of U.S. fruits and vegetables are produced in the West, including 40 percent in California. Florida is the most important fruit and vegetable state east of the Mississippi River, and the major producer during the winter months, when there is little production of similar crops elsewhere in the United States.

Instead, Florida fruits and vegetables often compete with those grown in the Caribbean and Mexico. This tends to make Florida farmers protectionist, seeking to limit imports of competitive Latin American crops. Florida sugar is protected from imports of cheaper sugar produced in Brazil and the Caribbean, and Florida oranges and tomatoes are protected from cheaper Brazilian and Mexican crops, respectively.

About 80 percent of Florida's almost $8 billion annual farm sales are from crops, most of which require seasonal workers to harvest. Florida has traditionally been home to large numbers of seasonal workers who pick the state's crops during the winter months and migrate northward during the summer months, following the sun to harvest fruits and vegetables along the eastern seaboard.

Three crops dominate Florida agriculture. Between the 1940s and 1990s, sugarcane was in the spotlight because of its reliance on guest workers from sugar-producing Caribbean islands. Oranges have long been Florida's most important fruit, but urbanization, freezes, and trade are shrinking and moving the groves. These factors, combined with rising wages, may spur the mechanization of the state's orange harvest. Florida produces most of the fresh tomatoes grown in the United States during the winter months, and an organization of workers is locked in a battle with growers and fast-food firms to raise the piece rate wage they pay tomato pickers.

SUGARCANE AND GUEST WORKERS

Sugarcane production began in the 1930s in south-central Florida when a few large landowners realized that they could grow the perennial grass in the area's subtropical climate. Obtaining harvest workers was a problem, in part because local workers knew of the debt peonage that sometimes occurred on sugar plantations.[1] In 1942, the U.S. Sugar Corporation and four of its managers as well as the sheriff of Hendry County were indicted by a federal grand jury for violating federal peonage statutes by holding workers by force until they repaid their debts.[2]

Sugar mills wanted a labor force that could not leave the fields for other jobs. They found such workers in Caribbean islands such as Jamaica, and imported them as guest workers. Caribbean cane cutters were admitted first under exceptions in U.S. immigration law and later with H-2 and H-2A visas. In 1942, after the U.S. and Mexican governments negotiated the first of the bracero agreements, the War Food Administration negotiated memorandums of understanding (MOUs) with the British West Indies to recruit farmworkers for Florida and other eastern states. A peak 16,000 Jamaicans were admitted in 1944.

After World War II ended, the guest-worker program continued, with the British West Indies Central Labor Organization (BWICLO) representing the governments of the islands that were home to farmworkers headed to the United States. BWICLO and island governments tightly controlled the list of workers from which U.S. employers could make their selections, and required selected workers to sign supplemental agreements that deducted some of their earnings and forwarded them to government-controlled banks in Jamaica and other islands.

The H-2 Program was created by the omnibus Immigration and Nationality Act (McCarran-Walter Act) of 1952, enacted over President Truman's veto.[3] Section 101 (a) (15) (H) outlined procedures to admit three types of temporary workers: persons of distinguished merit and ability, other temporary workers, and trainees.[4] The other temporary workers were eligible for H-2 visas if they had "a residence in a foreign country" that they had "no intention of abandoning" and were "coming temporarily to the U.S. to perform other temporary services or labor, if unemployed persons capable of performing such services or labor cannot be found in this country."

The attorney general was given the authority to deal with employers seeking H-2 visas for foreign workers "after consultation with the appropriate agencies of the government." In practice, this meant that employers had to obtain a certification from the U.S. Department of Labor that U.S. workers were not available to fill the jobs for which the employer was seeking H-2 workers and that the presence of H-2 workers would not adversely affect U.S. workers who were "similarly employed." Unlike the wartime MOUs and the Bracero Program, which were begun to deal with specific wartime labor shortages, the H-2 Program was a permanent part of U.S. law, although most contemporary observers believed that it would be used to admit foreign farmworkers only in exceptional circumstances, not on a routine basis.

However, Jamaicans with H-2 visas were admitted year after year to harvest Florida's sugar crop. As sugarcane harvesting was mechanized in Louisiana, Australia, and other countries, there were calls to mechanize the Florida harvest, but the mills argued that the muck soil could not support the weight of machines. However, after suits were filed on behalf of cane cutters in the early 1990s alleging that the mills underpaid the cutters and a court initially agreed that the cutters were owed more than $100 million in back wages, the Florida harvest was mechanized within five years. The Florida sugarcane story highlights the need for skepticism when farm employers assert that "there is no alternative to imported farmworkers."

SUGAR CONSUMPTION AND PRODUCTION

The United States is the world's largest consumer of sweeteners such as sugar and high-fructose corn syrup. Sugar, a sweetener, preservative, and bonding agent in food, has 16 calories per teaspoon; nutritionists consider them "empty calories" because sugar lacks vitamins and minerals.

The United States is one of the few countries that produces sugar from both beets and cane, a total of 8 million tons a year, and imports another 1.2 million tons of sugar from developing countries, some of which send migrants to the United States.[5] The United States provides quotas to foreign sugar producers, and favors three countries with higher-than-world prices: the Dominican Republic, Brazil, and the Philippines.[6] The world's leading sugar producers include Brazil, which produced 29 million tons of the global 144 million tons in 2005–2006; India, which produced 18 million tons; and China, producing 10 million tons. In North America, the United States produced 6.8 million tons of sugar in 2005–2006, Mexico 6 million tons, and Cuba 1.5 million tons.

Sugar is produced in 120 countries. Most developing countries can grow sugar from cane more cheaply than it can be produced in the United States from cane or beets (the sucrose from beets and cane is identical). The world price of sugar averaged $0.08 a pound between 2000 and 2005, while the U.S. price averaged $0.21. The U.S. price is higher than the world price because the U.S. government restricts imports of lower-cost sugar, meaning that if there were free trade, U.S. sugar production would shrink and sugar imports would rise.

Sugar beets are similar to red beets in shape, but they are inedible. They are planted annually in a variety of climates, from the Imperial Valley of California to upper midwestern states such as the Red River Valley of North Dakota and Minnesota, which has half of U.S. sugar beet acreage. Most beets are harvested in the fall, and areas with cold winters can store harvested beets for processing without loss of sucrose. The sugar recovery rate from beets is about 14 percent, so that 7 tons of beets make a ton of sugar. Yields average 22 tons of beets an acre or 3 tons of raw sugar.

Sugarcane is a perennial grass native to Asia that grows to a height of 8 to 12 feet in tropical and semitropical environments, and is usually the only crop grown on a plantation-type farm (monoculture). Florida produces more than half of the U.S. sugar that comes from cane, Louisiana a third, and Hawaii and Texas the rest. The sugar is in the cane's stalk, which is 80 percent water. Cane fields are burned to eliminate the leaves before harvesting so that the grinding mills have less trash to eliminate.

The sugarcane harvest has an otherworldly feel. Burning cane fields, black workers outfitted with leg and arm guards and wielding machetes, and the presence of snakes prompted one writer to assert "The most perilous work in America is the harvest of sugarcane in south Florida."[7] The association of sugarcane with plantations and slavery, debt peonage, and other poor labor conditions completes a picture of sugarcane production as a nasty business.[8]

Cane deteriorates rapidly after harvest, so it is grown close to a mill that takes the stalks and grinds them to extract the juice. The juice is clarified, boiled, and crystallized, producing a thick syrup. When the syrup reaches the molasses stage, it is dropped into centrifuges to be spun into raw sugar crystals that are 96 to 99 percent pure. Refineries wash raw sugar, melt it into syrup, filter the syrup, and dry and package the resulting sugar. Most sugar refineries are located near ports to give them easy access to imported sugar for blending.

Green cane is cut into short segments and planted in the fall in rows 5 feet apart. The first harvest a year later is the plant-cane crop, the second harvest is called the first ratoon or first stubble, and the third the second ratoon or second stubble. While growing, the water level in Florida is raised and lowered with pumps and canals and kept at 18 to 24 inches below ground level; yields are highest on sandy soils.[9]

The United States levied a tariff on sugar imports in 1789 to raise revenue for the federal government; at the time, no sugar was produced in the United States. As the U.S. sugar industry developed, the tariff protected U.S. sugar producers. Under the Jones-Costigan Act of 1934 and successive sugar acts, the United States restricts sugar imports, charging a prohibitive tariff on imports above the tariff rate quota of 1.2 million tons a year,[10] so that U.S. consumers pay at least $1.5 billion a year more for sugar and products containing sugar (Government Accounting Office, 2000). U.S. sugar producers receive benefits worth $500 million to $1.5 billion a year from the sugar program, which also causes a deadweight loss of about $1 billion, since less sugar is consumed because of the high price.

Sugar production remains a major employer in the Caribbean, including Cuba, the Dominican Republic, and Jamaica. Jamaica's sugar industry employs 13,000 harvesters to produce about 200,000 tons of refined sugar a year, but production is shrinking, largely because of U.S. trade restrictions and the fact that Brazil can produce sugar cheaper than the Caribbean islands.[11]

BIG SUGAR IN FLORIDA

Florida's sugar production was limited until trade with Cuba was halted in July 1960. The Cuban embargo encouraged Florida's cane acreage to quadruple within five years and then to double between the mid-1960s and mid-1980s.[12] In 2005–2006, Florida harvested 13 million tons of cane worth $30 a ton or $390 million from 402,000 acres, mostly owned by large corporate farms. Flo-Sun, controlled by the Fanjul family of Palm Beach, had 150,000 acres of sugarcane in the early 1990s, followed by the United States Sugar Corporation with 140,000 acres, Talisman Sugar (a subsidiary of St. Joe Paper Company) with 48,000 acres, and Texas-based King Ranch with 20,000 acres.

The sugar industry is vertically integrated; the seven Florida mills that process the cane also harvest it. The mills own farmland and grow at least some of the cane they grind, called "administration cane," and they harvest their own cane as well as that of independent growers. The average mill capacity in the early 1990s was 16,400 tons a day, meaning that the industry could grind about 115,000 tons of harvested cane a day.[13]

Producing sugar in the United States is profitable. The U.S. Department of Agriculture (USDA) estimated the average gross value of sugarcane at $1,040 an acre in 1995, based on producing 34 tons an acre worth $30.60 a ton. Hired labor costs were $407 an acre, or $12 a ton. A University of Florida study concluded that gross revenues for a 640-acre cane farm were about $1,100 an acre in the early 1990s, and net returns $238 an acre, a 21 percent profit rate. Since most cane is raised for the mill that grinds it, the price the mill pays for the cane is somewhat artificial, since farming profits can be raised or lowered by having the mill pay less or more for the cane.[14]

The last major USDA review of the Florida cane industry cited four major issues: soil subsidence, yields, labor, and environment (Buzzanell, Lord, and Brown, 1992). Soil subsidence is the biological oxidation process through which an average 1.2 inches of soil in the Everglades area is lost each year as bacteria turn the organic residues into particles that are blown away. By keeping water levels higher, soil subsidence is reduced; some growers plant rice in the summer fallow months and flood the fields as well.

Cane yields were about 32 tons an acre from the 1960s through the 1980s, rising to 35–36 tons an acre in 1990–1991. New varieties have increased yields, and the three mainstay varieties of the industry—CP-72-1210, CP-70-1133, and CL-61-620—fell from more than 80 percent of all cane in the mid-1980s to less than 60 percent a decade later.[15]

Environmental and labor issues are of broader interest. The Florida sugar industry is mostly in the Everglades Agricultural Area (EAA), created in the 1930s and the 1940s by draining swamplands. After back-to-back hurricanes flooded most of south Florida in 1947, the Army Corps of Engineers was ordered to create both the EAA and the Everglades National Park. The organic or muck soils in the EAA were ideal for growing cane, with wet, warm summers and dry, freeze-free winters.

However, producing cane slowed the flow of fresh water entering the Everglades National Park during the summer months and added phosphates, enabling cattails to replace native saw grasses. The federal and state governments in the 1990s debated how to protect the Everglades "river of grass." The result is an $8 billion, 20-year project that involves government purchases of 250,000 acres of land surrounding the park, including 60,000 acres of farmland; cane growers will make a small contribution to the cleanup.[16]

The sugar industry's major concern during the debate about restoring the Everglades was to avoid paying for the cleanup. A state ballot initiative in 1996, Amendment 4, would have required sugar companies to pay a $0.01 per pound tax on the sugar they produce to raise $700 million to filter phosphorus-laden water before it enters the Everglades. The sugar companies spent $25 million to defeat Amendment 4, and fared better under the federal-state cleanup plan eventually enacted.

WAGES AND THE IRON TRIANGLE

Labor was the final challenge facing the sugar industry. Almost all Florida cane was cut by guest workers. The U.S. Department of Labor (DOL) routinely certified the need for more than 10,000 foreign cane cutters, agreeing with the mills that U.S. cane cutters were not available and that the presence of the H-2/H-2A cane cutters would not adversely affect similar U.S. workers. Employers were required to recruit U.S. workers, which they did by completing a DOL Form ETA 790, the so-called "job clearance" order that spelled out the wages and working conditions they were offering. These job orders were circulated or cleared throughout the United States so that workers seeking farm jobs could learn about them and respond.[17] The job order became a contract between the mills and any U.S. or H-2/H-2A workers cutting cane.

High-price sugar had led to a higher-than-usual wage for cane cutters. Sugar job orders in the late 1980s offered a government-mandated minimum wage—the Adverse Effect Wage Rate—of at least $5.30 an hour at a time when the federal minimum wage was $3.35 an hour. In fact, cane cutters earned a piece rate wage, which the mills called a task rate, and workers who could not cut fast enough to earn at least $5.30 an hour at this piece or task rate could be terminated and returned to their countries of origin. If the mills retained slower cutters, they had to "make up" their piece rate earnings so that all workers earned at least $5.30 an hour.

Workers who had not cut cane before needed an idea of how much cane they would have to cut in order to avoid termination, so the job orders included the phrase: "a worker would be expected to cut an average of eight (8) tons of harvest cane per day throughout the season." Mills reserved the right to test a worker's productivity any time after a seven-day training and break-in period. If a worker failed on three days to cut fast enough to earn $5.30 an hour at the mill-specified piece or task rate, the worker could be terminated and sent home.

The combination of the government-set minimum wage of $5.30 an hour and the mill-set productivity standard of a ton an hour or 8 tons a day created an iron triangle that should have automatically made the piece or task rate for cutting cane $5.30 a ton. For example, if the minimum wage was $10 an hour and the piece rate $10 to pick a bin of apples, the productivity standard is a bin an hour. A worker who picked only three-quarters of a bin in one hour would earn $7.50 at the piece rate wage but, because of the $10 minimum wage, the employer would have to "make up" $2.50. Most employers fire workers who cannot work fast enough at the piece rate they set to earn the minimum wage.

Most job orders specify all three parameters of the iron triangle—the minimum wage, the piece rate, and the productivity standard. The sugar mills' job order was unusual because it did not specify a piece rate, but instead a "task rate." This was explained on a handout given to cutters, most of whom had primary school educations, as follows: "The task, set for each day in terms of the number of feet of cane the worker is expected to cut in one hour, is based on the experience of the company over many years. . . . Over 95 percent of the cutters have made the task in the past, and it is considered a reasonable task and work standard by the company." "Making the task" meant cutting cane fast enough to earn the minimum wage.

The mills used task rates to save money. The mills, but not the workers, knew how many tons of cane were in 100 or 150 feet of cane because they could estimate cane yields accurately. They kept meticulous records, and set task rates that required workers to cut 1.3 to 1.7 tons of cane an hour. Supervisors, who were ex-cutters in the United States on H-2/H-2A visas, carried tape measures and "checked out" cutters who did not cut cane fast enough, ordering them to stop working and sit on the bus until the end of the workday. After three checkouts, a cutter could be terminated, which usually meant a quick return trip to Jamaica.

The key to understanding why the mills—but not the cutters—knew how many tons of cane were in the 100- or 150-foot task assigned to a worker lies in the fact that cane is planted in rows 5 feet apart and workers are assigned to cut two adjoining rows of cane, known as a cut row.[18] Since there are 43,560 square feet in an acre, the mills knew that a field yielding 43.56 tons an acre had a ton of cane in every 100 feet of cut row.[19] If the task rate required workers to cut 150 feet in one hour, the productivity standard was 1.5 tons an hour. The mills did not have to weigh the cane cut by each worker because they were very good at estimating yields. Since feet equals tons and vice versa, mills knew how many tons of cane workers cut because they knew how many feet of cane they cut.

The U.S. Department of Labor defines a piece rate wage as one that measures or weighs the work done by individuals. The mills argued that the task rate was not a piece rate because the work done by individuals was not measured in weight or volume, and DOL agreed. In 1982, migrant advocates sued the DOL because it failed to order employers to raise the piece rates they offered when the government raised the minimum wage, known as the Adverse Effect Wage Rate,, arguing that if the DOL did not require employers to raise their piece rates in lockstep with the AEWR, workers would have to work harder to earn the higher wage.[20]

The DOL accepted this logic, and in 1985 ordered farm employers to raise their piece rates as the AEWR rose.[21] However, under pressure from the sugar mills, the DOL concluded that the task rate in sugarcane was not a piece rate, thus exempting the mills from establishing a link between the minimum wage and their task rates. Migrant advocates sued the DOL, and a federal judge ordered the DOL to determine whether the task rate system was in fact a piece rate system. The DOL conducted two studies: the first concluded that the 8-ton statement was a productivity standard, but the political clout of the sugar mills was evident in the final report, which concluded that the task rate system was not a piece rate system.[22]

SUGAR SUITS AND MECHANIZATION

In 1989, class action suits were filed on behalf of cane cutters that asserted the 8-ton productivity standard and the $5.30 an hour minimum wage created a contract that promised cutters a piece rate of $5.30 per ton. The suit used the iron triangle argument: if the minimum wage was $5.30 an hour, and workers had to cut an average 8 tons of cane in an eight-hour day to be considered satisfactory,[23] then the piece rate for cutting cane must be $5.30 a ton.[24] The mills budgeted and paid workers much less, about $3.75 a ton, and the suits asked for back wages of $1.55 a ton or about $100 million with interest.

A Florida state judge in August 1992 found the iron triangle argument convincing, and ordered the mills to pay each cutter $1,000 to $1,500 in back wages for the several years of harvesting that were not excluded by the statute of limitations.[25] This decision prompted U.S. Sugar to adopt a "Labor Peace" program and to acknowledge that its task rate system was a piece rate. As a result, U.S. Sugar cutters were paid $5.10 per net ton, with the $0.20 difference reflecting the removal of trash from the stalk. Cutters were required to cut at least one gross ton of cane an hour,[26] and U.S. Sugar published its rate sheet, showing workers for the first time that feet of cane cut was the same as tons of cane cut. In July 1998, U.S. Sugar paid $5.6 million to settle the suits.[27]

The other mills appealed the judge's decision, and a state appeals court agreed that there should be a trial to determine whether the contract was "clear and unambiguous" about the $5.30 a ton piece rate. The first case involved Atlantic Sugar, one of the mills controlled by the Fanjul family.[28] A jury was to answer "should and could" questions: *should* the mills have paid cane cutters an average $5.30 per ton and *could* the companies have paid cutters $5.30 a ton without weighing each cutter's cane? Worker attorneys used the iron triangle argument to make the "should" argument, and company yield data to make the "could" argument.

The mills countered that they never promised to pay cutters $5.30 a ton, and bolstered their case by citing the DOL conclusion that the task rate was not a piece rate. Some cutters, testifying in Jamaican patois, said that their work assignment was to cut a certain number of feet, not a certain number of tons. The mills showed that they did not pay exactly $3.75 a ton; they paid slightly more in fields with recumbent or flattened cane and slightly less when the cane was straight and easier to cut.[29]

The jury decided that Atlantic did not promise cutters $5.30 a ton, but also concluded that "Atlantic Sugar consistently misrepresented to the cutters the incentive features of their task system of payment. It was shameful." Juries reached similar verdicts absolving Okeelanta and the Sugar Cane Growers Cooperative, agreeing that, if the mills said the task rate was not a piece rate and the DOL agreed, workers could not expect to be paid $5.30 a ton. Instead, workers could expect to earn $5.30 an hour if they worked fast enough to complete their assigned task.

The cutters did not get back wages, but the mills began to mechanize when they realized that successful cutter suits could raise their labor costs by 40 percent. Talisman Sugar, a mill not involved in the cutter suits, mechanized cane harvesting in the early 1980s. Citing "unfounded legal hassles" associated with the H-2A Program, the Sugar Cane Growers Cooperative of Florida mechanized harvesting after the 1991–1992 season. U.S. Sugar was the last mill to mechanize, after the 1995–1996 season. In Louisiana, where U.S. blacks rather than H-2A workers cut sugarcane, the harvest was mechanized in the 1950s and 1960s.

LESSONS FROM SUGAR

Sugar is widely acknowledged to be the poster child for farm policies that slow economic development in migrant countries of origin and increase immigration to the United States. The reason there is a sugarcane industry in south Florida is because of trade barriers that keep lower-cost sugar out of the United States. For years, cane growers argued that they could not find U.S. workers and could not mechanize the harvest because of the unique soil conditions. This "migration in place of trade" continued for five decades, until worker suits alleging underpayments spurred mechanization.

One lesson from the sugar experience is skepticism about grower claims that there are no alternatives to imported farmworkers. The speedy mechanization of the harvest when faced with the prospect of sharply higher wages belied assertions that there were no alternatives to hand harvesters. A second lesson concerns the H-2A Program. Once employers become accustomed to guest workers, it is very hard to revert to U.S. workers, since recruitment and supervision take on a "foreign" flavor that makes any U.S. workers who apply for jobs feel out of place.

Third, the H-2 Program can give employers extreme control over workers. Some of the mills fired a few slower cutters early in the season to inspire remaining cutters to work faster. The mills reasoned that, even if they had to pay return transportation for workers who were fired, getting remaining cutters to work faster reduced the total number needed. Workers did not know how much cane they cut, but company records show that some of those terminated early in the season cut more than a ton an hour, but not the 1.5 tons an hour required by the task rate.

Sugarcane and the H-2A Program have given Florida's "sugar cities" of Pahokee, Belle Glade, and South Bay a distinct third-world feel. Edward R. Murrow filmed part of *Harvest of Shame* (1960) in Belle Glade, which had 15,000 residents in 2000. More than half were black, reflecting the fact that some H-2 cane cutters were able to settle in the United States.[30] According to the census, a third of Belle Glade residents had incomes below the poverty line, prompting the *Palm Beach Post* in a December 11, 2005, editorial to demand that the Fanjul family, major beneficiaries of U.S. sugar and labor migration policies, contribute to improving life in the sugar cities.

FLORIDA ORANGES

Citrus worth $1.6 billion accounted for 20 percent of Florida's farm sales in 2005, 85 percent of which was oranges. Orange harvesting is one of the most layered farm labor markets in the United States, meaning that there are often entities between orange pickers and processors. For example, the owner of a citrus grove may hire a farm management company to care for the ripening fruit and a contractor to harvest it and haul it to a packer or processor. The labor contractors who hire farmworkers to harvest oranges and other crops have been associated with some of the most abusive slavery and involuntary servitude cases in contemporary America.

Florida has more farm labor contractors than any other state; some 2,848 were registered with Florida's Department of Business and Professional Regulation in 2005. These contractors, who organize crews of 20 to 30 workers, are diverse. Some provide only harvest workers and the ladders and bags needed to harvest oranges, while others also provide the bins into which workers dump the oranges they pick and the trucks to haul oranges to processors. Some contractor-harvesters buy the orange crop on the tree, taking responsibility for getting it to processors and earning the difference between what they receive from the processor and what they paid for the on-tree crop.

There were 14 slavery and involuntary servitude cases involving farm labor contractors in Florida between 1996 and 2006.[31] When abusive contractors are discovered, the operators of the farms to which they brought workers are generally not punished. Most farmers argue that relying on a contractor to get oranges picked is analogous to a home owner hiring a painter. Just as the home owner is not responsible for how the painter treats his workers, so the farmer is not responsible for the contractor's treatment of the crew. Grower Jim Griffiths summed up this attitude: "I wouldn't have the slightest idea who any of them [workers] were or where they are from. Theoretically, you can be fined or penalized for that [hiring unauthorized workers]. But it doesn't matter to me because I don't ever see them or know anything about them. . . . That's the responsibility of the guy [contractor] hiring them to determine whether they're legal or not. The liability goes back to him."[32]

Cases involving contractors who abuse unauthorized or U.S. workers can make for chilling tales. Contractor Juan Ramos was sentenced to 15 years in prison in May 2004 for keeping 100 Mexican workers under guard near Lake Placid until they repaid smuggling debts from their earnings. Ramos, arrested in May 2001, charged workers a $1,000 smuggling fee. His attorney asked the judge for leniency because: "This business of harboring illegal immigrants is widespread" in the citrus industry.[33]

Ramos provided workers for Lykes Brothers, which said "it is too expensive" to hire workers directly: "We find it is a lot more efficient to use a contractor to provide the labor." In sentencing Ramos, U.S. District Judge K. Michael Moore said: "Others at another level in this system of fruit-picking, at a higher level . . . are complicit. . . . They rely on migrant workers, and they create a legal fiction or corporation that insulates them . . . so that they can be relieved of any liability for the hiring of illegal immigrants. And yet they stand to benefit the most."[34]

Contractor Abel Cuello Jr. pleaded guilty to federal charges of conspiring to violate U.S. laws barring involuntary servitude after federal agents in April 1999 freed 27 migrants from two trailers in Immokalee, a farmworker city in southwestern Florida. Like Ramos, Cuello kept the migrants under guard until their smuggling fees were repaid in wage deductions. Cuello was sentenced to 33 months in 1999. However, after being released, Cuello became a crew leader for Ag-Mart, grower of the Santa Sweets brand of grape tomatoes.[35] Cuello, who lost his contracting license when he was convicted, applied for and received federal and state labor contractor licenses in 2005.[36]

Contractor Ronald Evans Sr. preyed on black men that he recruited from homeless shelters, and kept them in debt peonage in rural Florida and North Carolina. A series of articles in the *Miami Herald* prompted federal investigators to raid the Evans farm labor camp in June 2005.[37] They discovered that workers paid Evans $50 a week for room and board but made much of his money charging workers for alcohol and crack cocaine, which kept them in debt. Evans, who supplied workers to Tater Farms, owned by a past chairman of the Florida Fruit and Vegetable Association, was sentenced to 30 years in federal prison in January 2007.[38]

Florida has about 500,000 acres of Valencia oranges, the official state fruit, and produces about 80 percent of the oranges that are processed into the orange juice consumed in the United States. Acreage peaked at 625,000 in the mid-1990s, and has been shrinking because of urbanization, hurricanes, and disease (citrus canker and greening). Tropicana, owned by PepsiCo Inc., and Minute Maid, owned by Coca-Cola, account for two-thirds of the retail orange juice revenue.

Like most farm commodities, orange industry revenues fluctuate. An acre of oranges yields 300 to 400 90-pound boxes of fruit worth $5 to $6 or $0.05 to $0.06 a pound.[39] Harvesters receive $0.75 to $0.80 for each box picked and dumped into a plastic field bin, or less than a cent a pound. Hand harvesters pick an average 9–11 boxes an hour, earning $7–$8 by climbing ladders, picking oranges, and dropping them into a picking sack that weights 60 to 70 pounds when full. The sacks are emptied into field tubs or bins that hold about 900 pounds of oranges. A "goat truck," often a school bus with the sides and roof cut off to resemble a flatbed truck, takes the bins to a trailer that hauls the fruit to a juice concentrate plant.[40]

Most fruits that are processed rather than consumed fresh are harvested mechanically. Florida researchers are seeking to make hand harvesting easier and to develop harvesting machines. Harvesting aids include hydraulic lifts or "people positioners" that eliminate the need for workers to climb ladders and handle full bags of oranges, reducing falls and injuries, but they are generally not used because of the extra expense and the availability of workers willing to climb ladders. Mechanical harvesting is more promising, and is spreading on new plantings with smaller trees.[41] If farmworker earnings doubled to the $17 average nonfarm wage across the United States, the harvesting of Florida's processing oranges would likely be mechanized quickly.

Machines that harvest fruits and nuts growing on trees grasp tree trunks and shake plums, peaches, and almonds from the limbs, and one vein of research is adapting them to harvest oranges.[42] Another machine uses a rotating device that resembles spinning car-wash brushes to remove oranges as it travels up and down rows of trees, while another uses a "pull-and-catch" machine with 900 eight-foot metal arms that reach into the tree and remove oranges with spring-loaded plastic fingers.

Mechanization is spreading slowly because machines require large acreages of evenly spaced and carefully pruned trees, and this is best accomplished in new plantings. Most new plantings are designed for machine harvesting, but there are relatively few because freer trade could increase imports of low-cost Brazilian juice. The Brazilian state of São Paulo produces 45 percent of the world's orange juice, more than the 40 percent produced in Florida, and

Brazilian processors can deliver a pound of frozen concentrated orange juice in the United States for under $0.75, compared to $0.99 in Florida. A tariff of $0.29 a gallon keeps Florida orange juice competitive, but raises the question of whether the United States should allow the recruitment of foreign workers to harvest a commodity that could be imported at lower cost.[43]

Mechanization and trade are likely to reduce the number of hard-to-regulate contractors who now assemble crews of orange pickers. With Brazil the low-cost producer of oranges for juice, and with Florida's groves shrinking for reasons that range from urbanization to weather and disease, public policy shapes the demand for migrant orange pickers via imigration and trade policies.

TOMATOES: THIRD-PARTY PRESSURE

Tomatoes are a fruit but considered a vegetable in the United States because of an 1893 US Supreme Court ruling. China produced a quarter of the world's 124 million tons of fresh tomatoes in 2005, the EU 15 percent, the US nine percent, Turkey eight percent, and Egypt and India, six percent each. The three leading fresh tomato exporters are Spain (one million tons), Mexico (900,000 tons), and the Netherlands (775,000 tons). U.S. fresh tomato production rose about 25 percent between the early 1990s and 2007–08, faster than the 20 percent rise in the U.S. population, but imports rose even faster, so that a third of U.S. fresh tomatoes are imported.

Florida produces about 1.3 billion pounds of tomatoes and California 1.1 billion pounds—these two states account for almost 60 percent of US fresh tomato production. Florida's tomato production is concentrated in the Bradenton-Palmetto region, south of Tampa, and in the southwestern corner of the state around Immokalee. There are 16 major Florida growers, and they grow and pack tomatoes that have sales of about $500 million a year between November and April, when the major competitor is Sinaloa, Mexico.

Florida's tomatoes are picked "green" and ripened with ethylene, a gas that turns them red and produces the hard "slicing tomato" desired by U.S. fast-food chains. Green tomatoes are picked into 32-pound buckets for piece rate wages of $0.40 to $0.45, about a cent and a half per pound. Growers receive $0.36 a pound, less than 20 percent of retail prices that range from $1.50 to $2 a pound during the winter months.[44] Most tomato pickers earn $50 to $100 per day, or $7,000 to $9,000 during the six-month Florida season.

The tomato picking piece rate did not rise during the 1990s, prompting the Coalition of Immokalee Workers (CIW) to organize a hunger strike in

December 1997 in an effort to raise wages.[45] The month-long hunger strike ended when ex-President Carter offered to act as a mediator between the CIW and the growers, who rejected Carter's offer.

The CIW then turned to the fast-food chains that buy Florida tomatoes, adopting a strategy pioneered by the Farm Labor Organizing Committee (FLOC) in Ohio and North Carolina of focusing on buyers vulnerable to consumer boycotts. After threatening boycotts, the FLOC persuaded Campbell's (Vlasic), Heinz, and Mt. Olive to require growers who produced cucumbers for them to recognize the FLOC as bargaining agent for their farmworkers and raise the price paid to growers enough to cover the higher wages that these pickle processors agreed to pay FLOC-represented workers.

The CIW followed a similar strategy, beginning with Taco Bell, which has outlets on many college campuses. After a four-year "fair-food" campaign that involved noisy demonstrations, Yum Brands, the owner of Taco Bell, agreed to raise its payments to tomato growers by a cent a pound so that the piece rate for pickers could be raised to $0.75 a bucket. Under the March 2005 agreement, Taco Bell sent the CIW weekly reports on the tomatoes it bought from two Florida suppliers, and a third party issued checks that added $10 to $30 a week to picker wages, costing Taco Bell $100,000 a year.

The CIW then turned to McDonald's USA, which in April 2007 agreed to follow the example set by Taco Bell and raise prices to tomato growers so that they could raise wages for pickers. McDonald's is developing a reputation as a leader in setting labor standards for its suppliers. For example, McDonald's requires U.S. growers of the fruits and vegetables it buys to hire workers directly rather than through contractors, a policy that makes 11 of the 16 major Florida tomato growers ineligible to be McDonald's suppliers. McDonald's USA buys about 15 million pounds of Florida fresh tomatoes a year, making the cost of the CIW agreement $150,000 a year.[46]

The successes with Taco Bell and McDonald's encouraged the CIW to turn its attention to Burger King in fall 2007. Burger King resisted, arguing that since it does not employ farmworkers and does not buy tomatoes directly from growers, it could not ensure that tomato pickers would receive any additional wages that could be paid from higher prices to growers. The CIW, citing its agreements with other fast-food chains, held rallies across Florida to put pressure on Burger King.[47]

After April 2008 congressional hearings and the revelation that a Burger King vice president hired Diplomatic Tactical Services to infiltrate student groups that supported the CIW, Burger King CEO John W. Chidsey in

May 2008 announced an agreement with the CIW to require the growers of its tomatoes to pay their pickers 1.5 cents a pound. One cent will go to workers, and growers will receive a half cent to cover their additional costs as a result of the agreement. Burger King estimated that its costs would rise by $300,000 a year under the agreement.

The southwestern Florida city of Immokalee continues to serve as a port of entry for the rural poor of Mexico and Guatemala. According to the 2000 census, more than 70 percent of Immokalee's 20,000 residents were Hispanic and 80 percent spoke a language other than English at home. More than 75 percent of adults had not completed high school, making it hard to attract employers offering higher-wage nonfarm jobs. A third of Immokalee's families had incomes below the poverty line, including half of those with children under age five. Immokalee's fields and orchards continue to attract migrants to fill seasonal farm jobs, but these jobs do not promise an easy path to upward mobility for immigrant farmworkers and their children.

Chapter 5 Meat and Poultry

Americans consume almost 300 pounds of meat and poultry (carcass weight) a year, three times the global average of 100 pounds a year.[1] Since 1975, Americans have reduced their consumption of red meats, such as beef and pork, and increased their consumption of poultry. Per capita consumption of chicken first surpassed pork and beef in the early 1970s, when red meat prices were very high because of increased demand and high commodity prices. Chickens are much more efficient than cattle at turning feed into meat, and innovations in poultry production, such as cut-up chicken, have been popular with consumers.

The $70 billion U.S. meat slaughtering and processing industry, the largest manufacturing industry in rural America, employs more than 500,000 workers to turn cattle, hogs, sheep, and poultry into meat and other products.[2] Meatpacking is the only part of the U.S. food manufacturing industry that is projected to add jobs by 2012 (see table 5; Drabenstott, Henry, and Mitchell, 1999).

Meat packers hire nonfarmworkers, some of whom are ex-farmworkers. Livestock accounts for more than half of annual

Table 5 U.S. Food Manufacturing Employment, 2002–2012

	Employment	Change 2002–2012(%)
Total	1,525	5
Animal Slaughtering and Processing	520	15
Bakeries and Tortilla Manufacturing	295	3
Fruit and Vegetable Preserving and Specialty Food Manufacturing	182	−1
Other Food Manufacturing	152	2
Dairy Product Manufacturing	137	−9
Sugar and Confectionery Product Manufacturing	83	−3
Grain and Oilseed Milling	62	−1
Animal Food Manufacturing	52	1
Seafood Product Preparation and Packaging	44	−8

Source: U.S. Department of Labor, www.bls.gov/oco/cg/print/cgs011.htm.

U.S. farm sales, and cattle, hogs, and broilers account for two-thirds of live-stock sales.[3] The production of both red meat and poultry meat has been rising, which reflects an increasing demand from American and foreign consumers; the United States is a net meat exporter.

THE MEATPACKING INDUSTRY

Meat processing has changed in scale and location. Compared to the 1970s, there are fewer and larger farms, feedlots, and meat processors, reflecting the consolidation of agriculture and food manufacturing. Meat processing has shifted from urban areas near consumers to rural areas closer to cattle and poultry producers, as from Chicago, Illinois, to Garden City, Kansas. The share of meat processing employees in nonmetro counties rose from less than half in 1980 to 60 percent by 2000.[4]

Meatpacking shifted from urban to rural areas for several reasons, including the cost of land, wages, and transportation costs. Many of the newer rural plants are larger than the older urban plants they replaced, making land costs and often fewer environmental restrictions important considerations in plant site decisions. Some researchers attribute the shift to rural areas almost entirely to the search for lower labor costs (Melton and Huffman, 1995). Rural plants, which are less unionized than urban plants, are often larger than the urban plants they replaced, and include workers who cut up, cook, and sometimes season meat products for retail sale . . . Most of the workers in rural meatpacking plants are less skilled than the butchers in retail stores that they replaced.[5] Finally, animals convert feed into meat, and transportation costs are lower if meat is transported rather than animals from the areas in which they are raised.

Meatpacking has been expanding while the other major food processing industry, fruit and vegetable preserving, has been shrinking. During the 1960s, meatpacking wages were higher than cannery wages, but the meatpacking wage premium has disappeared, and cannery wages were higher than meatpacking wages in the 1990s, because most fruit and vegetable plants are in high-wage states such as California. However, the characteristics of meatpacking and cannery workers have converged, with Hispanics dominating in both sectors (see table 6).[6]

Table 6 U.S. Meatpacking and Cannery Employment and Earnings, 1990–2004

	Production Worker Employment (1000s)			Hourly Earnings, Production Workers		
	Meatpacking	Cannery	All Food Mfg.	Meatpacking	Cannery	All Food Mfg.
1990	368	181	1,165	7.87	9.00	9.04
1991	372	185	1,174	8.03	9.44	9.32
1992	376	182	1,182	8.24	9.72	9.59
1993	385	180	1,195	8.41	10.08	9.82
1994	392	180	1,200	8.62	10.21	10.00
1995	409	179	1,221	8.88	10.50	10.27
1996	419	174	1,228	9.04	10.72	10.50
1997	422	172	1,228	9.26	10.97	10.77
1998	428	170	1,228	9.56	11.30	11.09
1999	438	166	1,229	9.88	11.60	11.40
2000	440	164	1,228	10.27	11.90	11.77
2001	445	159	1,221	10.53	12.32	12.18
2002	445	149	1,202	10.91	12.81	12.55
2003	446	152	1,193	11.30	12.79	12.80
2004	438	151	1,181	11.53	12.86	12.98
1990–1995	11%	−1%	5%	13%	17%	14%
1996–2000	5%	−6%	0%	14%	11%	12%
2000–2004	5%	−13%	−4%	28%	20%	24%

Source: http://www.bls.gov/ces/home.htm

Notes: Cannery is NAICS 3114, fruit and vegetable preserving and specialty; meatpacking is NAICS 3116, animal slaughtering and processing.

The Economic Census of 2002 reported that 86 percent of the more than 500,000 employees in meat processing establishments were production work- ers.[7] They earned an average of $22,400 in 2002 or $10.80 an hour. Half worked in red meat plants and half in poultry plants, and red meat workers had higher earnings because more were in the Midwest, where unions are stronger. Meatpacking work is "hard and dangerous, and wages are low by manufacturing standards, although often high compared with alternative em- ployment in the rural communities in which plants are concentrated" (see table 7; Craypo, 1994, 85).

The U.S. poultry processing industry is the world's largest,[8] and the United States is the second-largest exporter of poultry meat (after Brazil), exporting 15 percent of U.S. production. The poultry industry developed, which after the red meat industry, has been marked by rapid innovation, with new products ranging from chicken nuggets to poultry luncheon meats that allow pro- cessors to obtain higher prices for meat that was once consumed at much lower prices, such as chicken wings.[9]

Table 7 U.S. Meat Processing Industry, 2002

NAICS	Companies	Establishments	100+ Employees
311611 Animal (Except Poultry) Slaughtering	1,776	1,869	179
311612 Meat Processed from Carcasses	1,193	1,335	258
311615 Poultry Processing	311	536	319
Totals	3,280	3,740	756

	Production Workers		Average		
	Workers	Hours	Wages	Annual	Hourly
311611 Animal (Except Poultry) Slaughtering	134,444	300,059	3,375,196	25,105	11.25
311612 Meat Processed from Carcasses	79,494	165,264	2,033,078	25,575	12.30
311615 Poultry Processing	216,405	428,047	4,218,578	19,494	9.86
Total/Average	430,343	893,370	9,626,852	22,370	10.78

Source: Economic Census of 2002, www.census.gov/econ/census02.

Note: This table excludes the small rendering and meat by-product processing sectors.

Poultry was the first vertically integrated meat industry. This means that poultry processors supply farmers with chicks, feed, and instructions on how the chickens are to be raised. Farmers own the buildings in which the chickens are raised and supply labor to raise them. Under their contracts, the farmers receive the difference between the value of the chickens they raised and the cost of the chicks, feed, and antibiotics supplied by the processor.

The United States has the world's largest beef industry and the largest feedlot industry producing grain-fed beef. The beef industry has two distinct segments. Cow-calf operations with less than 100 head typically graze cows and their calves on land that is not suitable for growing crops; calves are then sold to feedlots and are fed grain for about 140 days until they are slaughtered.[10] More than 80 percent of U.S. cattle are from feedlots that have 1,000 head or more. The United States is a net importer of beef, exporting high-value grain-fed cuts and importing low-value grass-fed meat that is often turned into ground beef.

LABOR AND EMPLOYMENT

Food manufacturing today pays less than the average wage in the U.S. private sector, and meatpacking pays less than the average wage in food manufacturing. However, food manufacturing workers tend to work more hours per week than other private-sector workers, 40 hours in meatpacking in 2002 versus 34 hours in all of manufacturing, and the longer work week narrows the earnings gap. The median hourly earnings of meatpacking workers were $9.80 an hour in 2002 for slaughterers and meat packers and $8.47 for meat, poultry, and fish cutters and trimmers. According to the economic census, about 18 percent of meatpacking workers belonged to unions, with especially low rates of unionization for southeastern poultry workers (see table 8).

Meatpacking is one of the most dangerous manufacturing jobs. Muscular trauma, repetitive motion disease, and cuts and strains are among the common injuries. One reason for more injuries is faster disassembly lines. During the 1950s, Chicago slaughterhouses lines often handled 50 cattle an hour. By the 1980s, slaughterhouses in the rural Midwest processed 200 cattle an hour, albeit with technology such as electric knives that increased worker productivity. Today, many plants process 400 cattle an hour, raising the question of whether migrant newcomers, most of whom have not worked in meatpacking before, are expected to work too fast.

Table 8 Average Earnings ($), Production Workers, Food
Manufacturing, 2002

	Weekly	Hourly
U.S. Private Industry	506	14.95
Food Manufacturing	**497**	**12.54**
Grain and Oilseed Milling	802	18.14
Beverages	684	17.38
Dairy Products	639	15.83
Sugar and Confectionery Products	597	15.08
Fruit and Vegetable Preserving and Specialty	514	12.83
Other Food Products	503	12.77
Bakeries and Tortilla Manufacturing	453	12.30
Animal Slaughtering and Processing	442	10.91
Seafood Product Preparation and Packaging	334	9.70

Source: U.S. Department of Labor, ww.bls.gov/oco/cg/print/cgs011.htm.

The Bureau of Labor Statistics (BLS) conducts an annual survey of workplace injuries to develop an injury incidence rate, which is the number of injuries and illnesses reported per 100 full-time equivalent workers.[11] In 2006, there were 111 million private-sector workers, and the injury-incidence rate was 4.4 percent, meaning that 4 out of 100 full-time workers had a reportable injury or illness. The incidence rate was 6 percent in manufacturing, 7.4 percent in food manufacturing, and more than 9 percent in animal slaughtering and processing (higher in red meat and lower in poultry).

Meatpacking in the 1960s was a union stronghold, with a master agreement that kept meatpacking wages 15 percent above the average manufacturing wage. In 2007, average earnings in US manufacturing were $17 an hour, far above the average $11 an hour in meatpacking. If the 1960s meatpacking wage premium had still been in place, meatpacking workers would have earned almost $20 an hour.

One reason meatpacking wages were so high in the past was because most plants were in cities, where meat packers had to pay high wages to keep workers from moving to other jobs. There were strikes and protests in the 1970s as urban meat packers asked for wage cuts to keep plants open,[12] but most urban plants closed even as meatpacking wages slipped below the average for manufacturing workers in the mid-1980s.

Meatpacking's transition from urban to rural areas was eased by innovations that allowed the use of lower-skilled workers. However, despite casting a wider net for workers, many rural meatpacking plants could not recruit enough workers, especially to staff second or evening shifts. This made recruiting workers a top priority of rural plants, which they did by attracting refugees being resettled in the United States and recruiting workers in south Texas and other U.S. areas known for persisting high unemployment (Stull and Broadway, 2003).

The labor watershed for meat packers was the Immigration Reform and Control Act of 1986 (IRCA), which legalized more than 2 million Mexicans. Legalized Mexicans who were a common sight in California and Florida realized that they could move to the Midwest and work year-round in meatpacking plants. With two earners and year-round work, many could buy homes in the small towns with plants that processed hogs and cattle.

Profiles of the internal migration that occurred in the late 1980s and 1990s demonstrate that meatpacking was a step up the U.S. job ladder for many seasonal farmworkers. Six brothers from Michoacan migrated to Oxnard, California, and became seasonal strawberry pickers. They were legalized under the IRCA, and soon moved to Arkansas to work for Tyson Foods, where their annual earnings rose from $8,000 to $20,000 a year. With low-cost housing available, the brothers and their families became home owners, a goal that eluded them in California.[13]

Employer preferences speeded up this ethnic change in the meatpacking labor force. Meatpacking is a high-turnover job, meaning that it is not uncommon for a firm to hire 200 workers in the course of one year to keep 100 jobs filled. Human resource managers, whose job was to keep the disassembly lines fully staffed, soon learned that they could use network recruitment to hire and train good workers; in other words, once a Latino immigrant was hired, he or she would be asked to bring friends or relatives to fill vacant jobs. Many meat packers offered $150 to $300 to anyone who referred workers who were hired and stayed on the job 60 or 90 days. Network recruitment had many advantages for firms, since current workers who knew what the job required did not refer workers who could not do the job, and often trained the workers they brought into the plant.

It took time for network recruitment to efficiently acquire additional workers, allowing recruiters to play a key role in the Latinization of meatpacking. Usually acting as independent contractors, these recruiters found workers in areas such as south Texas. After screening the workers for drugs and work authorization papers, the recruiters put them on buses headed north to the plants. Problems with recruiters were soon apparent, prompting Iowa and other states to enact laws that required employers who recruited out-of-state workers to cover the cost of return transportation to the place of recruitment if the worker was not hired or did not stay on the job.[14] Meatpacking plants evaded such laws by adopting a "don't know" attitude toward recruiters— they paid a recruitment bonus to anyone who referred workers, from current workers to recruiters, and they did not want to know how it was done.

An example of how paid recruiters operated was provided by a reporter who went to south Texas and was recruited to work at Hudson Foods in Missouri. Located just outside the 1,200-resident city of Noel, this poultry processor paid $175 to anyone who referred workers who stayed on the job at least two months.[15] Hudson employed 1,200 workers to process 1.3 million chickens a week, but turnover was so high that 50 new workers a month were hired, equivalent to replacing half of the workforce in the course of the year.[16]

In south Texas, a recruiter found workers, verified their work authorization papers, administered a drug test, and then sent them by bus to Missouri. Newcomers were offered housing in the Ginger Blue Motel for $45 a week, and the hotel manager helped new arrivals to apply for food stamps.[17] Workers went to work right away, beginning on the part of the semiautomated "disassembly" line where they were least likely to slow down faster workers.

The Hudson plant was outside the city limits, so it paid no property taxes to Noel. As the number of non-English-speaking students in grades K–12 rose, Hudson did not contribute for language aides. Instead, Hudson's human resources director explained that its hiring policies generated larger benefits: "There's a large number of jobs that very few citizens in the United States want to do, but they are here and they need to be done. . . . One of the social goods the poultry industry provides is employing people who would otherwise have a great deal of trouble getting employed."[18]

The question is: What happens next in the meat towns and cities of rural America? Worker turnover in meat and poultry processing remains high, as workers move on to better jobs and their U.S.-educated children avoid the plants. The immigration treadmill that brings a constant inflow of newcomers to staff the plants also creates jobs in the service economy for former meat workers and their children. However, most children educated in meatpacking towns will imitate local youth and leave for more opportunities. This means that attracting immigrants to staff meatpacking plants may create another port of entry for the rural poor of Mexico and other countries, who move on to other jobs as soon as they can.

IMMIGRATION ENFORCEMENT

Aware that many of the workers brought into plants by recruiters and networks are unauthorized, immigration enforcement authorities have targeted the meatpacking industry several times. An estimated 25 to 35 percent of meatpacking workers are unauthorized (GAO, 1998; Passel, 2005). Those who enforce immigration laws believe that reducing the employment of unauthorized workers will open jobs for U.S. workers by forcing meatpacking firms to raise wages and improve working conditions. There have been three significant efforts to reduce the employment of unauthorized workers in meatpacking, with mixed results.

The first enforcement action, Operation Vanguard, was launched in Nebraska in 1998–1999. Vanguard was a response to criticism that Immigration and Naturalization Service (INS) agents who periodically surrounded plants and checked on the legal status of workers disrupted production and prompted migrants to risk injuries as they tried to escape. Instead of plant raids, the INS subpoenaed employee data from meatpacking plants and checked them against Social Security and immigration databases.

These checks of employee data found that some of the plants appeared to have only legal workers. However, in 60 of the 111 plants checked, typically the larger ones, there were discrepancies for about 20 percent of the workers. The INS told employers which employees' data was suspect, and the employers asked these employees to clear the discrepancies before INS agents arrived to interview them. Most of the 4,500 suspect employees quit before the INS agents arrived, but 1,000 were interviewed and 34 arrested.

This database-checking strategy, which the Department of Homeland Security (DHS) attempted to revive in August 2007, was roundly criticized. Meat packers argued that there should not be targeted enforcement in Nebraska, where the unemployment rate was under 3 percent. Farmers complained that the targeted enforcement was slowing speeds on the slaughter line, contributing to low beef and pork prices. Then Governor, and Senator since 2000, Ben Nelson (D-NE) combined these arguments: "It was ill-advised for Operation Vanguard to start out in a state with such low employment and an already big problem with a shortage of labor. . . . There has been an adverse economic impact on agriculture because of this."[19]

Migrant and enforcement advocates also united in criticism of Operation Vanguard. Most of the workers who had discrepancies quit their jobs but did not leave the United States, prompting migrant advocates to complain that

Vanguard was denying parents the jobs they needed to support their U.S.-citizen children.[20] The National Council of La Raza sent a letter to President Clinton asking that Operation Vanguard be stopped because it increased discrimination against Latinos.[21] Enforcement advocates, on the other hand, condemned Vanguard for not removing unauthorized workers from the United States, noting that Vanguard mostly shuffled unauthorized workers from one employer to another.

The backlash from meat packers, unions, farmers, and migrant and enforcement advocates prompted the Social Security Administration (SSA) to stop checking subpoenaed employee data. The INS in Omaha found a private data processing firm to check employee records, and offered to send only questionable records to the SSA, but INS headquarters did not allow Vanguard to resume. The INS agents who thought they developed an effective enforcement strategy were dismayed. They reported that during the six months that Vanguard was most active in 1999, they spent $528,000 to remove 3,500 unauthorized workers from meatpacking jobs. By comparison, some $234,000 was spent on one 1992 raid on a Monfort plant in Grand Island that resulted in 307 arrests.[22]

After the raids, then-Nebraska Governor Mike Johanns appointed a task force to evaluate the effects of Vanguard. It acknowledged that the INS had the responsibility to detect and remove unauthorized workers, and recommended a fine-tuned enforcement strategy, such as checking the status of workers only at plants suspected of having unauthorized workers. It also urged state and local governments to do more to integrate immigrants and their children in meatpacking towns to avoid an underclass, "a cycle of working poverty, 'drop outs,' lack of hope, and lack of civic engagement."

A second type of enforcement involved using undercover agents to indict Tyson Foods for conspiring to recruit and transport illegal workers to several of the company's 57 poultry processing plants in the Midwest and the South. According to the indictment, some of Tyson's plant managers arranged with smugglers to pick up newly arrived workers in south Texas and transport them to plants in Tennessee, receiving $100 to $200 a worker in "recruitment fees" paid with corporate checks.[23] The smugglers also charged the migrants fees to cross the border and get jobs at Tyson (Tanger, 2006).

Tyson is the largest meat processor in the United States—with 120,000 employees at 130 locations—and generates revenues of $11 billion a year. If found guilty of smuggling, harboring, and employing unauthorized workers in order to hold down the wages of U.S. workers and increase profits, as the indictment charged, Tyson faced fines of up to $100 million, triple the profits it allegedly earned by its unlawful activities. The assistant U.S. attorney in Chattanooga explained why the INS worked several years to bring charges against Tyson: "It's much more productive, we think, to attack the source, the companies that recruit these illegals, than to pursue endless prosecutions of illegals at the border."

Tyson countered that it took reasonable steps to ensure that the workers it hired were legally authorized to work. Tyson and most other meat packers voluntarily use the Basic Pilot Program (renamed E-Verify in 2007) to check the data provided by new hires against government databases. In some of its Tennessee plants, the indictment alleged that "Tyson utilized workers that were hired and provided to Tyson by temporary service agencies that did not utilize the . . . Basic Pilot Program, well knowing that most of these workers were unauthorized for employment within the United States."

Government prosecutors aimed to make an example of Tyson, calling top managers "pinstriped coyotes" who knew what plant managers were doing. They alleged that Tyson had a "corporate culture" that encouraged the hiring of illegal aliens to cut costs. Tyson said the federal government offered to settle the case for a $100 million fine, based on the assumed excess profits earned by Tyson because it could pay lower wages by hiring unauthorized workers. Noting that the highest fine paid for hiring unauthorized workers before 2001 was $1.9 million, Tyson refused to settle.

A Chattanooga jury acquitted Tyson after a seven-week trial in 2003. Instead of a corporate conspiracy, the jury agreed with Tyson that a few rogue managers broke company policy by paying recruitment fees to INS agents posing as smugglers, but that top management was not involved in local recruitment and hiring decisions. The jury believed Tyson, which argued "It is not the fault of this company that there are approximately eight million undocumented workers in the United States. It is not our fault that the systems that the government has set up for hiring employees are not perfect. If the prosecutors and the government want a perfect system, the government ought to be designing it."[24]

The acquittal did not end Tyson's troubles over hiring unauthorized workers. Private attorneys filed a class action suit on behalf of some of Tyson's legal workers under the federal Racketeer Influenced and Corrupt Organizations Act (RICO) law, which allows plaintiffs to recover triple damages if offenders conspired to violate federal laws. The attorneys cited the evidence assembled by the government, viz, that Tyson's corporate culture made "the hiring of illegal alien workers [necessary] to meet its production goals and cut its costs to maximize Tyson profits."

Most RICO suits against employers that allege a conspiracy to hire unauthorized workers to reduce wages and increase profits are settled because of the risk of triple damages. However, Tyson elected to fight the private attorneys, and persuaded a federal district judge to dismiss the RICO suit in July 2002; the judge noted that Tyson's workers were covered by a collective bargaining agreement so that the union, not the workers, would have to pursue the claim that Tyson held down wages by hiring unauthorized workers. The 6th U.S. Circuit Court of Appeals in June 2004 reversed this decision, saying that the U.S. workers were entitled to try to convince a jury that their wages had been lowered by Tyson's hiring of unauthorized workers. However, just before the trial scheduled for March 2008, the federal judge once again dismissed the RICO suit, concluding that lawyers for the U.S. workers failed to prove that Tyson's employment of unauthorized workers depressed the wages of legal workers.[25]

In contrast to Operation Vanguard (an effort to keep unauthorized workers out of meatpacking jobs without workplace raids) and the Tyson indictment (an effort to hold top management accountable for the recruiting policies of its managers), immigration enforcers returned to workplace raids on December 12, 2006. On that day, more than 1,000 Immigrations and Customs Enforcement (ICE) agents surrounded six Swift & Company beef and pork processing plants, screened most of the 7,000 employees at work on the day shift, and arrested 1,282 unauthorized workers, including 170 who were accused of identity theft for using valid Social Security numbers belonging to other people to get their jobs.[26] ICE Director Julie Meyers hailed the Swift raids, the agency's largest-ever workplace enforcement effort, and said that it "should send a clear message to employers: Hiring illegal workers is not acceptable."

The Swift raid was widely condemned. Swift emphasized that it had been submitting data on newly hired workers to the government for verification since 1997, so the fact that unauthorized workers were found in its plants highlighted the shortcomings of government databases.[27] Swift reported that it paid a $200,000 fine when Worthington, Minnesota, plant managers asked Latino job applicants to provide additional proof of their legal status, the largest employment discrimination fine based on immigration status by 2002. Swift portrayed itself as caught between competing federal laws—sanctions laws aimed at keeping unauthorized workers out of jobs and antidiscrimination laws limiting the questioning of worker-provided documents. Swift was not fined, but reported losing $20 million because of the raid; Swift was acquired by Brazil's JBS for $225 million plus the assumption of $1.2 billion of debt in 2007 .[28]

The United Food and Commercial Workers International Union (UFCW), which represented workers at five of the six Swift plants, also complained about the raids. The UFCW, like the American Federation of Labor and Congress of Industrial Organizations (AFL-CIO), opposes the enforcement of employer sanctions laws, arguing that: "Worksite raids are not an effective form of immigration reform. They terrorize workers and destroy families." The UFCW argued that only the workers sought for identity theft should have been detained and interviewed, not Swift's U.S. citizen and legal immigrant workers. Migrant advocates emphasized that the Swift raid disrupted families and may have pushed some U.S.-born children of migrants into the welfare system.

The Vanguard, Tyson, and Swift enforcement actions demonstrate the difficulty of enforcing laws against hiring unauthorized workers in meat and poultry processing. In each case, enforcement was stopped after an outcry from employers, unions, and migrant advocates, allowing the status quo to resume. Months after the targeted enforcement, the employment of unauthorized workers using false documents resumed.

This is what happened at chicken processor Crider Inc. in Stillmore, Georgia, almost 200 miles southeast of Atlanta. Crider was raided by ICE agents over Labor Day weekend in 2006, and lost 75 percent of its 900-member workforce.[29] Crider was not fined, and responded to the raid by increasing its starting wage by up to 50 percent.[30] Crider also asked the Employment Service office to send workers looking for jobs, and hired half of those referred. But Crider's major effort to replenish its workforce was to turn to a labor recruiter, Peacock Poultry, which recruited rural blacks throughout the state and offered them housing in Crider-owned dorms in Stillmore.[31]

Blacks soon dominated Crider's labor force, and the raids appeared to be a successful example of opening jobs for local workers. But the new hires soon complained about wages and working conditions. Blacks were only 15 percent of the workforce before the raids, and Crider's president explained that Hispanics were hired because "We want people who want to work and are willing to work every day."[32] Blacks complained that supervisors accustomed to Hispanic workers returning to work quickly after slips and falls found them to be poor workers when they took time to recuperate. The workforce became more diverse as Crider began hiring felons on probation from a nearby state prison, residents of a homeless mission in Macon, and Hmong from Minnesota and Wisconsin.

The Crider case illustrates the changes in personnel policies that can occur when employers become accustomed to a seemingly endless supply of migrants. Crider was able to find local workers after it raised wages, but they were not as "good" as the migrants they replaced. Supervisors accustomed to the obedience of newcomer immigrants soon clashed with U.S. workers who asserted their rights. The supervisors' preference for Hispanic workers prompted Crider in 2007 to turn to a Hispanic recruiter, and the Latino share of the workforce is rising again.

Data matching, undercover agents, and workplace raids failed to slow the rising share of Latinos in the U.S. meat and poultry processing industry. After the Senate failed to enact comprehensive immigration reform in May–June 2007 that was strongly supported by President Bush, the DHS announced a return to a Vanguard-type data-matching enforcement strategy. Under a strategy announced in August 2008, the DHS would have had the SSA include a notice advising U.S. employers receiving no-match letters to fire workers who cannot clear up discrepancies within 90 days or face fines for "knowingly" hiring unauthorized workers.

The background for this no-match strategy is straightforward. SSA sends no-match letters to employers who pay taxes on behalf of 10 or more workers for whom names and Social Security Numbers (SSNs) do not match SSA databases. The letters to be sent in September 2007 dealt with discrepancies for employer-reported wages in 2006. However, the DHS's strategy was challenged by a coalition that included the AFL-CIO, the U.S. Chamber of Commerce, and the American Civil Liberties Union, and this coalition won a court injunction that blocked the distribution of the DHS notice with the SSA's no-match letters because of acknowledged errors in the SSA database; the judge agreed with unions and employers that these errors could lead to "irreparable harm to innocent workers and employers" who may be fired because of errors.[33] The DHS said it would respond to the judge's concerns so that the no-match enforcement strategy could go into effect, but the concrete result so far is that there were no letters sent dealing with 2006 mismatches.

Even if the DHS notices are eventually included with no-match letters, and employers react by firing workers who cannot clear up discrepancies to avoid possible fines, the effect may be to shuffle unauthorized workers between employers, as Vanguard did. Under current procedures, it takes almost two years after a no-match worker is hired for the SSA to determine that there is a discrepancy and notify employers. Workers then have 90 days to deal with it, which they could do by quitting and returning to the same employer with another identity, winning another two years of employment, or changing employers using their old identities and working another two years. Under this scenario, no-match enforcement would promote the circulation of unauthorized workers between employers rather than decreasing their employment.

COMMUNITY IMPACTS

Enforcement has been unable to slow the hiring of unauthorized workers in the expanding meatpacking industry. There are no reliable time series data on the share of unauthorized workers in meatpacking, but the Equal Employment Opportunity Commission (EEOC) data on the sex and race or ethnicity of employees of private employers shows that the percentage of Hispanics classified as laborers in meat processing rose from 44 to 57 percent between 1999 and 2005, and laborers were 55 percent of the industry's employees in 2005 (see table 9).

What does Latino immigration mean for the often small towns and cities with meatpacking plants? A Government Accounting Office study examined the effects of immigration in 16 midwestern counties with large meatpacking plants and found largely benign effects. It acknowledged that there were rapid increases in the number of pupils who spoke limited English, Medicaid recipients,[34] and reported crimes in counties with meatpacking plants, but there were also faster-than-average increases in taxable sales or per capita incomes (GAO, 1998).

Table 9 Race/Ethnicity of Meatpacking Laborers, 1999–2005

	1999	2001	2003	2005
White	24%	21%	20%	17%
Black	27%	24%	22%	21%
Hispanic	44%	50%	53%	57%
Asian	5%	4%	4%	4%

Source: Equal Employment Opportunity Commission, www .eeoc.gov/stats/jobpat/jobpat.html.

Note: SIC 201 Meat Products until 2002; NAICS 3116 Animal Slaughtering and Processing after 2003.

The GAO noted that the quality of housing in communities with large meatpacking plants was generally adequate, but the effort of many workers to remit some of their earnings, and others to accommodate relatives, sometimes led to overcrowding (GAO, 1998, 14). Rents often rose sharply, as workers moved into areas with a limited supply of rental housing, and some workers paid high rent for poor-quality housing. The complaints of community leaders often focused on the behavior of men in the United States without their families, including drinking and driving without licenses and insurance. Activists say that some migrants turn to methamphetamine (crack) to keep up with the disassembly line.

Many community studies of meatpacking towns focus on the hopes and dreams of migrant families (Anrig and Wang, 2007; Gozdziak and Martin, 2005; Zúñiga and Hernández-León, 2005). These ethnographic studies emphasize that a combination of employer attitudes, community economic circumstances, and migrant attitudes and experiences combine to shape the integration of newcomers in meatpacking towns.

One undercurrent in these studies is the stark choice facing many small towns, which is to accept the diversification that comes with immigrants or risk depopulation as plants close (Kandel and Parrado, 2005). Over the past 50 years, rural counties without a city of at least 2,500 people lost more than a third of their residents in 11 Great Plains states,[35] with farm-based counties away from interstate highways losing the most people. Remaining residents are disproportionately elderly: 97 of the 99 U.S. counties with the highest percentage of residents older than age 85 were in the Great Plains, according to the 2000 census, making it difficult to attract new businesses and retain young people. If meatpacking towns do not find workers, some plants would close, which could accelerate population decline.

Three examples illustrate the challenge of integrating immigrants in meatpacking towns. Beardstown highlights the tensions between settled residents and newcomers, Storm Lake demonstrates local acceptance of newcomers, and Dodge City presents a mixed picture. The Beardstown Ladies Investment Club put the Illinois city of 7,000 on the map in the 1980s,[36] and immigration accelerated after a local meatpacking plant that closed in 1986 was reopened in 1987. Beardstown wanted the jobs, and privately owned Cargill was allowed to receive state tax benefits for its meatpacking subsidiary Excel without opening its books under a special exception to the usual rules.[37]

Excel reduced the starting wage from $8.75 an hour paid by previous meat packer Oscar Mayer to $6.50 an hour. Excel hired former Oscar Mayer workers but, as they moved onto other jobs because of the lower wage, Excel used recruiters in south Texas to acquire more workers, offering $150 for each new hire who stayed on the job at least three months. Some of the new hires were unauthorized, presenting false documents to get hired, which prompted Beardstown Mayor Bob Walters to accuse Excel of operating "in the gray area. They don't violate the law, but they sure don't play by the book, either." Excel said it "follows the government's I-9 requirements for verifying employment eligibility." The newspaper series concluded that Beardstown is "propped up by one major employer, a partially undocumented work force and uneasy residents."

Storm Lake, Iowa, was spotlighted during the presidential primaries in 2000, when organizations advocating less immigration ran ads asserting that the "quality of life is but a memory" in Storm Lake because meat packers recruited immigrants to work in pork processing plants. Then Governor Tom Vilsack said, "We deplore this propaganda campaign" and George W. Bush, then the governor of Texas, said the ads reflected "the xenophobic, dark side of American politics." Many Storm Lake residents said they preferred the diversity associated with immigration to the depopulation that would likely follow the closure of the pork plants. Storm Lake's school K–12 enrollment rose 17 percent in the 1990s, even as 70 percent of Iowa's schools were losing students (Millard and Chapa, 2004).

Some Iowa meatpacking communities have embraced immigration, forming sister-city relationships with migrant areas of origin. For example, half of the 1,900 meatpacking workers in Swift's Marshalltown, Iowa, plant are from Villachuato, Mexico,[38] and the two cities have a sister-city program that includes an exchange of teachers (Grey and Woodrick, 2005). The Marshalltown Chamber of Commerce welcomes the immigration that keeps the Swift plant operating, saying "economic development is about attracting people," and notes that immigration has returned the city's population to its 1980 level of 26,000.[39] Iowa's state government designated Marshalltown a "model community" for immigrant integration.

Dodge City, Kansas, was founded in 1872 as a trailhead for cattle driven north from Texas; its sheriffs included Bat Masterson and Wyatt Earp (and the fictional Matt Dillon). Today, Dodge City is often described as a place that sends local youth away for education and jobs and attracts Mexican immigrants to fill jobs in its meatpacking plants.[40] Hispanics are 75 percent of the workforce at the city's two largest meat packers, and most arrived after 1990. Their impact is especially noticeable in the schools, which had a majority of

Hispanic students within a decade after immigrants were recruited for the meatpacking plants.

Meatpacking plants that moved from urban to rural areas could move again in the future, searching for animals, low-cost labor, and friendly environmental and other regulations. As with farmers who plant crops and assume that the government will make affordable workers available to harvest them, meat packers assume that they will be able to find a workforce willing to work for the wages they offer, even in small towns and cities that are losing people.

Migrants can stabilize or revitalize meatpacking towns, filling homes that might otherwise be vacant and sustaining businesses that might otherwise close. By beginning their American journeys in places that offer one of the fastest paths to the American dream of home ownership and better opportunities for their children, migrants fill low-wage and undesirable jobs. However, if the children of meat packers do not follow their parents into the plants, meatpacking towns can develop the same immigration treadmill apparent in the fields of California and Florida.

Part Three Migrant
Integration

A typical newly arrived seasonal farmworker is a 25-year-old man from rural Mexico not authorized to work in the United States. Most seasonal farmworkers are employed 1,000 hours a year at wages of $8 to $9 an hour, half as many hours as a full-time worker at half the average hourly earnings in the United States, which explains why farmworker earnings of about $8,500 a year are a fourth of average U.S. earnings. Seasonal farmworkers who transition to a year-round job in agriculture or meatpacking earn higher hourly earnings and, with year-round work, annual earnings double to $18,000.

Many immigrant farmworkers form or unite families in the United States, resulting in U.S.-citizen children. This means that immigrant families are often mixed, in the sense that some members of the family are unauthorized, some are legal immigrants, and others are U.S. citizens by birth. Eligibility for and use of public services are uneven. Regardless of legal status, all children are obliged to attend grades K–12, but only some members of farmworker families may be eligible for means-tested benefits such as food stamps, Medicaid, and other assistance. However, most federal programs that provide supplemental education and health-care services targeted to migrant and seasonal workers and their families do not check the legal status of their clients.

The chapters in this section deal with two important aspects of migrant integration. Chapter 6 examines movements in and out of the farm workforce in California. There is no database that tracks farmworkers over time, but the evidence from data that employers report to state tax authorities suggests that most seasonal workers harvest crops for less than a decade. Some seasonal workers are able to find longer-season or even year-round jobs in agriculture, as irrigators and equipment operators or as dairy and livestock workers, but most move into nonfarm jobs that result in higher earnings. A few ex-seasonal farmworkers move down the job ladder, moving from jobs picking fruit and vegetables that paid more than the minimum wage to minimum-wage jobs in gardening and other sectors that may be as seasonal and uncertain as farm jobs.

Chapter 7 reviews the targeted assistance programs launched in the 1960s to serve migrant farmworkers and their children. At the time, there were three major justifications for these programs. First, farmworkers were excluded from many of the federal labor laws that protected most private-sector workers, notably minimum wage and union laws. Second, most welfare assistance before the War on Poverty was provided by states and cities, and they often imposed residency requirements on applicants seeking benefits, such as requiring applicants to live in the state or city at least six months before receiving cash assistance. Migrants who crossed state lines to do seasonal farmwork were often ineligible for welfare benefits in both sending and receiving areas because they did not satisfy these residency requirements, making them (and American Indians) of special concern to the federal government.

The third reason for federal farmworker assistance programs was the belief that most farmworkers would soon be displaced by machines. The exploits of engineers who sent a man to the moon were expected to turn to more mundane issues, such as mechanizing the harvesting of fruits and vegetables. American workers who moved from place to place, and their children with interrupted educations, were believed to need federal assistance to make the transition to nonfarm jobs.

Chapter 6 Seasonal
Worker Mobility

For most people, seasonal farmwork is a job, not a career. It is very hard to paint an accurate portrait of farmworkers and the farm labor market because newcomers are constantly replacing those who leave the farm workforce and some farmworkers also have jobs in other industries. Under most definitions, people who do farmwork for wages at any time during the year are considered farmworkers for that year.

This chapter examines movements into and out of the farm workforce using data reported by employers when paying their unemployment insurance (UI) taxes in California. Since 1978, almost all employers have been required to report the number of hired farmworkers and their earnings. The data do not provide demographic information on farmworkers, but they do illuminate the three key concepts that define farm employment: average, peak, and total employment.

Employment can be measured either at one point in time, as an average over time, or by counting the total number of individuals who were employed over some period of time. In nonseasonal labor markets with little turnover, the three employment concepts yield similar results—if 100 workers are employed during each month and there is no worker turnover from month to month, then point-in-time, average, and total employment is 100. However, agricultural employment during the six summer months may be 150 versus 50 during the six winter months, and employers may have hired 300 workers to keep the average 100 job slots filled; consequently, peak (150), average (100), and total (300) employment counts differ.

Average employment is the most commonly used reference point in any labor market. If the employment of workers on farms is recorded in periodic snapshots, summed, and divided by the number of snapshots, the result is average employment. Employment snapshots, taken monthly for most nonfarm employees and quarterly for hired farmworkers, find that employment of hired farmworkers averages almost 1.1 million and has been remarkably stable for the past quarter century; it was 1.3 million in 1977 (see table 10; U.S. Department of Agriculture, quarterly).

Peak employment can be estimated by determining which snapshot has the highest employment. In U.S. Department of Agriculture (USDA) surveys, peak employment is usually in July, when about 1.3 million hired workers are employed on U.S. farms; this employment reaches a low of less than 800,000 in January.

The total number of workers employed for wages on farms sometime during the year must be larger than peak employment, but there is no national data source that measures how much larger. During the 1970s and 1980s, questions were attached to the monthly Current Population Survey in December that asked if anyone in the household did farmwork for wages during the preceding 12 months—the theory was that migrant workers would be at

Table 10 Average U.S. Farm Employment (1000s), National Agricultural Statistics Service, 2005

	Direct Hire	Agricultural Services
January	589	185
April	746	232
July	936	408
October	840	289
Average	778	279
Average Total	1,056	

Source: Farm Labor,
http://usda.mannlib.cornell.edu/reports/nassr/other/pfl-bb/.

their U.S. homes during December, a theory that became less credible as the share of immigrant farm workers rose.[1] This procedure identified 2.5 million unique individuals who worked for wages on U.S. farms sometime during the year, suggesting that the average year-round job slot was filled by two unique workers.

All seasonal industries have a total workforce that exceeds average employment because of peaks and troughs, but agriculture has among the highest worker-to-job ratios. There are several reasons why at least twice as many farmworkers are employed sometime during the year than there are year-round job slots. First, agriculture has a biological production process, so that nature dictates peak and trough periods of employment. Second, employers do not incur significant penalties for hiring workers only when they are needed, so they have few incentives to stabilize employment, for example, by arranging their operations to keep workers employed longer. However, seasonal employment is a major reason why workers tend to seek nonfarm jobs offering higher wages or more hours of work. Statistical databases do not track farmworkers as they change industry and occupation, which is why special surveys, administrative data, and case studies are the basis for most of what we know about farmworkers.

TRACKING FARMWORKERS

Some of the best administrative data to assess movements into and out of the farm labor market is in the files of the California Unemployment Insurance (UI) system. California employers who pay $100 or more in quarterly wages are required to obtain a unique number from the Employment Development Department (EDD), which assigns each employer or establishment "reporting unit" to a four-digit Standard Industrial Classification (SIC) that reflects the employer's major activity (since 2001, employers have been assigned a six-digit North American Industry Classification System or NAICS code). In agriculture, major farming activities are enumerated in considerable detail, for example, SIC 01 is assigned to farms that produce crops, 017 to farms that produce fruits and nuts, and 0172 to farms that produce grapes.

Employers report the Social Security Numbers (SSNs) and earnings of the workers they hire each quarter, as well as employment during the pay period that includes the 12th of the month. This allows analysis of all farmworkers or SSNs reported by employers with agricultural codes. In the analysis that follows, all workers (SSNs) reported by farmers in California in 1991, 1996, and

2001 were considered farmworkers, and their farm and nonfarm employment and earnings records were compiled to examine how many farm and nonfarm jobs they had, their earnings, and whether the workers reported in 1991 were still employed in 1996 and 2001.

While these data should include all workers employed in California agriculture, they may not, for several reasons. First, some employers are classified as nonfarm establishments even though they hire farmworkers, as when a winery hires vineyard workers. Second, some farm employers hire both farmworkers and others, such as clerical staff on a large farm; no one knows if the exclusion of farmworkers hired by wineries offsets the inclusion of nonfarm clerical workers on farms. Third, some workers have multiple SSNs, while in other cases several workers are employed under a single SSN; no one knows if these multiple-SSN workers cancel out cases of several workers sharing one SSN. For the analysis in this chapter, we excluded any SSNs and jobs that seemed dubious—such as one SSN that was associated with more than 300 farm employers.[2]

JOBS AND WORKERS

Average employment in California agriculture rose faster than nonfarm employment between 1991 and 1996, but fell between 1996 and 2001 as nonfarm employment expanded. Table 11 shows that the major reason for the rapid growth in farm employment in the early 1990s was the surge in farm services

Table 11 California: Average Employment and Unique Social Security Numbers: 1991, 1996, and 2001

California	1991	1996	2001	1991–1996	1996–2001
Payroll Employment	12,701,000	13,151,700	15,084,600	4%	15%
Farm	342,000	408,300	388,000	19%	−5%
Farm Production	218,200	225,700	220,100	3%	−2%
Farm Services	123,800	182,600	168,000	47%	−8%
Unique Farmworker SSNs	907,166	966,593	1,086,563	7%	12%
SSN/Employment Ratio	2.7	2.4	2.8	—	—

Source: Current Employment Statistics (CES) estimates (www.calmis.cahwnet.gov/file/indhist/cal$hws.xls) and analysis of wage records by the Labor Market Information Division of the Employment Development Department.

employment, up from an average 124,000 to 183,000 or almost 50 percent. One reason for the upsurge in farm services employment is that some of the farmworkers legalized under the Immigration Reform and Control Act (IRCA) in 1987–1988 became labor contractors. In the early 1990s, a period of widespread unauthorized migration, many farmers turned to contractors to get farmwork done. There was a shakeout in the late 1990s, however, as some contractors went out of business.

In 1991, there were 2.7 workers or unique SSNs for each year-round equivalent job. The number of farmworkers rose slower than the average number of farm jobs in the first half of the 1990s, so that the worker-to-job ratio fell to 2.4. The number of jobs shrank in the late 1990s while the number of workers rose to almost 1.1 million, increasing the worker-to-job ratio to 2.8, which means that each worker averaged 4.3 months of farmwork.

These statewide patterns are mirrored in the San Joaquin Valley, which has more than half of the state's farm jobs. There was an extraordinary 60 percent increase in farm services employment in the Fruit Bowl in the early 1990s, followed by a 15 percent reduction in the late 1990s. The number of farmworkers rose, but not as fast as the number of farm jobs, so that the ratio of workers to year-round jobs fell from 2.1 in 1991 to 1.9 in 2001. In the Central Coast Vegetable Bowl, by contrast, most firms continued to hire workers directly, a pattern likely explained by the growth of strawberry production and the tendency of small growers to hire workers directly rather than via contractors. By 2001, there were almost four workers per year-round job in the Central Coast area.

Since farmwork is seasonal, it is often assumed that workers change employers and migrate from farm to farm.[3] This does not happen as often as imagined. Statewide, more than half of the unique workers or SSNs were reported by one farm employer, rising to more than 60 percent in the Fruit Bowl and more than 75 percent in the Central Coast. Very few farmworkers were reported by more than three farm employers (see figure 7).

EMPLOYEES, JOBS, AND EARNINGS

The total number of workers reported by agricultural employers rose by a third between 1991 and 2001—there were 1.3 million SSNs reported in 1991, 1.4 million in 1996, and 1.7 million in 2001.[4] Some of these workers were reported by more than one farm employer, so the number of unique SSNs rose from 907,000 in 1991 to 966,000 in 1996 and 1.1 million in 2001. The number

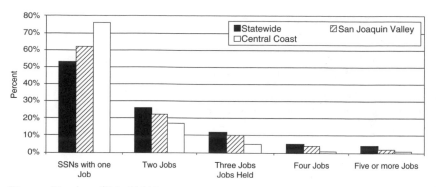

Figure 7 Number of Jobs Held in 2001
Source: Analysis of wage records by the Labor Market Information Division of the Employment Development Department.

of workers or unique SSNs increased faster in the Central Coast Vegetable Bowl than in the San Joaquin Valley Fruit Bowl (see table 12).

The significance of this rising number of unique workers reported by farm employers is that a separate survey of farm employers, the Current Employment Statistics Program, found much smaller increases in farm employment. If we compute the ratio of workers to average employment, we see that more farmworkers are "sharing" fewer year-round equivalent jobs. There are several explanations for the rising number of farmworkers and stable average employment. It may be that there are more unauthorized workers who change SSNs each time they change jobs, so that the uptick in workers is an artifact of rising unauthorized migration, or it may reflect ever more seasonality, with employers hiring workers from an ever-larger pool, only when they are needed.

The workers reported by California agricultural employers had a total 1.5 million farm jobs in 1991, 1.7 million in 1996, and 1.8 million in 2001. Most workers were reported by only one farm employer, meaning they had only one farm job. A quarter of the farmworkers were also reported by a nonfarm employer, generally in services and trade. Regional patterns follow expectations about mixing farmwork and nonfarmwork. In the San Joaquin Valley, which accounted for half of the state's farm jobs, farmworkers were much less likely to be reported by nonfarm employers, while in the Central Coast, which has a tourism industry in the Monterey area, 40 percent of farmworkers were also reported by a nonfarm employer.

The total earnings of California farmworkers were $11.1 billion in 1991, $12.0 billion in 1996, and $15.8 billion in 2001 (all in 2001 dollars).[5] The share

Table 12 Total Employees and Farmworkers (Unique Social Security Numbers), 1991, 1996, 2001

California	1991	1996	2001	1991–1996	1991–2001
Total Farmworkers	1,283,646	1,374,858	1,696,309	7%	32%
Farmworkers (Unique SSNs)	907,166	966,593	1,086,563	7%	20%
Share	71%	70%	64%		
San Joaquin Valley					
Total Employees by SIC	519,672	533,749	564,249	3%	9%
Farmworkers (Unique SSNs)	424,987	452,508	467,716	6%	10%
Share	82%	85%	83%		
Central Coast					
Total Employees by SIC	198,224	239,362	282,562	21%	43%
Farmworkers (Unique SSNs)	140,883	171,509	188,053	22%	33%
Share	71%	72%	67%		

Source: Analysis of wage records by the Labor Market Information Division of the Employment Development Department.

of total earnings from agricultural employers was 77 percent in 1991 and 1996, but fell to 71 percent in 2001, indicating more earnings from nonfarm jobs. Wages are lower in the San Joaquin Valley, which explains why the Fruit Bowl has half of the state's farmworkers and jobs but accounts for only a third of farmworker earnings.

California farmworkers earned an average $9,300 in 2001, but earnings varied by commodity. As expected, annual earnings were highest for workers employed primarily on livestock farms, $14,800, and lower for workers employed in agricultural services and crop production, $8,500. San Joaquin Valley workers earned an average $7,100 in 2001.

However, the most interesting comparison is between workers hired directly by crop farmers and those brought to farms by agricultural services establishments such as labor contractors. In the San Joaquin Valley, workers employed directly by crop farmers earned an average $6,100 in 2001, 50 percent more than the $4,000 earned by employees of agricultural services firms. In the Central Coast, there was a higher 75 percent earnings premium for workers employed directly by crop farms, $10,900, than for workers brought to farms by contractors and other service providers, $6,200.

These data hold two guidelines for workers. First, workers seeking the highest annual earnings should look for employment on livestock farms, which tend to offer year-round work. Second, earnings are higher for workers employed directly by a crop farm than for workers brought to a farm by an agricultural services employer such as a labor contractor. The fact that agricultural services' wages are lower may help to explain their rising share of the farm labor market.

PRIMARY FARMWORKERS AND JOBS

The 1.7 million unique SSNs reported by California farm employers in 2001 had a total 2.5 million jobs, including 1.8 million farm jobs and 700,000 nonfarm jobs, 28 percent. They included 564,000 workers reported by San Joaquin Valley farm employers, who had a total 972,000 jobs, 90 percent with agricultural employers.[6]

Farmworkers were assigned to a "primary" SIC based on where they had their highest earnings. For example, 92 percent of the workers reported by San Joaquin Valley farm employers in 2001 had most of their earnings from agriculture, including 148,000 who had most of their earnings reported by crop employers, 35,000 whose highest earnings were reported by livestock employers, and 250,000 whose highest earnings were reported by agricultural service employers. Illustrating the importance of the Fruit Bowl for California farmworker employment, 49 percent of the farmworkers with the highest earnings in crops were in the San Joaquin Valley, as were 70 percent of farmworkers with the highest earnings in livestock and 50 percent of the farmworkers whose highest earnings were in agricultural services.[7]

The major change in the San Joaquin Valley between 1991 and 2001 was the increase of 44,000 unique SSNs, which likely reflects the shift from the direct to the indirect hiring of farmworkers. There was a drop of 20,000 workers reported by crop employers, an increase of 6,000 workers reported by livestock employers, and an increase of 58,000 agricultural services workers, 83 percent of whom were reported by farm labor contractors. In other words, almost all of the increase in farmworkers in the San Joaquin Valley between 1991 and 2001 can be accounted for by rising contractor employment.

Most workers were reported by only one agricultural employer. In 2001, 303,000 workers in the San Joaquin Valley were reported by one agricultural employer and 97,000 were reported by two or more agricultural employers. Few farmworkers had nonfarm jobs—only 19,000 were reported at least once by an agricultural employer and a nonfarm employer, and 14,000 were re-ported by at least two agricultural employers and one nonfarm employer. In 1991 and 1996, the pattern was similar—68 percent of workers were reported by one agricultural employer, 23 to 25 percent by two agricultural employers, 4 percent by at least two agricultural employers and one nonfarm employer, and 4 percent by one farm and one nonfarm employer.

The workers reported by agricultural employers can be distributed into more detailed commodity subcategories. For example, there were 503,760 workers statewide in 2001 who had most of their earnings with agricultural services employers, and two-thirds of them had jobs only in agricultural services. Patterns of job holding conform to expectations, so that 80 percent of primarily dairy workers were employed only by dairy employers, while less than 60 percent of those who earned more from grapes than any other commodity were employed only in grapes. In citrus, tree fruits, and vegetables, 55 to 65 percent of the workers who had most of their earnings in these commodities worked only in these commodities.

EARNINGS AND HOURS WORKED

Agricultural employers in the San Joaquin Valley paid a total of $3.3 billion to farmworkers in 2001, while agricultural employers in the Central Coast paid $2 billion. Average statewide earnings for all persons reported at least once by an agricultural employer were $10,200, but were lower in the San Joaquin Valley, $7,107, and higher in the Central Coast, $10,838. Statewide, workers employed primarily in crops earned an average $8,500, those employed primarily in livestock $14,800, and those employed primarily in agricultural services $5,000.

If we focus only on workers employed primarily in agricultural services, we find considerable variation. Workers primarily employed in soil preparation services (SIC 0711) earned an average $15,900 in 2001, followed by $10,100 for crop preparation services for market (custom harvesters, SIC 0723), and only $2,900 for employees of labor contractors. The average earnings of farmworkers vary significantly, even within detailed four-digit commodity codes, with a high standard deviation around the mean wage.[8]

If farmworkers in the San Joaquin Valley are ranked from the lowest to the highest paid, the lowest 25 percent generally earned less than $3,000 in 2001. For example, among workers primarily employed in vegetables and melons in 2001 (SIC 0161), the first quartile or 25th percentile annual earnings were

$1,600, meaning that a quarter of workers earned less than this amount.[9] The 25th percentile earnings line was lowest for those employed primarily by contractors, only $394 or equivalent to 63 hours of work at the then minimum wage of $6.25 an hour. The highest 25th percentile mark was in beef cattle feedlots and mushrooms (food grown under cover) (see table 13).

Farmworkers in the Central Coast had higher average earnings but more variability. Median annual earnings in this region ranged from less than $2,000 for those reported by tree fruit farms to more than $21,000 for those reported by employers who grew food under cover, generally mushroom farms. This variability in earnings partly reflects seasonality, since the region's apple pickers have fewer hours of work than the mushroom workers. The 75th percentile of earnings, the highest earnings that a nonsupervisory worker could normally expect to achieve, ranged from $4,100 for those primarily employed by contractors to $21,300 for those employed in crop preparation services for market.

WORKER RETENTION

Data on workers and jobs show that almost three individuals share the equivalent of one year-round farm job in California agriculture, and few of these farmworkers return year after year. Only 24 percent of the farmworkers (unique SSNs) reported by agricultural employers in 1991 were also reported in 1996 and 2001, and retention rates were even lower in the San Joaquin Valley and Central Coast. Retention rates were higher in shorter five-year periods. For example, about 40 percent of the farmworkers reported in 1991 were also reported in 1996, and almost 40 percent of those reported in 1996 were also reported in 2001 (see table 14).

There is significant variation in worker retention rates by commodity and region. San Joaquin Valley worker retention rates were much higher in flower and nursery product establishments than for workers employed by citrus growers. Central Coast worker retention rates were higher for vegetables than fruits, suggesting that commodities that offer longer periods of employment have higher worker retention rates (see tables 15 and 16).

Some commodities have complementary harvesting seasons. For example, in the San Joaquin Valley, navel oranges and table grapes are grown in the same areas, and the oranges are harvested in the winter months while the grapes are harvested in the summer. While workers who harvest both crops could have a longer period of employment, few directly hired citrus workers

Table 13 California: Earnings of Primary Employees ($), 2001

Industry Title	SIC	Primary Workers	Mean Earnings	Std Dev	Median Earnings	Hours Worked 8.02/hr[1]	25th Percentile Earning	Hours Worked 6.25/hr	75th Percentile Earning	Hours Worked 10/hr	Total Earnings (mils)
Cotton	0131	7,409	15,156	15,705	12,243	1,527	3,692	591	21,622	2,162	112
Vegetables and Melons	0161	55,052	11,518	13,721	8,107	1,011	3,036	486	15,226	1,523	634
Berry Crops	0171	32,018	7,958	8,756	6,735	840	3,486	558	10,029	1,003	255
Grapes	0172	66,199	8,799	13,287	4,662	581	1,518	243	10,572	1,057	583
Tree Nuts	0173	12,453	10,654	13,084	6,278	783	2,160	346	15,274	1,527	133
Citrus Fruits	0174	5,367	11,923	13,612	7,597	947	2,665	426	17,480	1,748	64
Deciduous Tree Fruits	0175	23,220	6,116	8,082	3,960	494	1,530	245	7,633	763	142
Fruits and Tree Nuts,	0179	12,523	9,275	11,237	5,972	745	2,226	356	12,960	1,296	116
Ornamental Nursery Products	0181	49,635	17,753	19,872	13,357	1,665	5,410	866	21,252	2,125	881
Food Crops Grown Under Cover	0182	6,109	22,764	18,227	20,504	2,557	9,491	1,519	29,465	2,947	139
General Farms, Primarily Crop	0191	41,211	9,633	13,176	5,444	679	1,710	274	13,274	1,327	397
Beef Cattle Feedlots	0211	1,120	17,205	16,281	14,796	1,845	5,678	908	22,985	2,299	19
Dairy Farms	0241	20,167	17,767	12,099	18,030	2,248	7,990	1,278	25,150	2,515	358
Soil Preparation Services	0711	2,630	21,069	23,021	12,886	1,607	5,684	909	29,740	2,974	55
Crop Preparation Services for Market	0723	54,416	12,707	17,608	7,445	928	2,921	467	15,432	1,543	691
Farm Labor Contractors	0761	225,934	4,385	6,171	2,650	330	634	101	6,172	617	991
Farm Management Services	0762	15,974	11,991	16,304	6,724	838	2,265	362	16,500	1,650	192
Lawn and Garden Services	0782	109,402	14,454	15,131	11,264	1,404	4,615	738	18,934	1,893	1,581

Source: Analysis of wage records by the Labor Market Information Division of the Employment Development Department.

Note: 1. The U.S. Department of Agriculture, National Agricultural Statistics Service, reported that a hourly average earnings of field and livestock workers in 2001 were $8.02; the state's minimum wage was $6.25 an hour in 2001.

Table 14 Statewide and Regional Retention Rates

	Statewide, All Agricultural		San Joaquin		Central Coast	
	Matched SSNs	Retention Rate	Matched SSNs	Retention Rate	Matched SSNs	Retention Rate
SSNs In 1991–1996–2001	215,686	24%	91,050	21%	28,091	17%
SSNs In 1991–1996	363,875	40%	156,812	36%	55,261	33%
SSNs In 1991–2001	252,462	28%	107,475	25%	33,993	20%
SSNs In 1996–2001	374,959	39%	167,131	36%	57,421	29%

Source: Analysis of wage records by the Labor Market Information Division of the Employment Development Department.

were also reported by grape employers, and few workers reported by grape employers were also reported in citrus.

For example, in 1991, 1996, and 2001, only 6 to 8 percent of workers reported by citrus employers in the first quarter were reported by grape employers in the third quarter. There are several reasons why workers do not move between commodities in ways that would reduced the total number of workers needed to harvest both crops. First, the absence of benefits such as health

Table 15 San Joaquin Valley and Statewide Commodity Specific Retention Rates

	Nursery SSNs	SSNs Matched	Retention	Citrus SSNs	SSNs Matched	Retention
Statewide						
SSNs In 1991–1996–2001	56,443	9,203	16%	12,765	1,120	9%
SSNs In 1991–1996	56,443	17,482	31%	12,765	2,781	22%
SSNs In 1991–2001	56,443	10,312	18%	12,765	1,311	10%
SSNs In 1996–2001	61,239	19,091	31%	15,293	2,533	17%
San Joaquin Valley						
SSNs In 1991–1996–2001	9,363	1,371	15%	7,835	411	5%
SSNs In 1991–1996	9,363	2,607	28%	7,835	1,232	16%
SSNs In 1991–2001	9,363	1,499	16%	7,835	534	7%
SSNs In 1996–2001	8,463	2,143	25%	8,177	896	11%

Source: Analysis of wage records by the Labor Market Information Division of the Employment Development Department.

Table 16 Central Coast and Statewide Commodity Specific Retention Rates

	All Fruits	SSNs Matched	Retention	Vegetables and Melons SSNs	SSNs Matched	Retention
Statewide						
SSNs In 1991–1996–2001	258,302	35,707	14%	81,883	8,962	11%
SSNs In 1991–1996	258,302	77,790	30%	81,883	21,227	26%
SSNs In 1991–2001	258,302	45,986	18%	81,883	11,648	14%
SSNs In 1996–2001	271,694	72,660	27%	94,267	20,644	22%
Central Coast						
SSNs In 1991–1996–2001	28,860	3,532	12%	26,823	3,908	15%
SSNs In 1991–1996	28,860	7,652	27%	26,823	8,402	31%
SSNs In 1991–2001	28,860	4,268	15%	26,823	4,788	18%
SSNs In 1996–2001	28,230	6,585	23%	33,434	8,400	25%

Source: Analysis of wage records by the Labor Market Information Division of the Employment Development Department.

insurance and the presence of unemployment insurance (UI) benefits reduce incentives to work more hours by becoming proficient in the harvest of two commodities—workers gain little, both in benefits and in net income. Second, table grape pickers and packers include a significant share of women, but there are few women among the orange harvesters who must climb trees in cold weather. Third, there has been an ample supply of grape and orange harvesters, so employers have little incentive to develop mechanisms to encourage workers to shift between crops (see table 17).

These UI data on farmworkers, jobs, and earnings suggest that a large number of workers are employed on farms, but most have only one farm job

Table 17 Workers in Citrus and Grapes

	1991 SSNs	1996 SSNs	2001 SSNs
Worked in Citrus 1st Quarter	3,509	3,687	2,363
Worked in Grapes 3rd Quarter	57,623	61,238	55,670
Worked in Both 1st & 3rd Quarters	220	284	163
% of Citrus Who Worked in Grapes	6.27%	7.70%	6.90%

Source: Analysis of wage records by the Labor Market Information Division of the Employment Development Department.

and relatively low earnings. There are significant regional differences, with more workers employed by contractors and earning lower wages in the Fruit Bowl of the San Joaquin Valley than in the Salad Bowl of the Central Coast. The combination of seasonality and contractors is usually associated with more recently arrived and unauthorized workers as well.

Only a quarter of workers were reported in all three years of the 1991–2001 period, suggesting that the farm labor market is a revolving door. Newcomers enter at age 18 to 25 and accept the most seasonal and lowest-wage jobs with contractors. However, with experience in the U.S. labor market, most leave the farm labor market within a decade.

As the orange and grape example makes clear, if current farmworkers stayed in the farm labor market longer, there would be less need to constantly replenish the farm labor force. The UI data suggest that policies to help current farmworkers work more hours a year, and to do farmwork for more years, could increase their earnings and provide employers with a more experienced workforce.

Chapter 7 Migrants: The Integration Challenge

Agriculture is the major port of entry for the least-educated immigrants arriving in the United States. The average immigrant farmworker has less than eight years of native-country schooling. These immigrant farmworkers and their U.S.-born children begin their American journey near the bottom of the U.S. job ladder, often in places that offer pyramid-shaped labor markets, with a broad base of entry-level jobs and fewer higher-wage jobs, schools that have lower than average test and graduation rates, and where there are fewer social services and nongovernment organizations (NGOs) to help with integration.

The federal government spends at least $1 billion a year on programs that assist farmworkers and their children. As a nation of immigrants that believes immigrants help themselves while enriching the United States, the federal government does not have a tradition of providing immigrant integration services, as in Canada and many European countries. With the exception of federal funds and programs for refugee resettlement, most newcomers are expected to integrate with the help of their U.S. relatives and employers, and their children who attend U.S. schools are expected to perform as well as other U.S.-educated children (see table 18).

The United States experienced a "great migration" off the land between the 1940s and 1960s, as millions of white and black farmworkers, sharecroppers, and small farmers moved to cities, especially in the Midwest. Many achieved the higher wages and better opportunities that they sought, but many did not, especially as industrial jobs began to disappear. Migrant children educated in urban schools wanted the same opportunities as their classmates. Unlike their parents, they had no memories of the farmwork left behind, and their failure to find jobs lay at the core of some of the nation's urban riots in the mid-1960s.

Dealing with rural-urban migration as well as the rural poor left behind was a top priority of policy makers and economists during the 1960s. Schuh (1968, 183) estimated the demand for and supply of farmworkers, concluding that the best way to help farmworkers was to have full employment in the nonfarm economy so that farmworkers with little education would have a better chance of finding nonfarm jobs. Hathaway and Perkins (1968, 202) urged a clean break from farmwork, concluding that farmworkers who stay in rural areas and seek nonfarm work on a part-time basis "have the lowest probability of successfully moving out of farm employment."

Kain and Persky's (1968, 303) arguments about the urban stake in southern rural poverty could easily apply to rural Mexican poverty today: "The fortunes of [urban America] are closely linked to those of the rural [poor] though through migration. . . . [since] a substantial fraction of the [urban poor outside

Table 18 Federal Farmworker Assistance Spending, Fiscal Year 2005 ($ millions)

	Fiscal Year 2005
Migrant Head Start	266
Migrant Education	390
High School Equivalency Program	19
College Assistance Migrant Program	16
Disabled Farmworkers	2
Migrant Education Even Start	8
Migrant Health	144
NFJP	76
Total	**921**

Source: Data from the program web sites

Note: NFJP = National Farmworker Jobs Program

the South] were born and educated in the rural south." They argued that the two poor groups most difficult to assist in urban areas, rural blacks and Appalachian whites, should be helped in their areas of origin rather than after they arrive in urban areas, just as many argue today that the solution to Mexican rural poverty lies in Mexico rather than the United States (303).

It was in this context of helping farmworkers to succeed in the nonfarm labor market that federal assistance programs began. However, as the farm workforce changed from U.S. citizens to immigrants, migrant assistance programs evolved into immigrant-integration programs for some of the least-educated newcomers and their children. In this sense, migrant assistance programs that help farmworkers and their children to get out of farm jobs might be considered to have helped poor newcomers to take their first step up the U.S. job ladder.

Some federal migrant assistance programs target farmworkers, who can also participate in other assistance programs. For example, most farmworkers have incomes low enough to make them eligible for federal and state welfare assistance, ranging from food stamps and Medicaid to cash assistance, although some of these programs restrict eligibility to legal U.S. residents. There are no data on how many immigrant farmworkers participate in such general assistance programs, but in agricultural areas, they are likely to be a significant share of the clientele. There may also be hard to estimate follow-on effects of immigrant farmworkers on nonfarm welfare recipients, as when the U.S.-born children of farmworkers reject their parents' jobs in the fields, are eligible for welfare assistance, and supplement their incomes by providing services to newcomer farmworkers in agricultural areas.

EVOLUTION OF MIGRANT AND SEASONAL
FARMWORKER (MSFW) PROGRAMS

Even before the War on Poverty was launched by President Lyndon B. Johnson during his State of the Union address on January 8, 1964, migrant farmworkers were a special concern of both the Democrats and Republicans. Both parties' political platforms in 1960 called for action to deal with the problems faced by migrant farmworkers,[1] and the House and Senate had subcommittees on migratory workers that held hearings on the plight of migrant farmworkers.

These hearings produced a consensus that U.S. citizens who crossed state lines to harvest crops deserved federal assistance because most state and local governments refused to assist short-term residents, fearing some would settle and increase their welfare burden. After the urban riots of the mid-1960s, which often involved the children of farmworkers and sharecroppers who had moved to cities in the 1940s and 1950s, agricultural economists reported that there were still too many farmworkers, and that the lives of migrant workers could be improved only if the federal government helped more of them to find nonfarm jobs. They also urged the federal government to provide education, health, and other services so migrant children would not be "trapped" in agriculture (Jones and Christian, 1965).

There were significant partisan differences on exactly how to help farmworkers. The Democratic majority in Congress thought that the most efficient way to help migrants and their children was to halt the admission of Mexican braceros; tighten restrictions on children working in agriculture; give farmworkers collective bargaining, minimum wage, and other labor rights; and regulate farm labor contractors. However, there was strong Republican and sometimes rural Democratic opposition to these suggested farm labor reforms. With War on Poverty funds readily available in the mid-1960s, it soon became apparent that it would be far easier to fund services for migrant workers and their children than to extend federal labor laws to agriculture.

This substitution of assistance funds for labor laws explains the launch of the first federal program for migrant farmworkers, Migrant Health, in September 1962. It was followed by the Migrant Education Program in 1966 and later job training and Head Start Programs. These 1960s migrant assistance programs were expected to be transitional, helping the generation trapped in farmwork and their children to find nonfarm jobs. At the time, it was believed that, with mechanization rapidly displacing migrant and seasonal farmworkers, farmworker poverty would largely disappear within a decade.

Migrant farmworkers and their problems did not disappear, but their characteristics and needs changed remarkably. The black and white U.S. citizens who followed the ripening crops from south to north became eligible for subsidized housing, job training, and health care in the 1960s, and their children for supplemental educational services and Head Start Programs. However, most US citizen farmworkers left farmwork before these federal assistance programs were fully operational. Instead, as farm employment stabilized in the 1970s, immigrant farmworkers arrived, and today almost all those being served by migrant assistance programs have some connection to immigration, as when a U.S.-citizen child in Head Start has an immigrant parent.

Migrant service providers face a Herculean task that must often feel like the toils of Sisyphus, who was condemned forever to push a boulder uphill in Hades, only to see it roll back to the bottom each time. In America's fields, as fast as farmworkers and their children move up the U.S. job ladder by getting out of farmwork, they are replaced by newcomers with even greater needs. Incentives can be perverse. For example, if migrant assistance programs succeed in persuading parents that they should not move their children from place to place as they do farmwork, the children may lose their eligibility for special assistance because they do not move with their parents.

THE BIG 4 MSFW PROGRAMS

Migrant and seasonal farmworkers are generally seen as strangers in the fields where they work. The original justification for federal migrant assistance programs was the interstate mobility of farmworkers and its disruptive effect on families, as when the schooling of children who follow the crops with their parents is interrupted. Community leaders in areas receiving migrants feared that providing services to migrants would encourage them to settle and compete with local disadvantaged residents for limited welfare funds, explaining the gap that required federal assistance.

Migrant assistance programs did not pay a great deal of attention to definitions and eligibility criteria during the 1960s; most simply assumed that anyone who did farmwork was eligible. However, as the number of farmworkers stabilized in the 1970s and federal budgets tightened in the 1980s, definitions and eligibility criteria became more important to set priorities for the agencies that used federal funds to serve migrant farmworkers and their families.

One legacy of this history of first assuming that all farmworkers were eligible for services, and later trying to target limited resources to the neediest farmworkers and their children, is that each major assistance program has a unique definition of who is eligible for services. For example, migrant assistance programs differ in the border that must be crossed to be considered a migrant, the type and amount of qualifying farmwork that must be done to be considered a migrant, and how long a person or dependent can continue to receive services after he or she has stopped migrating. As new needs were identified, new programs were begun, and today there are a dozen federal programs for farmworkers and their dependents. Services are delivered by both public and private agencies (see table 19).

Table 19 Federal Programs for Farmworkers and Dependents

	Program	Services	Destination of Federal Funding
U.S. Department of Education	Migrant Education Program (MEP)	Provides academic support services to assist migrant children in meeting state standards and in preparation for the workforce or postsecondary education.	State Education Agencies
	High School Equivalency Program (HEP)	Provides academic support services for migrants or their children to obtain the equivalent of a high school diploma to obtain employment or to begin postsecondary education.	Institutions of Higher Education, Nonprofit Organizations
	College Assistance Migrant Program (CAMP)	Provides support during the first year of undergraduate studies at an institution of higher education.	Institutions of Higher Education, Nonprofit Organizations
	Migrant Education Even Start Program (MEES)	Provides family literacy services including early childhood education, adult basic education or English language instruction, and parenting education.	Local Education Agencies, Nonprofit Organizations, State Education Agencies
	Migrant and Seasonal Farmworkers w/ Disabilities (Rehab. Act)	Makes comprehensive vocational rehabilitation (VR) services available to migrant or seasonal farmworkers with disabilities.	State Agencies
U.S. Department of Health and Human Services	Migrant Health	Provides primary and preventative health care to workers and their families as well as referrals for specialized services.	Local Community Health Centers
	Migrant and Seasonal Head Start (MSHS)	Provides child care and early childhood development services for workers' children up to age five.	Local Agencies, Nonprofit Organizations

(continued)

Table 19 (*continued*)

	Program	Services	Destination of Federal Funding
U.S. Department of Labor	National Farmworker Jobs Program (NFJP)	Provides basic education, job training, placement services, and a wide range of supplemental services.	Nonprofit Organizations

Source: Department of Education, Migrant Education Directory.

Differences in eligibility and mode of delivery means that each farmworker assistance program has a distinct target population, its own outreach workers and intake forms, and usually separate facilities to provide services. The result is a mix of programs and eligibility standards that would likely not be replicated if the federal government were developing an overall strategy to help migrants and their families today. However, migrant programs are generally fearful of a wholesale redesign of the programs in an era of tight budgets and concern about providing services to unauthorized migrants.

Most farmworker assistance programs serve only a fraction of what they estimate to be their target populations. It is very hard to assess claims that less than half of the migrant children receive supplemental education or healthcare services, primarily because there is no reliable statistical system to estimate the universe of farmworkers and their dependents.

There are two broad approaches to estimating target farmworker populations—top-down and bottom-up (Martin and Martin, 1993). A top-down approach uses a national database such as the Census of Agriculture, which enumerates jobs on farms but not the people who fill them, and tries to determine how many farmworkers could have been employed to fill these jobs.[2]

The bottom-up approach, by contrast, begins with eligible farmworkers, and tries to estimate their total number. There are two major variants to bottom-up estimation. The first multiplies the number of eligible farmworkers and their dependents identified by some factor to estimate the total number of eligible persons, as when a migrant agency estimates it serves a third of the farmworkers, and is often used by migrant agencies to justify funding requests. The other variant follows the farm production approach, beginning with the acreage of various crops and estimating for each the hours needed to tend and harvest these crops. Analysts then make assumptions about how

many of these hours are provided by eligible farmworkers and how many dependents they have to estimate the eligible population.

There are strengths and weaknesses in each approach. The top-down approach begins with the best data, but must make assumptions to convert the
labor expenditures reported by farmers into workers. Bottom-up approaches,
on the other hand, generalize from limited samples to estimate the universe or
ignore the very real variation in how crops are produced in different areas.

MIGRANT EDUCATION PROGRAM

Since 1966 the Migrant Education Program (MEP; www.ed.gov/programs/
mep/index.html) has provided grants to state and local education agencies
that identify children between ages 3 and 21 who moved with their parents
across school district lines so that their parents could work in agriculture.[3] In
the 1960s, the program served mostly white and black children. Today, about
90 percent of the children served are Hispanic, mostly immigrants and children of immigrants, and almost all are limited English proficient (Kuenzi,
2002, 2).

Migrant Education provides services to children who have moved with
their parents, currently or formerly, and currently migratory children are to
"be given priority in the consideration of [MEP] programs and activities."
Children are considered to be currently migratory if their parents made a
qualifying move in the past 12 months, and formerly migrant if the qualifying
move was 12 to 24 months earlier, so that supplemental education services can
be provided to children up to 36 months after the last qualifying move.[4]

Most of the children in Migrant Education Programs are formerly migrant,
meaning that their parents did not make a qualifying move within the past
year. Many qualify for assistance from other federal programs as well, including free school lunches and assistance provided under programs that target
poor children. Indeed, Migrant Education is sometimes described as the "supplement to all other supplements," since school administrators have considerable flexibility to determine how Migrant Education funds are spent.

State education agencies usually hire recruiters to identify children eligible
for Migrant Education services. Some 854,872 eligible children were identified
in the 2000–2001 school year, and 737,684 received some type of service paid
for in part by Migrant Education funds. It should be emphasized that identification of eligible children and providing services are inclusive concepts, so
that a child who is identified as eligible may receive a service in a state for one

day that the family is passing through, but that day counts as one child served in the state that year.

In 1999–2000, California identified 241,000 eligible children, Texas 126,000, and six other states identified at least 20,000 each: Florida, Washington, Oregon, Kansas, Kentucky, and Georgia. The distribution of MEP funds among states reflects eligible children counts—in fiscal year 2005, California received 33 percent of Migrant Education funds, Texas 15 percent, Florida 6 percent, and Washington 4 percent. The top five states received 62 percent of MEP funds. About 87 percent of Migrant Education children were Hispanic, compared with 16 percent of all K–12 students.

Migrant Education funding has been fairly stable, so that identifying more eligible children means fewer funds per child. The Migrant Education Program has expanded eligibility criteria several times, for example, including children who crossed school district lines so their parents could be employed in meatpacking and other food processing jobs that have high worker turnover. However, these are nonfarm jobs, and the workers employed in them are covered by federal labor laws, but the broader definition allowed more eligible children to be found in Midwestern states.

The Migrant Education Program was added to the Elementary and Secondary Education Act of 1965 in 1966.[5] In deference to the tradition of local control over education, state education agencies were given considerable discretion in deciding exactly how to use these supplemental federal funds. For this reason, MEP funds can be used to provide tutoring, additional aides, medical and dental services, nutritional programs, transportation, counseling parents, and special summer schools. In fact, the only restriction on Migrant Education funds is that they do not provide basic educational services, which are to be funded from state and local sources.

There are three ways a child can become eligible for Migrant Education Programs. First, the parent can cross school district lines to find a temporary farm job such as harvesting apples, conforming to the migrant worker stereotype. Second, a parent can make the child eligible by asserting that he or she will be employed in a farm job temporarily, as when jobs in an apple or potato packinghouse are year-round, but the parent who moves over school district lines will be employed in the packinghouse only seasonally (the employer can confirm that the parent will be employed in the job only temporarily). Third, children are eligible if their parents cross school district lines to fill jobs in a food-related business such as meatpacking that have worker turnover rates of at least 60 percent over 18 months.[6]

States apply for Migrant Education Program funds each year, and each state's share of the total available funds depends on the number of eligible children identified and how long they are in the state.[7] In recent years, the federal government provided about 40 percent of the state's average per-pupil expenditure for each full-time equivalent migrant child identified, with the actual amount varying from 32 to 48 percent of the average U.S. per-pupil expenditure (Kuenzi, 2002, 4).

The Migrant Education Program raises a number of issues. The first is the expanding definition of eligibility for services despite pleas of insufficient funds. Instead of making more children eligible for services, some argue that limited program resources should be focused on the neediest children of farmworkers, including those whose parents move longer distances, perhaps at least 100 miles away from a usual residence, to work in seasonal farm jobs.[8]

The second issue is whether funds should continue to be allocated based on children identified as eligible rather than served by MEP-funds. Distributing funds according to eligible children identified helps to explain why Migrant Education recruiters swarm the south Texas families who stop in the Hope Migrant Complex near Hope, Arkansas, en route to Michigan, Wisconsin, and other northern states.[9] By identifying eligible children on their way north, Arkansas can be credited for their presence until they are recruited in another state.

Third is the question of who among those deemed eligible should be served. Migrant Education Programs can serve children from the ages of 3 to 21, but only those 5 to 21 are counted for funding purposes. After the parents stop migrating, there is also a question of how long the children should remain eligible for supplemental education services that are targeted for migrant farmworkers.

Despite the elastic definitions of children who are eligible for Migrant Education services, the major issue in recent years has revolved around funding. The fact that state shares of MEP funds depend on the number of eligible children identified gives local recruiters incentives to declare ineligible children to be migrants.[10] In Connecticut, four of the state's Migrant Education Programs were found to have enrolled mostly ineligible children, prompting school districts in New Haven, Danbury, and New London to cancel their programs. In Waterbury, the six full-time employees reported 300 eligible children between 2002 and 2004, but an audit found that fewer than 10 percent had in fact made qualifying moves.[11] The $867,000 in MEP funds received was spent on classroom aides, parenting classes, and tutors, but for children whose Hispanic parents were painters, construction workers, and mechanics, not farmworkers.[12]

Eligibility issues are arising across the United States. An audit in Georgia found that 35 percent of the children identified as eligible for MEP services in 2005 were not.[13] The state of Maine took over several local programs in 2004 after discovering that some school districts hired private firms that were paid according to how many children they found who were eligible for Migrant Education services; perhaps not surprisingly, they enrolled ineligible children. For example, only 39 of the 900 children deemed eligible for Migrant Education in Portland were in fact eligible.[14]

Migration means movement, and migrant children changing from school to school do not always take their school records with them. In an effort to ensure that a child's records were readily available to his or her new school, Migrant Education funds were used to establish the Migrant Student Record Transfer System (MSRTS) in 1974. The theory was that schools would submit migrant children's records to a central database so that they could be accessed by any new school in which the child enrolled. The MSRTS never lived up to its promise, and was discontinued in 1994. The No Child Left Behind Act of 2001 (Public Law 107-110) may revive a national migrant student record transfer system, since it provided $10 million to "assist the States in developing effective methods for the electronic transfer of student records and in determining the number of migratory children in each State" (Kuenzi, 2002, 4).

The Office of Migrant Education in the Department of Education also oversees several other programs that serve the children of farmworkers, including Migrant Education Even Start (MEES; www.ed.gov/programs/mees/index.html), the High School Equivalency Program (HEP; www.ed.gov/programs/hep/index.html), and the College Assistance Migrant Program (CAMP, www.ed.gov/programs/camp/index.html). The MEES web site notes that grants of $8 million a year are available to schools and nonprofits that offer services "designed to break the cycle of poverty and improve the literacy of migrant families through a unified program of family literacy services [that include] early childhood education, adult basic education or English Language instruction, and parenting education."

HEP provides about $19 million a year to colleges and universities or NGOs that work with them to help migrant farmworkers or their dependents who are at least 17 years old to obtain high school equivalency diplomas. CAMP provides $16 million a year to assist several thousand farmworkers or their children during their first year at a four-year college, devoting part of these funds to outreach and recruitment of those farmworkers "who meet the minimum qualifications for attendance at a college or university," that is, be a migrant farmworker or have a parent who did at least 75 days of farmwork in the previous two years.

A profile of three sisters studying at California State University, Sacramento, with CAMP support highlights the challenge facing these assistance programs. The girls' father, a Watsonville strawberry worker of seven, used his U.S. earnings to build a seven-bedroom home in Michoacan. The sisters reported that their family treated their eight or nine months a year in the Watsonville area as work time, and the three or four months in Michoacan as a time to relax, so they did not attend school from January through March. The combination of having parents who do not value education (especially for girls) and the lack of classes in Mexico or the United States for children who miss part of every school year, can make it very hard for the children of farmworkers to graduate from high school and enroll in college.[15]

With 20 percent of U.S. children either immigrants themselves or children of immigrants, and almost 30 percent of them low-income, education is the most expensive U.S. immigrant integration program. The influx of immigrants with little education strains all school systems, but especially those in rural and agricultural areas. If these schools can educate immigrant children to achieve their American dreams, worries about importing poverty along with farmworkers are misplaced. If the schools cannot give these children the skills needed to climb the U.S. job ladder, a rural underclass could develop that would be hard to extirpate.

The most significant recent development in federal education policy is the No Child Left Behind Act (NCLB), which requires schools to identify, serve, and be held accountable for the performance of all children, including those who have limited English proficiency (LEP). The NCLB mandates standardized tests in grades 3–8 to measure the progress of students, and requires schools to report the scores of all students, with sanctions on schools whose students do not show improvement.

It is not clear what effect the NCLB's testing requirements are having on schools that enroll large numbers of children of farmworkers. However, it is often reported that some schools encourage low-performing students to drop out so that their low test scores do not have to be reported. If this is correct, then a testing system aimed at encouraging schools to invest more in low-performing students could have the opposite result.

MIGRANT HEAD START

The Migrant Head Start Program (MHS) may be the best-loved federal farm-worker assistance program.[16] Migrant Head Start receives more than $250 million a year to serve about 33,000 children up to age five in 475 MHS centers scattered across 38 states. These centers, some of which operate only seasonally, are sometimes open from dawn to dusk so that parents can work long hours in the fields. About two-thirds of the children in Migrant Head Start programs are under age three, a group not served by regular Head Start.

Project Head Start was launched by the Office of Economic Opportunity in 1965, and is now administered by the Administration for Children and Families in the Department of Health and Human Services (HHS). The Head Start Program provides "comprehensive preschool development services" for children in low-income families, providing education, nutrition, and parental involvement so that the children in it are as prepared for grades K–12 as other children.

As with other 1960s antipoverty programs, Head Start made special provisions for migrant farmworkers and Native Americans. Migrant was not defined, although regulations in 1992 codified the practice of giving priority to the young children of parents who move to do farmwork in the fields. Today, children eligible for Migrant Head Start must have changed their residence with the parent during the previous 12 months, the parents must work in crops, and the family's income must derive "primarily" from crop work. In 1998, Migrant Head Start began to serve the children of poor seasonal farmworkers as well, that is, children of farmworkers employed less than year-round who do not move.

Parents do not pay for Migrant Head Start services, and demand for care exceeds supply. Most Migrant Head Start centers have a first-come, first-served policy, which benefits farmworker families who know about the program and are in the area when seasonal centers open. Interviews with families whose children were being served in Migrant Head Start centers in 2003–2004 found that the average household had six people, including two parents, two children, and one or two other relatives. All the parents whose children were in Migrant Head Start spoke Spanish, and about half also spoke some English. These parents had a median seven years of U.S. farm-work experience, and reported less than $5,000 in earnings from farmwork in 2003, which was significantly less than the earnings of most farmworker families.

MIGRANT HEALTH

The Migrant Health Program is the oldest of the Big 4 Migrant Service Programs. It receives almost $150 million a year to provide services to almost 750,000 farmworkers and their dependents, and often works closely with Migrant Health Centers, caring for the children in them.

The Senate Subcommittee on Migratory Labor in the early 1960s was deadlocked over bills that would have granted collective bargaining rights to farmworkers and required farm labor contractors to obtain federal licenses. Unable to overcome the opposition of farm employers who did not want more federal regulation of the farm labor market, Senator Harrison Williams (D-NJ) suggested that Congress appropriate funds to provide health care for migrant farmworkers and their families. Williams's proposal was accepted, and in September 1962, Section 310 was added to the Public Health Service Act (PHSA) to provide finds for "part of the cost of . . . family health service clinics for domestic agricultural migratory workers and their families" (Johnston, 1985, 135–139).[17]

Migrant Health Programs initially emphasized immunizations and health education, and many clinics relied on volunteers to offer services at accessible locations and on evenings and weekends. Migrant Health Programs later hired doctors and nurses to provide services rather than relying on volunteers, and became much more sophisticated about seeking funding. Most clinics today receive a combination of federal, state, and private funds, and many serve both farm and other workers.[18]

Like other farmworker assistance programs, the Migrant Health Program expanded its definition of eligibility for services over time. Initially, only migrant farmworkers and their dependents were served, but seasonal workers and their dependents became eligible in 1970 under the rationale that they faced many of the same health problems of migrants. Today, migratory or seasonal agricultural workers and their dependents whose "principal employment" is in agriculture on a seasonal basis can receive health-care services. Migrants who establish "a temporary abode" in order to be employed in agriculture and were employed in farmwork within the last 24 months get priority for services.[19]

Migrant Health Centers apply for federal funds by documenting the number of eligible workers and their families in their service area, and available funds are normally allocated accordingly. This funding formula has prompted several efforts to estimate the number and distribution of those eligible for health-care services, but none of these estimates are widely accepted.

For example, a bottom-up estimation procedure developed state profiles that relied on a three-step procedure to estimate the number of farmworkers and their dependents. As with other bottom-up studies, analysts had to make assumptions on everything from how many hours per acre were typically required to produce crops, how many of these hours were performed by eligible farmworkers, how many hours a typical farmworker was employed, and how many dependents they had.[20] The assumptions used in these bottom-up studies likely produced estimates of too many farmworkers and too many dependents.

Migrant Health clinics usually have long lines of people seeking services, reflecting the lack of affordable health care. The fact that clinics in areas with farmworkers receive funds from several sources means that it has not been a top priority that the federal Migrant Health funds precisely reflect the distribution of eligible farmworkers.

MIGRANT JOB TRAINING

The National Farmworker Jobs Program (NFJP) spends about $75 million a year to provide English and job-training services to economically disadvantaged migrant and seasonal farmworkers (www.doleta.gov/msfw).[21] Like other farmworker assistance programs, the jobs program is a unique federal program that targets farmworkers. However, unlike the other migrant assistance programs, most of which have expanding budgets, President Bush proposed eliminating the NFJP every year between 2001 and 2008, arguing that there is no justification for a federal farmworker jobs program in the twenty-first century. The Bush Administration believes that farmworkers could be served alongside other disadvantaged workers in the 1,900 One-Stop centers funded by the federal government via the Workforce Investment Act of 1998.

Congress has not agreed with President Bush,[22] and the NFJP funds provide some type of service to 30,000 farmworkers year. A third of these farmworkers receive the most costly service, training, while the others receive skills assessment, job search assistance, and similar services. The NFJP appears successful in raising the earnings of participants. In 2004, more than 85 percent of the farmworkers served were employed after exiting the program, 75 percent maintained this postprogram employment at least a year, and annual earnings rose by an average of $4,500 in the year after receiving NFJP services.[23]

Like other farmworker assistance programs, job training for migrant and seasonal farmworkers originated in the Office of Economic Opportunity in the mid-1960s. Farmworker job-training programs were transferred to the

U.S. Department of Labor (DOL) in 1973, and the Comprehensive Employment and Training Act of 1974 specified a federal farmworker training program in Section 303, which was transferred to Section 404 of the Job Training Partnership Act of 1982. Along the way, the focus of federal job efforts shifted from creating subsidized jobs in the public sector, favored by many Democrats, to training workers for jobs identified by local governments and private industry councils.

The DOL allocates farmworker training funds to states based on the number of eligible farmworkers in each state.[24] The formula for distributing farmworker training funds has been controversial, in part because of the detailed eligibility criteria. Those seeking federal farmworker training services must be at least 14 years old and have been a migrant or seasonal farmworker[25] and "disadvantaged" during any consecutive 12-month period within the 24-month period preceding their applications.[26] Unlike other farmworker assistance programs, federal farmworker training programs must ensure that they serve only U.S. citizens or foreigners who are authorized to work in the United States. Finally, males seeking training must have registered with the Selective Service.

The purpose of the NFJP is to "break the cycle of poverty" by helping economically disadvantaged farmworkers raise their earnings by obtaining better farm or nonfarm jobs. The program appears to achieve this goal, but perhaps because of creaming.[27] Training programs that know their continued funding depends on having participants achieve higher earnings can select those most likely to raise their earnings with or without training (Bell and Orr, 2002).

The purpose of farmworker and other job-training programs is to give the United States the educated and trained workforce it needs to compete in a globalizing economy. However, as Marshall and Tucker (1992) emphasize, job-training programs should be integrated into national economic policies to maximize employment and competitiveness. Employers need to invest in the training and upgrading of their workers, including farmworkers, but they are unlikely to do so as long as newcomers from abroad are readily available.

OTHER MSFW PROGRAMS

The Big 4 farmworker assistance programs aim to assist farmworkers and their dependents with education, health, early childhood, and job-training services.

Because each program has its own definitions of who is eligible for services, as well as its own recruiters and intake workers, there is much less coordination between these programs than most observers believe would be optimal. However, there is little enthusiasm for a comprehensive review of the programs aimed at developing a common definition of an eligible farmworker (Martin and Martin, 1993).

Farmworkers may receive assistance under many other federal programs, some of which target them. For example, the U.S. Department of Agriculture operates several programs under the Housing Act of 1949. Section 514 provided $32 million in loans to farmers (33-year loans at 1 percent interest) in fiscal year 2007 to buy, build, or improve housing for farmworkers, while Section 516 provided $10 million in grants to farmworker associations, NGOs, and public agencies to build or repair farm housing.[28] A recent review found almost 800 active projects providing 14,000 housing units for farmworkers, but noted that fewer new farmworker housing units are being constructed despite increases in overall funding (Housing Assistance Council, 2006).[29]

Additional funds for farmworker housing are available from the Department of Housing and Urban Development (HUD), which administers the Rural Housing and Economic Development and HOME Investment Partnerships Programs,[30] the U.S. Department of Labor's Migrant and Seasonal Housing Program, and the Low Income Housing Tax Credit. Despite these programs, the consensus is that there is a severe shortage of affordable housing for farmworkers, and that many live in substandard housing.

The most controversial farmworker assistance program provides legal services to migrant and seasonal farmworkers. Civil legal services, which were also an outgrowth of the War on Poverty, are provided to legal farmworkers and their families at no cost, with funding provided by the Legal Services Corporation (LSC) and other sources.[31] Representing farmworkers often means suing farmers, who complain that they are "harassed" by tax-supported lawyers (Issac, 1996). Farm employers on several occasions have tried to eliminate LSC funding for migrant farmworker programs. They failed, but their complaints have prompted repeated investigations of recipients of LSC funds, and Congress has restricted the ability of LSC grantees to file class action suits and to represent H-2A workers.[32]

One reason why farm labor disputes often become bitter legal contests is because many farmers believe there would be fewer complaints if there were no LSC-funded lawyers. Bill Beardall, former director of the Texas Rural Legal Assistance Program, believes that farm labor disputes often become bitter because:

"Unlike suing banks or landlords, there is a conflict not just of economics but a conflict of culture—a culture that is rooted in a different century—about what is the proper social relationship between poor workers and their employers."[33]

For example, when the California Rural Legal Assistance (CRLA) Program sued Gerawan Farms, the largest peach, plum, and nectarine farm in the United States, alleging violations of housing, wage, and transportation laws, Gerawan complained loudly enough to prompt a congressional hearing.[34] Gerawan, which employs 8,000 workers, considers itself a model San Joaquin Valley farm employer. As a result of the CRLA suit, Gerawan was found guilty on 2 of 11 counts in 1992 for, inter alia, underpaying overtime wages.[35]

Many farmworker legal assistance groups have established separate organizations that do not receive LSC funds to sue on behalf of other unauthorized and other farmworkers who cannot be served with taxpayer funds. One of these organizations, the Virginia Justice Center for Farm and Immigrant Workers, sued several employers to recover back wages for legal temporary foreign workers. The suit prompted Shores and Ruark Seafood Inc., a processor of oysters and blue crabs in Urbanna, Virginia, to complain that: "We had very few people who were dissatisfied until they found out they had something to be dissatisfied about." Shores and Ruark paid workers piece rates, but failed to record the hours they worked, and the suit claimed makeup wages so that workers earned at least the minimum wage.

The federal government's education, health, training, and legal service programs for farmworkers and their dependents aim to help them integrate successfully into the American economy and society. Almost all of those being served by these programs are immigrants or the children of immigrants, effectively making these assistance programs immigrant-integration programs. The best way to help farmworkers has not changed—help them to get out of farmwork, and ensure that their children do not begin to do farmwork. However, the success of farmworker assistance programs in helping farmworkers and their children escape from agriculture makes the assistance challenge for these programs ever larger, since the replacement farmworkers are often needier than the farmworkers who left. It is in this sense that federal farmworker assistance programs are engaged in "an endless quest" (Martin and Martin, 1993).

Part Four Whither Rural America?

If current trends continue, the farmworkers of tomorrow will continue to grow up today outside the United States. This raises both immigration and integration questions. Under what terms should farmers and farm-related businesses gain access to workers abroad, and what happens to foreign workers and their families when their U.S. farm jobs end?

The extremes of the policy debate—open and closed borders— are a convenient starting point to consider the alternatives. Those opposed to slowing or stopping the inflow of newcomers to fill farm and farm-related jobs usually make three arguments. First, sharply higher wages could disrupt rural economies. Land and other asset prices reflect the assumption that foreign workers will continue to keep labor costs from rising sharply, so sudden jumps in farm wages could force some farmers and farm-related industries to make costly adjustments. Some would likely go out of business, adding to the economic challenges of rural areas struggling to retain people and jobs.

The second argument concerns food safety and security. It is better to import the workers and keep fruit and vegetable production in the United States, this argument runs, than to allow production to shift to lower-wage countries, giving Mexico or China the ability to block exports or to ship produce that is not safe for Americans. The third argument is that guest workers are the "missing ingredient" for viable fruit and vegetable production. The United States has the land, water, and climate to produce fruits and vegetables and should not allow this production to shift abroad only because there are insufficient workers willing to work at "reasonable wages," especially because guest workers in the fields help to support better jobs in packing and processing plants.

There are counterarguments to these adjustment-cost, food safety and security, and missing-ingredient reasons for legalizing the farm labor status quo. First, farmers and landowners are among the wealthiest Americans, raising questions about the morality of importing guest workers who are willing to work for low wages so that the value of their farmland does not fall. Just as Americans might question the rationality of importing low-wage coal miners to keep coal mining towns viable, one can also question whether it makes sense to import low-wage farmworkers to keep fruit and vegetable production viable.

Second, the United States professes a belief in free trade, whose bedrock principle is that each country should produce those goods in which it has a comparative advantage, and trade for goods that other countries can produce relatively cheaper. Low-wage countries with a comparative advantage in the production of labor-intensive fruits and vegetables should be allowed to produce them so that their economies can grow faster and increase the demand for other U.S.-produced goods as well as reduce emigration pressures. Private firms and the U.S. government can inspect imported food to ensure that it is safe for Americans, as is currently done for bananas, coffee, and the other commodities that are almost entirely imported.

As these arguments for and against the continued arrival of low-wage farmworkers play out in Congress, migrants continue to arrive and to fill farm and farm-related jobs. Most leave seasonal farmwork within a decade, and their U.S.-educated children do not follow them into the fields and food factories. The result is an immigration treadmill in rural America—an economic system that requires a continuous infusion of newcomers to keep jobs filled, but which may lead to a new rural underclass. We know very little about ex-farmworkers and their children, but few believe the best way to assure successful integration into American society is to begin as a seasonal farmworker with an income that is below poverty level.

The three chapters in this section explain that we do not have to risk transferring rural poverty from Mexico to the United States. Instead, Chapter 8 shows that there is a time-tested alternative to low-wage farmworkers in machines. History is littered with predictions that there are no alternatives to slaves or guest workers to produce food and fiber. We know that these predictions turned out to be wrong, but there is a continued reluctance to believe that agricultural production systems adjust to higher wages and will continue to do so. The flexibility in farm labor markets has always been on the demand side of the market, meaning that higher wages are more likely to reduce the need for farmworkers rather than encourage U.S. workers to go into the fields.

Chapter 9 assesses past and pending U.S. immigration reforms, emphasizing the three phases of open doors, qualitative restrictions on who could arrive in the 1880s, and quantitative restrictions in the 1920s. U.S. immigration policy changed fundamentally in 1965 by shifting the major criterion for selection from a potential immigrant's country of origin to whether the immigrant had U.S. relatives. In 1986, illegal or unauthorized migration was tackled, and the result was the same as with 1965 reforms—the exact opposite of what was expected occurred, as the national origins of immigrants changed and as illegal immigration surged. The United States today is debating exactly how stepped-up enforcement and legalization for 12 million unauthorized foreigners should be implemented.

Chapter 10 examines the immigration reform proposals targeted on agriculture. Their origins lie in a decades-long effort by farm employers to legalize the status quo, under which they do not have to try to recruit U.S. workers under government supervision, provide out-of-area workers with housing, and pay a higher than usual minimum wage. Farmworker advocates worried about their declining clout under a Republican president, in 2000 reached a compromise with farm employers that offered farmers a new guest-worker program and advocates legalization of currently unauthorized workers. This compromise, the Agricultural Job Opportunity, Benefits, and Security Act (AgJOBS), has been pending before Congress for almost a decade. It would undoubtedly help the individuals and their families who were legalized, but would not change the farm labor system. We outline a variation of AgJOBS that would regularize the farm workforce and rationalize the farm labor market to ensure that farm labor problems do not recur.

Chapter 8 Labor Shortages, Mechanization, and Food Costs

One argument for legalizing the farm labor status quo is to prevent shortages of workers that could make fruits and vegetables unaffordable luxuries. This chapter addresses the farm labor shortage issue, explaining that there is no government or economic definition of persisting "shortage" because, in a market economy, prices and wages adjust to bring supply and demand into balance, for example, both for peaches and for peach pickers. If there were persisting labor shortages, one would expect wages to rise sharply, leading to labor-saving mechanization, mechanical aids that make higher-wage workers more productive, or decreased production and increased imports.

The usual response to higher wages is labor-saving mechanization. In less than 200 years, the share of U.S. workers employed on farms shrank from more than 90 percent to less than 2 percent. In many cases, necessity proved to be the mother of invention, as tractors spread after World War I when farm boys returning from the military had the option of working in higher-wage factories. Farmers and other contemporary observers were often unable to see that mechanization was possible, so that many of those who argued that braceros (Mexican laborers) were essential to U.S. fruit and vegetable production in the early 1960s honestly did not foresee the labor-saving changes on the horizon.

Mechanization in agriculture is often complex, and this chapter explains the very different pictures of demand adjustments envisioned by economists and farmers. The key to successful labor-saving mechanization in many fruit and vegetable crops is often an honest broker to coordinate between farmers, packers, and retailers, whose different economic interests can make it almost impossible for a single producer to change production methods. In the past, the government played an important role in subsidizing mechanization research and acting as an honest broker, and resuming these subsidy and broker roles could speed labor-saving mechanization in the twenty-first century.

The final question is: What does the farm labor debate mean for consumers' pocketbooks? The simple answer that reducing immigration will not raise prices of fruits and vegetables very much, but continuing to import the rural poor from abroad could lead to a new rural underclass. Americans have become accustomed to spending a small and shrinking share of their incomes on food. Fresh fruits and vegetables are important to a healthy lifestyle, but most Americans spend so little on them that farmworker wages have a negligible impact on consumer food spending. If farm wages rose 40 percent, as they did in the mid-1960s, and there was no mechanization in response to the higher labor costs, the average household's spending on fresh fruits and vegetables would rise by $8 a year, about the cost of a movie ticket.

FARM LABOR SHORTAGES

In recent years, there have been widespread media reports of farm labor shortages. Farmers blamed the crackdown at the border and state laws in Arizona, Georgia, and elsewhere that drove unauthorized workers away, and said they were so short of workers that they could not harvest lettuce and pick peaches. These assertions were reported widely, as when the *Los Angeles Times* in 2007 described "a nationwide farmworker shortage threatening to leave fruits and vegetables rotting in fields"[1] and the *Wall Street Journal* claimed that "farmers nationwide are facing their most serious labor shortage in years."

The *Wall Street Journal* emphasized that there had been several years of farm labor shortages, so that "20 percent of American agricultural products were stranded at the farm gate" in 2006, including a third of North Carolina cucumbers.[2] The editorial went on to predict that 30 percent of California crops would be lost in 2007 because of too few workers. This prediction proved to be false; the production of most California fruits and vegetables was higher in 2007 than in 2006.

One reason why there can be media reports of shortages while supermarket aisles are bursting with produce is that there is no economic or government definition of shortage. In a market economy, demand curves rank consumers by their willingness to pay a particular price for a commodity, and curve falls because more people are willing to buy at a lower price. Supply curves rank producers by their willingness to sell at particular prices, and these curves rise because producers increase production in response to higher prices. In the familiar demand and supply X-diagram, if demand exceeds supply, prices rise, reducing demand and increasing supply; if supply exceeds demand, prices fall.

Producers of fresh fruits and vegetables are very familiar with the price changes associated with these workings of the market, especially with shifts in supply that lead to higher or lower prices. When bad weather or pests reduce production in one area, producers who are not affected enjoy higher prices. However, when all areas have good weather and no disease problems, higher production often means lower prices.

In agriculture, it may take time for the demand and supply of farm commodities to adjust to changing prices. Growers of perennial crops such as apples and oranges must decide if high prices are likely to persist before making the investments necessary to increase production, since it may be three years between the time a tree is planted and the grower harvests a first crop. When prices are low, growers must decide whether they are likely to remain low enough to justify removing trees or vines, or whether the low prices are a passing phenomenon.

The labor market adjusts in the same way, as changes in the supply of and demand for labor prompt wage adjustments. Labor demand curves rank employers by the wages they are willing to pay to fill particular jobs, and labor supply curves rank workers by their reservation wages, the wages needed to induce them to fill particular jobs. As with farmers who must decide whether to plant more apple or orange trees in response to higher prices, there can be lags between changes in the demand for labor and a supply response. For example, an information technology (IT) boom can sharply increase the wages of computer programmers but not produce an immediate surge in programmers because it takes time to acquire the needed education and skills.

Government intervention, such as trade and social policies, can affect the speed and extent of labor market adjustments. Government trade policies that keep out lower-cost foreign commodities encourage production in the United States. If the workers hired behind this protection wall are foreigners, as in the Florida sugarcane industry, import barriers increase the U.S. demand for foreign farmworkers. Similarly, when U.S. trade negotiators succeed in persuading Japan and Korea to reduce barriers to U.S. apples and oranges, they increase the U.S. demand for farmworkers, which in the current labor market means more immigration.

A range of social policies, from education to welfare, affects the supply of farmworkers. For most of America's history, the dominance of farmers meant that school schedules were adjusted so that children were available to be seasonal farmworkers. The ready availability of adult immigrant farmworkers has reduced pressures, even in rural areas, to adapt school schedules to seasonal farm labor demands, and laws restricting child labor mean that school-age children are today a negligible part of the farm workforce. Similarly, farmers often complain that generous welfare benefits have reduced the farm workforce, but most of those receiving cash assistance are women with children who have never been a significant share of the hired farm workforce.

The most important policy that affects the supply of farmworkers is immigration policy. The U.S. Department of Labor's National Agricultural Workers Survey reported that 75 percent of the hired workers employed on U.S. crop farms were born in Mexico, and 53 percent were not authorized to work in the United States. A sixth of the hired farmworkers were in the United States less than a year when interviewed, highlighting the revolving-door nature of the farm labor market.[3]

How can we square farmer complaints and media reports of farm labor shortages with market adjustments? Most media reports are based on farm employers complaining that fewer workers are employed than they would prefer. For example, a farmer may say there is a labor shortage if a crew of 30 is picking peaches but a crew of 40 is preferred. Some definitions of farm labor shortage are harder to evaluate, such as the assertion of a Grand Junction, Colorado, peach grower that there is a labor shortage because: "There is no labor walking up and down the road like there was years ago."[4]

Economists who believe that supply and demand adjust in response to wage signals look not to what employers say, but to what they do in order to attract additional workers. In a market economy, too few workers should be associated with rising wages. Rising wages in turn, should prompt farm employers to try to attract new workers or retain existing workers by offering benefits such as housing and making farmwork easier with mechanical aids.

Many news reports explain that farmers do not raise wages when they face "shortages" because they "know" that higher wages will not produce more workers. For example, Phoenix-area vegetable farmer Will Rousseau asserted: "We know local folks won't take those jobs, at any price."[5] Rousseau is partially correct—raising wages from $8 to $10 an hour is not likely to send U.S. workers streaming into the fields, although wages of $16 an hour may bring U.S. workers. However, rising wages will reduce the demand for labor. Well before wages double, farmers are likely to "need" far fewer workers, either because they discover that some tasks can be mechanized, they decide to skip the third or fourth repicking of a field or orchard, or they reduce quality standards so that workers can pick faster.

Persisting labor shortages would be expected to reduce U.S. production of fruits and vegetables, but U.S. fruit and vegetable production is rising, not falling. Between 1980 and 2006, there was very little change in overall fruit production, about 25 million tons a year, reflecting stable levels of grape, apple, and peach production. But the production of two very labor-intensive fruits—strawberries and sweet cherries—rose by more than 50 percent, which would not be expected if there were persisting labor shortages. In other words, U.S. production data show that, if there is a market for labor-intensive commodities, U.S. farmers planted more and assumed that workers would be available for the harvest.[6]

Fruit production from trees and vines adjusts more slowly to changing prices and wages than vegetable production, where there can be as little as 60 days between planting and harvesting. U.S. production of fresh vegetables has been rising, up more than 50 percent between 1980 and 2006. As with fruit crops, the production of some fresh vegetables rose and others fell, reflecting changing tastes more than labor shortages. For example, the production of head lettuce has been falling, but the production of romaine and leaf lettuce has been rising, reflecting changing consumer preferences. The production of broccoli rose sixfold between 1980 and 2006, and the production of carrots doubled. The production of some fresh vegetables has declined in recent years due to rising imports, including asparagus and garlic.[7]

The plantings and production of fruits and vegetables in the areas generating the most complaints of labor shortages show stable or increasing production. Farmers in Arizona and California produce most U.S. fresh vegetables such as lettuce and broccoli during the winter months along the Mexico-U.S. border. They began to complain of labor shortages during the 2004 harvest, which peaks between December and April.[8] Most of the harvest workers in Yuma

County, Arizona, and Imperial County, California, are Mexican citizens with U.S. immigrant visas who live in Mexico and commute daily or weekly to U.S. farm jobs. These green-card commuters are aging, and the younger workers who sometimes join the crews are often unauthorized, using false documents to get across the border and find jobs. Border Patrol agents in 2004 checked some of the buses leaving ports of entry for the fields and removed unauthorized workers, an enforcement strategy that gives unauthorized workers little incentive to return to Mexico and risk being apprehended again. Instead, unauthorized workers kept going north to earn higher wages and reduce the risk of detection.

Stepped-up border enforcement is likely to continue, which should lead to higher wages and adjustments that reduce the demand for labor. But there are few signs in 2008 of the sharp wage increases that would lead to labor-saving changes. Instead, Imperial County farmers planted more vegetables and melons—13 percent more acres between 2003 and 2006—and the value of their produce rose almost 20 percent, as did the acreage, value, and production of lettuce, their most valuable vegetable (see table 20).

Table 20 Imperial County Vegetables and Melons, 2003–2006

	Acres	Value of Production ($ millions)	
2003	94,602	443	
2004	104,176	505	
2005	100,052	572	
2006	107,280	527	
Change	13%	19%	
Head Lettuce	Acres	Value of Production ($ millions)	Cartons (millions)
2003	14,343	59	8.8
2004	16,586	87	12.4
2005	17,116	77	11.9
2006	17,318	67	12.6
Change	21%	14%	43%
Leaf Lettuce			
2003	9,648	72	9
2004	11,856	80	10.8
2005	14,009	111	12.7
2006	15,553	80	12.8
Change	61%	11%	42%

Source: Imperial County Agricultural Crop and Livestock Report, annual.

One reason why vegetable production can increase amid labor shortage complaints is because many farmers have become accustomed to an oversupply of workers. In a casual labor market that hires workers on a daily basis, employers want plenty of workers so that there will be enough to fill all crews. Stephen Birdsall, Imperial County's agricultural commissioner, explained why growers "need" three times more workers than can be employed: "In Imperial Valley there is a need for at least 10,000 full-time workers a day for the [vegetable] harvest. But the reality is they actually need a pool of about 30,000 workers. For every one person that works they need three people, because one person will only work a third of the time. They will work for a couple of days and then not return and then the grower will need others to replace them."[9]

The unemployment rate in Imperial County averaged 24 percent between 1990 and 2004. Why don't unemployed local workers rush into the fields? There are a number of reasons, many reflecting the disorganization of the casual labor market. Most hiring for harvesting crews is done in the early morning hours at the border. Under current hiring arrangements, local workers would have to drive to the port of entry at 4 or 5 a.m. to be hired. Workers are not paid while they wait for the buses to leave, nor are they paid for the drive to the field, which may be an hour or more away. Finally, there may be eight hours of work one day, four the next, and none the third day. These factors explain why even average earnings of $12 an hour do not attract local workers.

During the summer of 2006, California pears were reportedly going unpicked for lack of harvest workers. The *New York Times* ran a front-page story showing a Lake County pear grower whose pears were on the ground for lack of pickers.[10] As with border-area vegetable production, the story of Lake County pears is more complicated. Some 2,400 acres of Lake County Bartlett pears yielded 47,400 tons in 2004, 2,300 acres yielded 28,700 tons in 2005, and 2,100 acres yielded 36,100 tons in 2006. Lake County is a small player in California pear production, as two-thirds of the state's Bartlett pears are grown in the Sacramento Delta Region, three hours to the southeast.

The simple explanation for the "labor shortage" in Lake County is that the Delta's large and late crop kept picking crews there longer in 2006, and they saw little reason to drive three hours northwest to harvest a smaller crop. The larger story is that pear production is declining, from more than 300,000 tons in 1999 to less than 100,000 tons in 2005, according to the California Pear Commission, reflecting declining demand, especially for canned pears.[11] There were an average 374 workers employed by 55 establishments in "other noncitrus fruit farming" in Lake County in 1990, and 172 employees of 22 establishments in 2006.[12]

Perhaps the most remarkable aspect of the Lake County labor shortage is that an industry that employs fewer than 200 workers and produces a small slice of a declining commodity can become front-page news. The missing harvesters were largely Mexicans, and the media reports did not point out that a third of U.S. pears are exported, usually to Canada and Mexico. If it is true that Lake County pear growers cannot remain competitive at wages high enough to draw seasonal workers to an area that offers few other farm jobs, we have a case of immigrant labor as the missing ingredient. In this case, a pear industry cannot survive without workers who are willing to work at about the minimum wage, raising the question of whether the U.S. government should allow farmers to import workers.

Between 2002 and 2007, a few vocal farmers in the San Joaquin Valley, California's agricultural heartland, have complained of farm labor shortages.[13] Many of the labor shortage reports came from raisin growers, one of whom wanted 110 harvesters but had only 50 and complained of a severe labor shortage. Manuel Cunha Jr. of the Nisei Farmers League asserted that raisin growers were "short" 20 percent of the workers needed for the harvest in 2005.[14]

What happened to raisin production? Despite the raisin harvest being delayed by an unusually wet spring in 2005, more (green) raisin grapes were harvested in 2005 than 2004—about 4.5 pounds of green grapes dry into a pound of raisins (see table 21).

The unusual combination of a larger raisin grape crop of 2005 and higher grower prices led to wage increases for some harvesters. Raisin harvesters are paid piece rate wages, usually $0.25 for each 25 pounds of green grapes cut and laid on a paper tray, plus a 25 percent overhead to the labor contractor to cover payroll taxes, toilets, record keeping, and profits. Some growers raised wages by a cent or two, while others adapted as economic theory would predict, using modified wine grape harvesters to knock grapes that had already dried

Table 21 California Raisin Grapes, 2003–2005

	Acres	Production (tons)	Value ($)
2003	255,000	2,220,000	374,167
2004	240,000	2,038,000	624,600
2005	240,000	2,306,000	567,140

Source: *California Agricultural Resource Directory,* 2006, 75.

into raisins from the vines. The prospect of rising wages has spurred labor-saving mechanization, so that a third of California's raisin grapes were harvested with some form of mechanical assistance in 2008. Rising wages and subsidized mechanization can put the raisin industry in a better position to compete with lower-cost producers in Turkey and China, while importing more workers to keep wages low could add to the pool of impoverished immigrants in cities such as Parlier.

WAGES AND LABOR MARKET ADJUSTMENTS

Agricultural history is a story of innovations that allow fewer people to produce food and fiber, and rising farm productivity also reduced the share of household income spent on food. Around the world, countries that have fewer than 5 percent of their workers employed in agriculture are rich, with their residents spending less than 15 percent of their incomes on food, while countries with more than 50 percent of their workers in agriculture are poor, and residents often spend half or more of their income on food.

Rich countries reduced the share of their workers in agriculture by developing and diffusing labor-saving innovations. Labor-saving innovations came first in countries where labor was relatively scarce and wages were rising; in countries with relatively little land, land-saving or yield-increasing innovations often took priority. In short, agricultural history shows that innovations are "induced" by the relative prices of workers, machines, and farmland, and agricultural systems fairly quickly adjust to save the relatively expensive input (Ruttan, 2001).

Higher wages prompt labor-saving changes, but substituting machines for workers can be a complicated process. Machines can damage fresh fruits and vegetables, giving them less eye appeal and a shorter shelf life. A major obstacle to labor-saving mechanization is the fact that most farmers send their produce to packers and processors equipped to handle hand- or machine-picked produce, but not both, making it hard for one farmer to mechanize in isolation.

Understanding how labor-saving mechanization occurs in agriculture is the key to highlighting the role of government in fostering it. Point "e" on figure 8 portrays California's farm labor market, employing a million workers, 90 percent of whom are immigrants. Suppose stepped-up border enforcement reduced the influx of newcomers, while interior enforcement and normal exits shrank the current workforce, so that the labor supply curve would shift to the left. Wages would rise due to the ever-smaller workforce, and eventually there

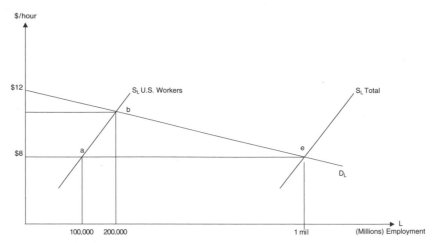

Figure 8 Smooth Adjustments to Rising Wages

would be a new equilibrium at "b," where more U.S. farmworkers were employed at higher wages, but with far fewer total farmworkers. The smooth adjustment illustrated in this figure highlights the union adage that "there is no shortage of workers, only a shortage of wages."

An alternative adjustment scenario is pictured in figure 9. Beginning from the same starting point at "e," border and interior enforcement as well as exits from the farm workforce shift the supply curve to the left. At first, fewer workers and higher wages reduce the demand for labor in the same manner as in figure 8, as farmers do not repick fields a second or third time. However, at a critical high wage signified by "a," there is a sharp drop in the demand for labor, from "a" to "c," due to mechanization or farmers shifting to other crops. In this discontinuous adjustment case, farm wages have risen sharply, as with the smooth adjustment case, but employment has fallen more, so that there are fewer U.S. workers employed than before the immigrant farmworkers were removed from the labor market.

The discontinuous adjustment labor market best describes labor-saving mechanization in California. For example, in 1960, braceros were 80 percent of the 45,000 peak harvest workers employed to pick California's 2.2 million tons of processing tomatoes. A decade later, almost all processing tomatoes were harvested mechanically. This rapid labor-saving mechanization was not anticipated. During the summer of 1963, while Congress debated whether to end the Bracero Program, the *California Farmer* asserted that "all agree that the state will never again reach the 100,000 to 175,000 acres [of processing

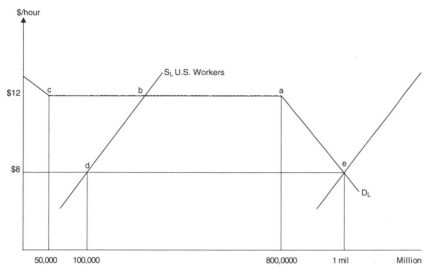

Figure 9 Discontinuous Adjustments to Higher Wages

tomatoes] planted when there was a guaranteed supplemental labor force in the form of the bracero. . . . The industry sees no hope of filling the [labor] gap in tomatoes from the domestic ranks even if competition for workers drives wages up to the average factory wage."[15]

Just like the growers who say they do not raise wages because they "know" U.S. workers will not rush into the fields, the *California Farmer* was speculating about how much higher farm wages would have to rise to induce Americans to pick tomatoes. But long before tomato wages reached factory levels, methods were developed to harvest tomatoes by machine. The fundamental lesson of the tomato harvester is that the flexibility in response to rising wages is primarily on the demand side of the labor market. This means that farmers figure out how to produce fruits and vegetables with fewer workers long before higher wages induce Americans to be farmworkers.

The mechanization of the processing tomato harvest also highlights the importance of government as midwife for mechanization. The keys to successfully mechanizing the harvesting of a crop usually lie in having the crop ripen at one time and developing machines to remove the crop without too much damage. In the case of processing tomatoes, federal and state funds supported the efforts of plant scientists to develop tomatoes that ripened uniformly, so they could be harvested in one pass through the field. Tax monies also subsidized the agricultural engineers who developed machines that cut the plant, shook off the tomatoes, and conveyed them past hand and electronic sorters before dumping them into trucks outfitted with tubs that hauled the tomatoes to processors.

Federal and state governments played key roles in subsidizing the science and engineering that made mechanization feasible, and they also played an honest broker role that facilitated adoption of the new tomato seeds and harvesting machines. Tomato farmers are paid by weight and quality, and have their payments reduced if there is too much "material other than tomatoes" in the tomatoes they deliver to processors.

Processing tomatoes were worth about $50 a ton in 2005, or 2.5 cents a pound. When hand-harvested tomatoes were delivered in 50-pound lugs or cartons, rejecting a lug cost the farmer $1.25. However, mechanically harvested tomatoes were delivered in 12.5-ton loads, and rejecting a load cost a farmer $625. The government hastened acceptance of mechanical tomato harvesting by establishing stations that took random samples of the harvested tomatoes to determine their quality. Without them, it is unlikely that tomato mechanization would have occurred so quickly.

There were many other labor-saving changes in the 1960s and 1970s in response to the end of the Bracero Program and rising farm wages, and many did not involve harvest mechanization. As with tomatoes, hand-harvested commodities were often placed in boxes or cartons that held 50 to 60 pounds of a fruit or vegetable and young men lifted these cartons onto trucks to take them to packinghouses. Rising wages prompted a shift to bulk bins in fields and orchards, and forklifts conveyed them to trucks, eliminating thousands of jobs. Another mechanical aid involved conveyor belts moving slowly down the field, allowing workers to pick a tray of strawberries or a melon and place it on the belt rather than collecting it in a bag and carrying it to a waiting truck. By making harvesting easier, women and older workers were more likely to remain in the crews.

The 1960s wave of mechanization came to a halt in the early 1980s. The most important reason was the upsurge in illegal immigration, which made workers readily available and dulled grower interest in labor-saving machines. But a second reason was the withdrawal of government subsidies for labor-saving mechanization research. The University of California (UC) was sued by the United Farmworkers Union and California Rural Legal Assistance in 1979 for using tax funds to mechanize the tomato harvest. The suit was eventually settled with UC agreeing to include worker representatives on advisory committees that evaluated proposals for mechanization research, but the publicity reduced federal and state funds for such research (Martin and Olmstead, 1985).[16]

Tomato harvest mechanization provides several lessons for contemporary debates about how agriculture would adjust to higher wages. First, those closest to the processing tomato industry were unable to predict the speed of the adjustments that occurred, casting doubt on assertions that there is no alternative to immigrant workers. Second, government played a critical role in speeding mechanization. Third, mechanization affects how a crop is grown and processed as well as the structure of the industry. Instead of tomatoes being one of several crops grown on diversified farms, processing tomatoes often became the major or only crop grown on larger and more specialized farms as farmers invested in harvesting machines.

PROSPECTS FOR MECHANIZATION

In the past, the basic research that led to labor-saving farm mechanization was often conducted at land-grant universities and perfected and diffused by private firms. Land-grant universities were founded in each state in the 1860s to teach agriculture and the mechanical arts to farmers and their families, with initial funding provided by the sale of federal lands in each state. Federal-state cooperation and funding created agricultural experiment stations to increase agricultural productivity and extension services to ensure that farmers knew about new technologies.

Agricultural engineers surveying the status of mechanization in particular crops often divide them into those that are consumed fresh and those that are processed (Sarig, Thompson, and Brown, 2000). Most nuts, below-ground vegetables such as potatoes and carrots, and tree fruits that are processed such as prunes (dried plums) and tart cherries are harvested by machine.[17] Shake-and-catch machines harvest most tree nuts such as almonds, and could be adapted for tree fruits such as cling peaches that are canned and Florida Valencia oranges that are processed into juice.

Machines usually harvest crops in one pass through the field, which encourages biologists to breed plants whose fruits and vegetables ripen uniformly. Machine-harvested crops are not as "clean" as hand-harvested commodities, but once they reach a packing or processing facility, hand and electronic sorters can remove bruised crops and foreign material. Advances in biology, engineering, and packing and processing have put several major crops on the verge of mechanization, including Florida's oranges and California's raisin grapes. Government decisions on immigration are likely to have major impacts on how quickly these and other commodities are transformed.

The key to faster labor-saving mechanization is rising wages. If reduced immigration led to rising farm wages, the result would be labor-saving mechanization and much higher productivity for the fewer workers who remain employed. There could also be increased imports of fruits and vegetables. Fruits and vegetables are mostly water, which in the past limited their sale to local markets. California pioneered the separation of production and consumption in the 1950s, a transition that was helped first by the interstate highway system and then by the deregulation of the trucking industry. Foreign producers are rapidly improving the quality of their fruits and vegetables, and by using the global transportation system are likely to increase their exports to the United States.

In some cases, higher wages may lead to mechanical aids rather than mechanization. Most of the workers who climb trees and pick apples and oranges are young men. Growers are planting more dwarf trees, and training them to grow so that they produce their fruit on a wall, making it easier to harvest apples and pears from platforms that can be raised and lowered with hydraulics, eliminating the need for ladders and the falls associated with them.

Economists who argue that higher wages will lead to labor-saving changes are often questioned by farmers who ask to see the machines that can harvest their apples, oranges, or strawberries. Such requests misunderstand the mechanization process. If machines were profitable at current wages, we would expect profit-maximizing farmers to already be using them. If wages were to rise, theory and experience suggest that machines will be developed and diffused quickly, often in ways that are hard to imagine before they occur.

One reason why many farmers cannot picture alternatives to current methods of production is that they often think in physical rather than profit terms. This means that they expect all 100 peaches that grow on a tree to be picked. A shake-and-catch machine, by contrast, may pick only 70 or 80 of the peaches, and may bruise or damage 10 or 20 of those delivered to the packinghouse. Agricultural engineers say that once fruits and vegetables are moved from fields into controlled environments, technology can be used to separate good and bad commodities.

Hand picking produces a higher pack-out rate than machine-picking, but if the goal is to maximize profits rather than peaches, machine picking is more profitable at higher wages. For example, mechanical tomato harvesting leaves some usable tomatoes in the fields. During the 1960s, some farmers hired workers to go through fields after they had been harvested because they did not want to see any of their tomatoes "go to waste." Despite studies showing that the value of the tomatoes recovered did not cover the minimum wage that had to be paid to the hand workers, some growers insisted on having hand crews follow the machines. Eventually, the practice was ended with improvements in the machines and fewer and larger tomato growers.

Growers need allies to mechanize harvesting. Most sell their commodities to packers and processors, who can encourage mechanization by establishing standards for machine-picked commodities or discourage mechanization by insisting on hand-picked quality. Retailers also play key roles. Stores that now offer 400 kinds of breakfast cereal, but only two types of a fruit or vegetable, such as organic and conventional, could be encouraged to offer consumers another choice—machine-harvested produce at lower prices and hand-harvested produce at higher prices.

Government can play a key role in bringing growers, packers, and retailers together to establish standards. Most fruits and vegetables must meet government-set standards, and inspectors visit fields and packinghouses to ensure that they do. Instead of reacting to what growers and packers propose, government could take the lead in setting standards that facilitate mechanization.

IMPLICATIONS FOR CONSUMERS

Many Americans believe that cheap farmworkers are the source of their cheap food. This is false—the United States has inexpensive food because it has a productive and largely mechanized agriculture. Farm wages and benefits play a very small role in the budgets of most American households because farmers do not receive much of the retail dollar spent on fresh fruits and vegetables, and farmworkers receive only a share of farmers' revenues. The bottom line is often a surprise—farmworker wages to produce fresh fruits and vegetables cost the typical American household about $21 a year.

Americans have relatively high incomes, and less than 13 percent of their spending is for food. Three sources of data link farm wages and retail food prices more precisely. The U.S. Bureau of Labor Statistics (BLS) conducts a Consumer Expenditure Survey that reports how much households spend on food, the U.S. Department of Agriculture reports on the farm share of average retail food prices for most commodities, and land-grant universities prepare cost-of-production budgets that show labor's cost of producing various commodities.[18]

The BLS refers to households as "consumer units," and there were 117 million in 2005, with an average of 2.5 persons, 1.3 earners, and two vehicles. The average annual income of a consumer unit before taxes was $58,700. After paying taxes and putting aside money for savings, average household expenditures were $46,400 a year or $892 a week, including $5,900 or $113 a week for food. To put food spending in perspective, the average household spent $15,200 for housing and utilities, $8,300 for transportation, $2,700 for health care, $2,400 for entertainment, and $1,900 for apparel.

Food spending has two components: food bought to eat at home and food eaten away from home. More than half of food spending, $3,300, was for food eaten at home ($63 a week), while $2,600 was spent on food away from home. Much of the cost of food eaten away from home reflects service and convenience, not the cost of the food, such as the ambience in restaurants or convenience at fast-food outlets. For this reason, labor-cost analysis focuses on foods eaten at home. Most of these foods have relatively small farm-wage cost components, including meat and poultry ($765), nonalcoholic beverages such as soft drinks ($610), and milk and cream ($145).

Household expenditures on fresh fruits ($182) and fresh vegetables ($175) totaled $357 in 2005, an average of $6.85 a week.[19] Although consumers often say they want to eat more fresh fruits and vegetables, the average household spends more on alcoholic beverages ($426) than on fresh fruits and vegetables ($357). The farm-wage cost of fresh fruits and vegetables is low because farmers receive less than 20 percent of consumer spending on them. Strawberries are picked directly into the plastic clamshells in which they are sold, and iceberg lettuce gets its film wrapper in the field, but farmers receive only an average 16 percent of the retail price of fresh fruits and 19 percent of the retail price of fresh vegetables.[20] This means that farmers receive only $62 a year from an average American household for the fresh fruits and vegetables consumed at home.

Most of what farmers receive covers the cost of land, seeds, fertilizer, and other nonlabor costs of production. The cost of farmworkers, including wages and benefits, is usually less than a third of farmers' revenue. With consumers spending $357 a year on fresh fruits and vegetables, which includes $62 for farmers, farmworker wages for fresh fruits and vegetables cost the average household $21 in 2005.

Rising farm wages are likely to prompt labor-saving mechanization, although the adjustment process may be discontinuous and the result may be fewer and larger farms. But what would happen to consumers if farm wages rose significantly, and there was no labor-saving mechanization? The average hourly earnings of farmworkers were $8.69 in 2005, about half the average earnings of factory workers. After the Bracero Program ended, farmworker wages rose 40 percent in the first contracts negotiated by the United Farm Workers (UFW).

What would happen to a typical American household if there were another 40 percent farmworker wage increase, and there was no labor-saving mechanization? Average hourly earnings would rise to $12.17 and, if passed on to consumers, this wage increase would raise the retail price of a pound of apples or a head of lettuce from $1 to $1.02.[21] For a typical household, spending on fresh fruits and vegetables would increase only $8 a year. However, the annual earnings of a seasonal farmworker would rise from less than $9,000 to more than $12,000 or from below the federal poverty line for an individual to above it.

Chapter 9 Reforming
U.S. Immigration Policies

Immigration policy is the central force influencing the number of farmworkers, their earnings and benefits, and whether farmworkers settle in the United States. Immigration policy also influences the production of farm commodities, affecting how and how many labor-intensive crops are produced in the United States.

U.S. immigration policies, which determine how many, from where, and in what status newcomers arrive, have gone through three major phases: laissez-faire until the 1880s, followed by 40 years of qualitative restrictions, and both quantitative and qualitative restrictions on who can immigrate since the 1920s. This chapter reviews the evolution of U.S. immigration policy, then turns to the current debate over how to reduce unauthorized migration and what to do about the 12 million unauthorized foreigners in the United States in 2008. Chapter 10 focuses on immigration and agriculture, assessing the proposal endorsed by worker advocates and farm employers and laying out an alternative that would both regularize the farm workforce and rationalize the farm labor market.

FROM LAISSEZ-FAIRE TO QUOTAS

During its first 100 years, the U.S. government had a laissez-faire policy toward immigration. This means that there were no limits on the number of immigrants who could be admitted, and federal, state, and local governments could adopt policies that encouraged immigration, which they did. For example, government subsidies for canal and railroad construction prompted employers to recruit immigrants who were willing to work for comparatively low wages under often harsh conditions. High tariffs discouraged imports of European manufactured goods, creating a demand for workers in American factories. There were few distinctions between immigrants and U.S. citizens, since the high cost of transportation meant that for most low-skilled migrants, the trip across the Atlantic was one way. This was one reason why immigrants were a third of the regular soldiers in the U.S. army in the 1840s, and they were an even higher proportion of many state militias (Briggs, 2001, 45).

There were no fees or admissions tests for arriving immigrants. However, beginning in 1820, the federal government required ship captains to report on the immigrants they brought to the United States. Most early immigrants eventually became U.S. citizens, and their children born in the United States were generally citizens at birth. The Naturalization Act of 1790 established requirements for naturalization whereby immigrants could acquire U.S. citizenship after several years of residence.[1]

There were fears that immigrants would alter the culture and customs of the evolving United States, but the neat match between Europeans seeking opportunity and an America in need of settlers kept the immigration door wide open. However, in the 1840s, an influx of Roman Catholics from Ireland and Germany prompted the first organized anti-immigrant movement, the "Know Nothings" who formed the American Party to elect candidates that shared their views on immigration. Protestant clergymen, journalists, and other opinion leaders of the Order of the Star Spangled Banner urged a stop to immigration from non–Anglo Saxon countries.[2] The American Party won 70 congressional seats in the federal election of 1854, but was unable to close the doors to the United States before the Civil War soon slowed immigration.

After the Civil War, those who wanted to restrict immigration took aim at particular groups they considered undesirable. In this way, Congress barred the entry of convicts and prostitutes in 1875. The Immigration Act of 1882 for the first time prohibited immigration from a particular country—China—as a result of pressure from white workers in California who felt threatened by "unfair competition" from the Chinese.[3] Eventually, U.S. qualitative restrictions on immigrants barred the entry of 30 types of foreigners, from Communists to homosexuals (some of these bars were later lifted).

Immigration from southern and eastern Europe increased in the 1890s. At the time, the United States was largely rural and Protestant, and many Americans feared that they would be overwhelmed by the influx of Jews and Catholics. Woodrow Wilson (later elected president) expressed their fears: "Immigrants poured in as before, but . . . now there came multitudes of men of lowest class from the south of Italy and men of the meanest sort out of Hungary and Poland, men out of the ranks where there was neither skill nor energy nor any initiative of quick intelligence; and they came in numbers which increased from year to year, as if the countries of the south of Europe were disburdening themselves of the more sordid and hapless elements of their population" (Wilson, 1901, 212–213)

Congress first reacted to this popular opposition to immigration with more qualitative restrictions, approving literacy tests on new arrivals beginning in 1897. However, literacy tests were vetoed by three presidents before Congress overrode President Wilson's veto in 1917 and required immigrants 16 years of age and older to be able to read in at least one language. To bolster the case for restricting immigration, Congress commissioned the 41-volume Dillingham report, named after Senator William Paul Dillingham (R-VT), the first major U.S.-government social science inquiry. It supported the restrictionists, concluding that immigrants from southern and eastern Europe had more "inborn socially inadequate qualities than northwestern Europeans," setting the stage for national origin quotas.[4]

When European immigration resumed after World War I, Congress imposed the first quantitative restrictions on immigration. The method was straightforward—the number of immigrants from any country could not exceed 3 percent of the number of foreign-born persons in the United States in 1910, and the base year was soon changed to 1890, before most third-wave immigrants arrived, to further limit arrivals from southern and eastern Europe. By 1927, there was an annual quota of 150,000 immigrants, plus accompanying wives and children, and each country had a quota that was "a number which bears the same ratio to 150,000 as the number of inhabitants in the United States in 1920 having that national origin bears to the number of white inhabitants of the United States."[5] This so-called national origins quota system ensured that 60 percent of the immigrants between 1924 and 1965 were from Britain and Germany. However, immigration from the Western Hemisphere was not affected by the national origins quota system.

Many Americans opposed the national origins system, seeing it as a discriminatory blot on a nation sacrificed to preserve democracy in World War II. President Harry Truman supported efforts to abolish the national origins system, but Congress preserved it in the basic U.S. immigration law, the Immigration and Nationality Act (INA) of 1952, by overriding Truman's veto. The INA is the law that made harboring unauthorized aliens a crime, but included the so-called Texas proviso at the behest of southwestern farmers, which specifically said that employing unauthorized workers was not harboring them.

In the early 1960s, immigration reformers tried a different tactic. Basic immigration law was left unchanged, but the national origins system for selecting immigrants was replaced by a family preference system, meaning that priority to immigrate would be given to foreigners with family members settled in the United States, plus a few foreigners desired by U.S. employers.

IMMIGRATION REFORMS: 1986–1996

By the 1980s, U.S. immigration law could be described as a complex system that changed once a generation. As immigration increasesd in the 1970s, the pace of immigration reform quickened in response to globalization and particular events that affected flows of foreigners to the United States.

The first major change was in the U.S. definition of refugees requiring resettlement. In 1951 the United Nations (U.N.) Refugee Convention defined a refugee as a person outside his or her country of citizenship who is unwilling to return because of a well-founded fear of persecution due to the person's race, religion, nationality, membership in a particular social group, or political opinion. The U.S. government did not adopt this definition, instead defining refugees as persons fleeing Communist dictatorships or political violence in the Middle East. The Refugee Act of 1980 adopted the U.N. definition, and required the president to determine the number of refugees to be resettled in the United States each year in consultation with Congress.[6]

The second major reform aimed to reduce illegal immigration. During the decade of the 1960s, the Border Patrol apprehended 1.6 million foreigners, a number that rose fivefold to 8.3 million in the 1970s. Federal commissions studying the effects of illegal immigration concluded that unauthorized workers adversely affected U.S. workers and undermined the rule of law. They recommended a grand-bargain compromise. For those whose priority was reducing illegal migration, impose sanctions on employers who hired unauthorized workers. For those whose priority was bringing unauthorized foreigners "out of the shadows," provide immigrant visas to the estimated 3 to 5 million unauthorized foreigners who had developed an "equity stake" through work or residence in the United States (Select Commission on Immigration and Refugee Policy, 1981).

The Immigration Reform and Control Act (IRCA) of 1986 implemented this grand bargain, but in a manner that increased rather than reduced illegal migration. The IRCA put amnesty first and enforcement second. There were two amnesty programs, one for foreigners who were illegally in the United States by 1982 and another for farmworkers who were employed illegally on U. S. farms in 1985–1986. The residence-based amnesty program legalized about 1.7 million foreigners who were in the United States at least five years, since five years was judged to be the time needed to develop an equity stake in the United States. The farmworker program took the opposite approach, legalizing 1.1 million foreigners who did farmwork in the year before its enactment, that is, recent arrivals.

The farmworker legalization program, known as the Special Agricultural Worker (SAW) Program, was riddled with fraud and contributed significantly to subsequent illegal migration. Most researchers estimated there were about 400,000 unauthorized farmworkers who satisfied the fairly generous rules for amnesty, doing at least 90 days of farmwork in 1986–1986 (Martin, 1994). The U.S. government, anticipating that some nonqualified workers would apply, initially printed 800,000 applications. However, more than 1.3 million foreigners applied for amnesty under the SAW Program, and the Immigration and Naturalization Service (INS) was not prepared to deal with this flood of applicants.

SAW Program rules had a unique feature. Farmworkers were portrayed as often helpless victims of employers who paid them in cash and did not issue pay stubs, so once a foreigner applied for amnesty, the burden was on the federal government to prove that the applicant was lying. Most SAW applicants attached one-sentence letters to their applications to prove that they had done sufficient qualifying work, typically a letter from a farm employer or labor contractor that said: "Jose Gonzalez picked tomatoes for 92 days in Fresno."

The INS did not have the expertise to know that the tomato picking season rarely exceeds 60 to 70 days, and approved more than 85 percent of the SAW applications. Adjudicators were able to reject some of the extreme cases, such as the applicants who claimed they picked strawberries and lettuce from trees, but most of those who knew how fruits and vegetables were grown were approved.

The SAW Amnesty Program began in May 1987, amid fears of too few strawberry pickers in Oregon. In response, Congress approved an amendment that allowed foreigners abroad who said they did qualifying U.S. farmwork as unauthorized workers in 1985–1986 but had no records to prove it, to come to the U.S. border with Mexico, and explain the farm work they did to an INS employee. Over 100,000 Mexicans entered the United States under this border-entry program, receiving permission to work legally while they assembled their SAW applications.

Word soon spread that the SAW Program was the "easy" amnesty program, prompting a rush to the border. At some ports of entry, "coaching" was available to those waiting for interviews to inform applicants how fruits and vegetables were harvested in the United States—the penalty for lying was not being admitted to the United States. Eventually, 750,000 Mexican men, a seventh of the adult men in rural Mexico in the mid-1980s, became U.S. immigrants under the SAW Program.[7]

The SAW Program taught rural Mexicans that they could become U.S. immigrants by asserting that they did qualifying U.S. farmwork, whether they did or did not. Another part of the IRCA sent a clear signal to farmers that they could continue to rely on foreign workers. Farmers feared that as soon as their workers were legalized, many would move into nonfarm jobs.

To avoid farm labor shortages, the IRCA included a Replenishment Agricultural Worker (RAW) Program that would open the border gates to farmworkers and allow them to float from farm to farm, so that farm employers would not have to undergo certification or be responsible for providing RAW workers with housing. Foreigners registered with the RAW Program could earn an immigrant visa if they did at least 90 days of farmwork in each of three years, testing the concept of earned legalization. The RAW Program was not implemented because the U.S. government determined that were no farm labor shortages.[8]

Farmers demonstrated their clout in Congress by insisting that the IRCA include both the SAW and RAW Programs. Even though it was clear that the IRCA's agricultural provisions were increasing illegal migration in the late 1980s (Commission on Agricultural Workers, 1993), many in Congress assumed that illegal migration was under control and turned to reform the legal immigration system. Some nonfarm employers complained of shortages of skilled and professional workers, and wanted Congress to approve more immigrant and guest-worker visas for such foreigners. The Immigration Act of 1990 (IMMACT) did so by more than doubling the number of immigrant visas available for foreigners (and their families) requested by U.S. employers to 140,000 a year. It also created the H-1B Program to easily admit to the United States foreigners with at least a college degree to fill jobs with that requirement.

Immigration remained a front-burner political issue in the early 1990s. When Chinese troops fired on protesters in Tiananmen Square in 1989, Chinese students in the United States were allowed to become immigrants, which subsequently increased immigration from China. The North American Free Trade Agreement (NAFTA), which went into effect in 1994, began the process of creating freedom of movement for American, Canadian, and Mexican professionals. California suffered a severe recession in 1990–1991, and Governor Pete Wilson won reelection in 1994 in part by endorsing Proposition 187, an initiative approved by a 59–41 percent margin that would have created a state-funded system to ensure that illegal migrants did not receive state-funded services, including K–12 schooling.[9] Proposition 187 was never fully implemented.

In 1996, Congress approved three immigration-related laws that dealt with terrorism, welfare, and foreigners who commit crimes in the United States. The Anti-Terrorism and Effective Death Penalty Act (ATEDPA) was a response to the foreigners responsible for the 1994 World Trade Center bombing. Some of those involved had applied for asylum, and the ATEDPA made it easier to turn back foreigners arriving at airports without proper documents and applying for asylum. If they could not convince an inspector that they had a "credible fear" of persecution at home, they could be turned away without having an immigration judge decide whether they needed asylum in the United States.

The Personal Responsibility and Work Opportunity Reconciliation Act (PRWORA) changed access to welfare benefits for both Americans and immigrants. President Clinton pledged to "end welfare as we know it" by requiring poor adults to work and putting time limits on cash assistance. The PRWORA made most legal immigrants who arrived after August 22, 1996, ineligible for federal means–tested welfare benefits, accounting for almost half of the projected savings from welfare reform. Henceforth, legal immigrants would have to naturalize (generally after five years) or work at least 10 years in the United States to qualify for cash assistance.[10]

The Illegal Immigration Reform and Immigrant Responsibility Act (IIRIRA), also enacted in 1996, aimed to reduce illegal migration by expanding the Border Patrol. However, in recognition of the failure of the IRCA's employer sanctions, which were easily evaded by unauthorized workers presenting false documents to their employers, the IIRIRA mandated several pilot programs under which U.S. employers could submit the data on newly hired workers to the government to confirm that they were legally authorized to work, the origins of what is now known as E-Verify. The IIRIRA also imposed new requirements on U.S. residents who sponsor their relatives for immigration visas, requiring them to sign legally binding pledges to provide financial support for the immigrants they sponsor.[11]

During the late 1990s, Congress regularized the status of Central Americans who had come to the United States during civil wars in the 1980s but had been refused asylum because of U.S. foreign policies. Despite the adoption of the U.N. definition of refugee, the U.S. government gave asylum far more often to Nicaraguans fleeing a regime that the United States opposed than to Salvadorans fleeing a government that the United States supported. Migrant advocates highlighted this discrepancy in court, and won injunctions preventing the removal of most Central Americans who applied for asylum, setting the stage for their legalization. However, the U.S. government did not end special treatment for Cubans. Both Cubans and Haitians arrive in Florida by boat. Under the so-called dry foot policy, Cubans who successfully reach U.S. land are allowed to stay as immigrants, while most Haitians who reach south Florida are returned to Haiti.

TERRORISM AND ENFORCEMENT: 2001–2004

On September 11, 2001, four commercial planes were hijacked by 19 foreigners. Two were flown into the World Trade Center towers in New York City, bringing them down and killing 3,000 people. President George W. Bush declared war on terrorists and the countries that harbor them, and Congress enacted legislation to fight terrorism, including laws that affected immigrants. The hijackers were able to plan and carry out their attack while living in the United States, and most obtained driver's licenses and identification cards in states that did not require proof of the applicant's legal status.

Congress aimed to change this with the Uniting and Strengthening America by Providing Appropriate Tools Required to Intercept and Obstruct Terrorism Act (USA PATRIOT) of 2001. USA PATRIOT, inter alia, gave the U.S. attorney general the power to detain any foreigner he or she designated a danger to U.S. national security. Some 1,200 foreigners were soon detained and held in secret after 9/11, but none were found to have terrorist links, and most were deported for violating immigration laws.[12] The Enhanced Border Security and Visa Entry Reform Act (EBSVERA) of 2002 required universities to keep better track of the foreign students they enrolled and heightened scrutiny of visa applicants from countries deemed to be sponsors of terrorism. EBSVERA required foreigners needing visas to be interviewed personally by U.S. consular officers abroad, with applications from most Middle Eastern countries checked against government databases to detect terrorists. Finally, the REAL ID Act of 2005 required states to check that applicants for driver's licenses are legal U.S. residents, and to reissue all driver's licenses by 2014 to ensure that only legal U.S. residents have the government ID most often used to fly and to enter federal buildings.

Perhaps the most important change after 9/11 was the creation of a new cabinet agency, the Department of Homeland Security, which absorbed the Immigration and Naturalization Service. The ex-INS was divided into three agencies, one dedicated to border enforcement and inspecting persons arriving in the United States, a second responsible for enforcement of immigration laws within the United States, and a third that deals with applications for immigration benefits, such as immigrant visas for foreigners inside the United States, and naturalization.

UNAUTHORIZED MIGRATION

Despite these news laws, illegal immigration rose after 9/11. With the federal government unable to agree on how to respond, state and local governments moved in different directions. Despite the REAL ID law, some state governments issued drivers' licenses to unauthorized foreigners under the theory that it is best if all drivers learn the rules of the road and are eligible for insurance. Other state governments required applicants for licenses to prove they were legally in the United States and trained their police to identify suspected unauthorized foreigners. Cities also moved in different directions. Some subsidized day labor markets where migrants sought jobs and others had local police arrest workers soliciting jobs on street corners.

Congress has been unable to approve legislation to deal with illegal migration because restrictionists and admissionists have been unable to compromise. Restrictionists argue that unauthorized foreigners violate U.S. laws and depress U.S. wages, and that the first priority of any twenty-first-century immigration reform is reducing illegal migration. Admissionists argue that unauthorized foreigners fill essential U.S. jobs and, as a nation of immigrants, the United States should be willing to legalize needed unauthorized workers.

President Bush generally sided with the admissionists, but sometimes argued for legalization to guest worker rather than immigrant status. In January 2004, Bush unveiled a Fair and Secure Immigration Reform Program that would permit unauthorized foreigners in the United States with jobs to become temporary legal residents for three to six years. As guest workers, they would be free to travel in and out of the United States and get both Social Security Numbers and driver's licenses. Bush's plan did not provide a path to legal immigrant status, prompting admissionists to warn that the unauthorized would not come forward and identify themselves to the government if they eventually would have to depart.[13]

Bush's plan was never formally submitted to Congress. Instead, the House and Senate, both controlled by Republicans, moved in different directions. In December 2005 the House approved the enforcement-only Border Protection, Antiterrorism, and Illegal Immigration Control Act (BPAIIC), which would have required all employers to participate in E-Verify and screen newly hired as well as existing employees to ensure that they were legally authorized to work in the United States. However, the BPAIIC was most notable for its effort to reduce illegal migration by mandating the construction of 700 miles of fence along the Mexico-U.S. border, prompting Mexican Foreign Secretary Luis Ernesto Derbez to assert that "Mexico is not going to bear, it is not going to permit, and it will not allow a stupid thing like this wall."

The BPAIIC did not include a guest-worker or legalization program, but nonetheless drew the support of President Bush. During the House debate, the White House released a Statement of Administration Policy that said: "The Administration strongly supports House passage of [BPAIIC] and . . . looks forward to working with Congress to improve certain provisions in the bill and to implement the many necessary reforms that this legislation provides." Bush seemed to side with those who believed that enforcement should be proven effective before additional migrant workers arrived legally and before the government deals with unauthorized foreigners in the United States.[14]

The BPAIIC was a shock to migrant advocates who believed that a consensus was developing in support of legalization, and the only question was whether unauthorized foreigners would become guest workers or immigrants. Unions, churches, some employer groups, and Hispanic activists organized massive demonstrations around the United States opposing the BPAIIC's enforcement-only approach, culminating in a May 1, 2006, "day without immigrants" protest. Perhaps a million workers did not report to work, and some meatpacking plants closed for the day. With hundreds of thousands of protestors, there was talk of a new "immigrant rights movement" that would repeat the successes of the civil rights movement in the 1960s and win legislation to help unauthorized foreigners.

The immigrants' rights protests may have had an impact in the Senate in May 2006, which approved the Comprehensive Immigration Reform Act (CIRA).[15] Like the House bill, the Senate's CIRA would have stepped up enforcement, both at the border and at U.S. workplaces. Unlike the House bill, the Senate's CIRA was sensitive to the fact that the government databases against which employers check the status of new hires could have errors that might lead to a legal worker being fired. Thus, the Senate's CIRA said that employers should retain workers who appeared to be unauthorized after database checks until the verification system was 99 percent accurate, and allowed workers wrongly fired to seek compensation.

The Senate's CIRA included a three-tiered earned legalization program that reflected the difficulty in reaching agreement on what to do about unauthorized foreigners. The unauthorized were divided into three groups based on how long they had been in the United States, so that those present at least five years could earn an immigrant status by continuing to work, paying taxes, and passing English and background tests. The unauthorized in the United States two to five years would have had to satisfy the same work, tax, and English requirements, but would also have had to return to their countries of origin and reenter the United States legally to become immigrants. Those in the United States less than two years would have been expected to leave the country.

Many advocates considered this three-tiered legalization program too complex and stingy, warning that only half of the unauthorized would qualify for immigrant status under the five-year cutoff, and that many foreigners would be dubious of a requirement to return home and reenter, fearing they could not return. Restrictionists, on the other hand, denounced the program as "amnesty" for lawbreakers, and vowed to resist any bill that allowed foreigners to "buy American citizenship."

Following the recommendations of President Bush, the Senate's CIRA included a new H-2C guest-worker program with two unusual features: the guests could have earned immigrant visas, and the number of guest workers could have fluctuated with market conditions. The admissions process would begin when U.S. employers "attested" to the government that they needed to hire migrants to fill vacant jobs and that the employment of migrant workers "will not adversely affect the wages and working conditions of workers in the United States similarly employed."[16] Employers would have sent government approvals to foreigners, and they would have paid $500 for six-year work permits.

Unlike past guest-worker programs, H-2C migrants could have become immigrants if their U.S. employers applied for immigrant visas on their behalf or foreigners could apply on their own after four years of U.S. work and passing an English test.[17] The market mechanism allowed the number of H-2C visas to increase if employers requested the total annual allotment of visas before the end of the year. For example, the number of H-2C visas was initially set at 325,000 a year. It could have been raised by 20 percent if employers requested all these visas within the first quarter (to 390,000) and, if employers continued to request all available visas right away, the ceiling would rise annually, to 970,000 in the seventh year, or about half of normal U.S. labor force growth. Unions strongly opposed to the prospect of almost a million new guest workers within seven years persuaded the Senate to reduce the starting number to 200,000.

The Senate's CIRA also included another new guest-worker program for agriculture. The Agricultural Job Opportunity, Benefits, and Security Act (AgJOBS) was modified slightly to allow up to 1.5 million unauthorized foreigners who did at least 150 days of farmwork during a 24-month period preceding enactment to obtain a blue-card probationary immigrant status, continuing the IRCA tradition of legalizing recent arrivals employed in farmwork. Blue-card holders who performed at least 100 days of farmwork each year for five years, or at least 150 days in three years, could earn a legal immigrant status for themselves and their families, reflecting the earned legalization concept of the never-implemented RAW Program. AgJOBS (examined more closely in Chapter 10) also would have made it easier for farm employers to hire guest workers.

Democrats won control of Congress in the November 2006 elections, raising the hopes of migrant advocates for an immigration reform that included more legalization and less enforcement. The Senate took the lead on immigration reform, debating a new version of the Comprehensive Immigration Reform Act in May–June 2007 that was negotiated privately by a dozen senators led by Senators Edward Kennedy (D-MA) and Jon Kyl (R-AZ), representing the admissionist and restrictionist wings in the debate, respectively.

The Senate's CIRA 2007 included more enforcement measures and less-generous legalization provisions, such as doubling the number of Border Patrol agents from 14,500 to 28,000 (New York City has about 36,000 police) and adding more fencing on the Mexico-U.S. border. However, the major new enforcement effort would have been in the workplace, which most experts agree is the key to deterring unauthorized workers. CIRA 2007 proposed that the Social Security Card become a fraud-resistant identity document that employees would have to present to their employers, who would be required to check the information via the Internet.

The Senate's CIRA 2007 also included an earned legalization program that would have allowed unauthorized foreigners to register for four-year renewable Z-1 visas that would have permitted them to live and work in the United States indefinitely. However, Z-1 visa holders could have "earned" a regular immigrant visa only by waiting at least eight years, passing an English test, paying a fine, and leaving the United States—they would have received immigrant visas at U.S. consulates in their home country and reentered the United States legally. As with previous legalization proposals, restrictionists argued that this "amnesty" rewarded lawbreakers, while migrant advocates worried that unauthorized foreigners would be reluctant to wait eight years and have to leave the United States in order to obtain an immigrant visa.

The Senate's CIRA 2007 also included a new market-based guest-worker program that would have issued Y-1 visas to low-skilled foreign workers filling year-round U.S. jobs. As with previous proposals, this new guest-worker program would have made it easy for employers to receive permission to hire migrant workers, and they would have sent the permission to the foreigners so they could receive Y-1 visas good for two years of U.S. work in their countries of origin. However, unlike CIRA 2006, these Y-1 guest workers could renew their visas a maximum of two times, for a total of six years of U.S. work. To avoid attachments to the United States, Y-1 guest workers would have to spend at least a year in their country of origin between their two-year U.S. work stints.[18]

The fourth component of CIRA 2007 was a change to the legal immigration system. Many restrictionist senators wanted to select more immigrants on the basis of points awarded to individuals for characteristics that are likely to assure economic success in the United States, including knowledge of English and having a college degree. Canada selects more than half of its immigrants under such a point system,[19] and some senators thought that more Americans would support high levels of immigration if they thought that immigrants were making significant contributions to the U.S. economy.

The point system proposed in CIRA 2007 would have required aspiring immigrants to earn at least 55 of the maximum 100 points. Individuals could have received up to 47 points for employment prospects (having a U.S. job offer), up to 28 points for their level of education, and up to 15 points for knowledge of English. Once an applicant achieved 55 points, he/she could receive another 10 points for having U.S. relatives, thus establishing a link between the new point system and the current family preference system. The proposed U.S. point system differed significantly from the Canadian system, since it would have awarded 16 of the maximum 47 employment points to foreigners filling "high-demand" jobs, whether as janitors or engineers. The Canadian system admits mostly college-educated immigrants, but the proposed U.S. point system could have also admitted low-skilled immigrants.[20]

Despite a strong push from President Bush, the Senate did not approve CIRA 2007. After the House Republican Conference voted by a 3–1 margin to "disapprove" of CIRA 2007, Bush challenged Republican restrictionists, saying that they "don't want to do what's right for America." Department of Homeland Security (DHS) Secretary Michael Chertoff and Commerce Secretary Carlos M. Gutierrez worked closely with the senators seeking its approval, but their efforts were not sufficient to overcome opposition from Republicans who opposed "amnesty" and Democrats who worried that more guest workers might depress U.S. wages.[21]

Immigration loomed large in both the Republican and Democratic 2008 presidential primaries. Among Republicans, only John McCain, the putative nominee, continued to embrace Senate-style comprehensive immigration reform of more enforcement and a path to legalization. However, under fire from more restrictionist rivals such as Representative Tom Tancredo (R-CO), who made opposition to illegal migration the centerpiece of his campaign, McCain disowned the CIRA 2006 that he championed, saying "Americans want the border secured first."

The likely Democratic candidate for president, Barack Obama (D-IL), supported the Senate's comprehensive immigration reform proposals in 2006 and 2007. Obama has emphasized enforcing labor laws to ensure that employers do not prefer to hire unauthorized workers because they are willing to work "hard and scared," expressed opposition to a large new guest worker program, and has pledged to encourage Congress to enact a generous path to earned immigrant status. However, as President Bush's experience makes clear, even a president committed to comprehensive immigration reform may not be able to overcome the strong resistance to "amnesty" in Congress and among Americans.

Chapter 10 Regularize and Rationalize Farm Labor

Rural America is on an immigrant labor treadmill. The farmworkers of tomorrow are growing up today somewhere outside the United States, making immigration policy a major concern of farmers, farmworkers, and agricultural communities. Unlike urban areas, which receive immigrants at the top and bottom of the education ladder, most of the newcomers in rural America have not finished high school. The question is whether these newcomers and their children will become a poor underclass of concern in the future.

The immigrants in rural and agricultural areas often lack both education and legal status. Almost 5 percent of the 150 million U.S. workers are believed to be unauthorized,[1] but the percentage of unauthorized farmworkers is higher, topping 50 percent of seasonal workers on crop farms. The share of unauthorized workers in other farm-related industries, from food processing to meatpacking, is generally thought to be about 25 percent, which is five times the U.S. average.

U.S. farm labor and immigration policies did not anticipate a rising tide of poorly educated and unauthorized workers in rural America. As we have seen, policy makers in the 1960s anticipated a wave of mechanization that would eliminate most farm jobs, making it their primary responsibility to help farmworkers and their children transition to nonfarm jobs. By the mid-1980s, it was apparent that the number of farm jobs was stable and the share of unauthorized workers filling them was increasing. The response to the unanticipated increase in unauthorized farm workers was an easy legalization program, which signaled to farmers that foreign workers would continue to be available. Increased plantings and ineffective enforcement opened the floodgates and allowed Mexico's rural poor to spread throughout rural America.

This chapter reviews the struggle for agricultural immigration reform and assesses the proposal currently before Congress—AgJOBS. It then outlines a strategy to regularize and rationalize that would better achieve the goals of providing rural America with a legal workforce and ensure that the number of farm jobs—and the problems associated with them—decrease over time. Finally, we ask what effects the status quo and proposed immigration reforms are likely to have on U.S. agriculture and rural communities.

THE ROAD TO AGJOBS

Farmers have long worried about whether there would be enough seasonal workers available to harvest their crops. Over decades, they convinced themselves and the federal government that the solution was to reach over borders and find workers for whom U.S. wages were a godsend. The alternative, allowing wages to increase enough to attract U.S. workers, would likely have reduced the demand for farmworkers well before U.S. workers stormed the fields.

The major program through which farmers could obtain guest workers, H-2 until 1987 and since then H-2A, presumed that most farmers could hire U.S. workers to fill their jobs. However, in the exceptional circumstances when U.S. workers are not available, the U.S. Department of Labor (DOL) could certify a farmer's need for legal guest workers.

Certification satisfied sugarcane farmers in Florida and apple growers along the eastern seaboard, where there were no farmworker unions and few groups opposing guest workers. However, growers in the western states feared that the United Farm Workers (UFW) and other unions would send workers in response to the recruitment efforts they were required to undertake, and they would be faced with the choice of hiring pro-union crews or being sued for not hiring U.S. workers. Thus, western farmers insisted on a noncertification path to hiring legal guest workers.

The divide between eastern and western farmers was evident well before the Immigration Reform and Control Act (IRCA) was enacted in 1986. In discussions about how immigration reforms might affect agriculture, eastern growers expressed concern about the minimum wage they had to pay to guest workers and the amount they could deduct from workers' wages to cover the cost of their food. Western growers, on the other hand, rejected the then H-2 Program, asserting that it was not adaptable in areas with large farms and a wide range of fruit and vegetable crops.

In what the *New York Times* called one of the top political stories of 1985, western farmers demonstrated that they had sufficient clout in Congress to block any immigration reform that did not create a noncertification guest-worker program. The result, as we have seen, was a reform of the H-2 Program that renamed it the H-2A Program and both the Special Agricultural Worker (SAW) legalization and the Replenishment Agricultural Worker (RAW) guest-worker programs. The resulting flood of unauthorized farmworkers allowed the RAW Program to expire in 1993 without being used.

Farmers who had worked hard to win the RAW Program did not want to see the concept of a noncertification guest-worker program die. However, with Mexicans pouring into the United States in the mid-1990s as a result of Mexico's economic crisis, it was hard to raise money from farmers worried about labor shortages to win support in Congress for a new guest-worker program.

Congressional hearings were nonetheless held on western farmers' proposals for alternative guest-worker programs. They featured testimony on the rising share of unauthorized workers, farmers explaining why they could not use the H-2A Program to obtain legal guest workers, and an outline of an alternative guest-worker program. Farmers appeared to be making enough headway in Congress to prompt the U.S. Commission on Immigration Reform (CIR) in June 1995 to assert that: "A large-scale agricultural guest worker program . . . is not in the national interest . . . such a program would be a grievous mistake." The CIR persuaded President Clinton to try to head off congressional approval of a new guest-worker program by issuing a statement that said: "I oppose efforts in this Congress to institute a new guestworker or "*bracero*" program that seeks to bring thousands of foreign workers into the United States to provide temporary farm labor."[2]

Western farmers were undeterred by this opposition. Representative Richard Pombo (R-CA) introduced a bill that would have permitted up to 250,000 guest workers a year to enter the United States outside the H-2A Program, but it was rejected by the House on a 242–180 vote on March 21, 1996.

Representative Bob Smith (R-OR) introduced a bill in August 1997 to create a 24-month pilot program administered by the U.S. Department of Agriculture (USDA) that could have admitted 25,000 guest workers with new H-2C visas "to perform temporary or seasonal agricultural services."[3] Instead of DOL-supervised recruitment of U.S. workers, farm employers could have hired these H-2C guest workers by attesting or asserting that they satisfied recruitment and wage obligations, just as employers of foreign professionals did under the H-1B Program.[4] One new feature of the H-2C proposal was the creation of a trust fund to encourage workers to return to their countries of origin. Employers would have deposited 25 percent of guest-worker earnings into a trust fund managed by the U.S. Treasury; these funds would have covered the government's cost of administering the program and then returned any remaining funds to guest workers in their countries of origin.

Worker advocates decried these new guest-worker proposals, asserting that they would undermine the worker protections that had been strengthened in response to events over decades in the H-2A Program. For example, the H-2A Program requires farmers to give U.S. and foreign workers written copies of wage and working condition promises, providing a starting point if there are wage disputes. However, the H-2C Program would have eliminated this written contract requirement, prompting worker advocates to warn that recruiters abroad would make outlandish oral promises to guest workers who might go into debt to be selected and then arrive in the United States and receive much lower wages. Their concerns prompted U.S. Secretary of Labor Alexis Herman to warn that "the Administration strongly opposes enactment" of the H-2C Program. If Congress were to approve it, Herman said she "would recommend that [Clinton] veto the bill."

Western senators also introduced bills that offered alternative guest-worker programs. Senator Larry Craig (R-ID) introduced the Agricultural Work Force and Stability Protection Act in January 1997 to shift the burden of recruitment from farm employers, as under the H-2A Program, to the government. Under Craig's bill, farmers would submit job offers to local Employment Service (ES) offices. They would have to refer "specific individuals who are able, willing, and qualified to work for the employer," or issue a "certification of need" that allowed the employer to employ guest workers. Craig's bill made two other changes desired by western farmers. First, it would have allowed farmers to offer their out-of-area U.S. workers and foreign workers a housing allowance instead of housing, since many western growers did not have farmworker housing available and did not want to incur the expense of building it. Second, it would have allowed farmers to pay guest workers the higher of the federal or state minimum wage or the "median rate of pay for similarly employed workers in the area of intended employment," eliminating the third and usually highest minimum wage, the Adverse Effect Wage Rate, that farm employers are required to pay guest workers.

Craig won support from other senators for this alternative guest-worker program, and reintroduced his bill a year later as the Agricultural Job Opportunity Benefits and Security Act of 1998 (AgJOBS). This first version of AgJOBS included a requirement that the U.S. Department of Labor create "registries" of legal U.S. workers seeking farm jobs, so that farmers could consult local registries and find workers or receive permission to hire guest workers.[5] AgJOBS included a trust fund to collect employer social security and unemployment insurance taxes on guest-worker earnings, and these funds would cover the cost of administering the guest-worker program. In a bid to soften opposition from worker advocates, guest workers admitted under AgJOBS who did at least six months of U.S. farmwork in each of four consecutive calendar years could apply for immigrant visas.

The Clinton administration strongly opposed AgJOBS. John Fraser, acting chief of the U.S. Department of Labor's Wage and Hour Division, said that it would: "increase illegal immigration, it will reduce job opportunities for legal U.S. farmworkers, and it will undercut wages and working conditions." Despite these objections, the Senate approved AgJOBS in July 1998,[6] but it was later removed from the bill in a conference committee with the House.

As western farmers demonstrated their growing clout in Congress to secure an alternative guest-worker program, the U.S. Department of Labor moved to "streamline" the H-2A Program in ways that made it easier for farmers to use. Under June 29, 1999 regulations, the DOL reduced the time from 60 to 45 days that recruitment of U.S. workers must begin before the employer-specified "need for workers" date, and promised to make decisions on whether a farm employer needed H-2A workers 30 days before the employer-specified need date, up from 20 days, so that employers had more time to recruit guest workers and obtain visas for them.

With farmers seemingly on an unstoppable drive for new guest-worker programs in Congress, both the Mexican government and some migrant advocates jumped aboard. During a March 1999 meeting of the U.S. and Mexican labor ministers, the Mexican labor minister requested a "legalized exchange of workers from Mexico to the United States." A think tank normally seen as sympathetic to migrants, the Carnegie Endowment, released a proposal in summer

1999 that echoed Craig's AgJOBS proposal, proposing registries to list and re-fer legal workers to farmers, endorsing housing vouchers in lieu of providing housing, and urging the creation of a farmworker trust fund to pay return bonuses (Papademetriou and Heppel, 1999).

The Mexican and think tank endorsements prompted western farmers to have AgJOBS reintroduced in the Senate in October 1999, but with a new twist—earned legalization. A path to an immigrant visa would be created by al-lowing currently unauthorized workers to register with local ES offices. Regis-tered unauthorized workers could then earn an immigrant status by doing at least 180 days of farmwork each year for five of the next seven years. However, in a somewhat contradictory effort to discourage registered unauthorized farm-workers from settling in the United States, they would have to leave for at least 65 days a year.

Western farmers made progress toward a new guest-worker program in Congress despite an ample supply of workers guaranteed by continued Mex-ico–U.S. migration. Farmers were elated with the elections of Vicente Fox in Mexico and George Bush in the United States, expecting a new guest-worker program in short order. Worker advocates were worried; they had demon-strated an ability to block new guest-worker programs in Congress, but were unsure what would happen under a Republican U.S. president who had en-dorsed a new guest-worker program and a Mexican president whose top for-eign priority was to have more legal Mexican workers in the United States.

These changing political currents prompted Representative Howard Berman (D-CA) to resurrect IRCA's RAW concept of earned legalization in December 2000. Under the never-implemented RAW Program, foreign guest workers em-ployed on farms could have earned immigrant status if they did farmwork for at least 360 days within six years. Earned legalization, which growers had ac-cepted in one version of AgJOBS, would give worker advocates what they wanted (a path to immigrant visas), and employers what they wanted (an end to certification—or the government in control of the border gate—as well as an end to the requirement to provide free housing and an end to the super-minimum wage, the Adverse Effect Wage Rate). In addition, the requirement that newly legalized farmworkers continue to do farmwork would slow exit from the farm workforce. However, Congressional Republicans who opposed "rewarding lawbreakers" with legal status, led by Senator Phil Gramm (R-TX), blocked approval of AgJOBS in the waning days of the Clinton administration.

Immigration reform was the central focus of Mexico-U.S. government relations in 2001, as Presidents Bush and Fox met and appointed cabinet secretaries to develop solutions to migration issues. In Congress, restrictionists such as Senator Phil Gramm (R-TX) proposed new guest-worker programs that would have permitted unauthorized Mexicans in the United States to obtain renewable work visas and allowed those filling seasonal farm jobs to return to the United States year after year, indefinitely. Gramm proposed that employer- and worker-paid social security taxes be used to create a trust fund to provide emergency medical care for guest workers, with any balance refunded to guest workers who returned to Mexico.[7] Other senators continued to encourage enactment of AgJOBS, refining the requirements to earn a legal immigrant visa but maintaining the three changes that western farmers had sought in new guest-worker programs since the mid-1980s, viz, attestation replacing certification, housing allowances in lieu of housing, and eliminating or freezing the Adverse Effect Wage Rate.

AGJOBS: NEW SOLUTION OR NEW PROBLEM?

The AgJOBS proposal has been pending in Congress since 2000. Farm employers and worker advocates drew attention to AgJOBS by encouraging representatives and senators to become cosponsors, and their advocacy persuaded many newspaper editorial boards to endorse AgJOBS as the most reasonable compromise to deal with farm labor. However, despite 60 senators listed as cosponsors of AgJOBS in 2004 and 2005, supporters were unable to attach AgJOBS to must-pass spending bills as planned.

Between 1998 and 2005, the major argument in favor of AgJOBS had been that both farmers and farmworkers wanted a legal workforce, and that these traditional enemies had worked out a compromise that was good for workers and employers. Beginning in 2005, a new argument appeared—farm labor shortages. Without the approval of AgJOBS, this argument ran, fruits and vegetables would rot in the fields and consumers would have to pay higher prices for produce. Senator Diane Feinstein (D-CA), who had earlier refrained from active participation, became an enthusiastic supporter of AgJOBS, and a leading voice of the labor shortage argument.

The 2008 version of AgJOBS[8] would allow up to 1.5 million unauthorized foreigners who did at least 150 days of farmwork during the 24-month period before enactment to apply for "blue-card" temporary legal resident status.[9] Blue-card holders could travel in and out of the United States and obtain work authorization for their spouses, and secure a legal status for their minor children who were in the United States. However, in order to become immigrants, blue-card holders would have complete more farmwork over the next five years.[10] To stress that unauthorized farmworkers must "earn" their immigrant visas, they would have to pay application fees as well as a $100 fine and any income taxes owed on their earnings.[11] While doing farmwork to earn an immigrant visa, blue-card holders would be eligible for unemployment insurance and Earned Income Tax Credits, but not federal means-tested welfare benefits such as Temporary Assistance to Needy Families and Food Stamps.

Blue cards give worker advocates what they want, a path to legal immigrant visas for unauthorized farmworkers and their families, but AgJOBS also makes three significant "employer-friendly" changes in the H-2A Program. First, employers would achieve their goal of having attestation replace certification, effectively giving employers control over the border gate because their assertions that they are paying appropriate wages are normally sufficient to open border gates to guest workers.[12] The U.S. Department of Labor would no longer circulate an employer's job offers, so unions would be less likely to learn about employer requests for guest workers and send workers to fill them. Finally, AgJOBS would make it easier for farmers to share guest workers, since an association could transfer guest workers between its farmer members.

Second, farmers under AgJOBS could pay a housing allowance rather than provide housing to guest workers, provided the state's governor agrees that sufficient rental housing is available. Guest workers would receive a payment equivalent to their share of the fair-market rent of a two-bedroom apartment, assuming that two workers share one bedroom.[13] Since most labor-intensive agriculture is in urban counties, these payments would likely be $200 to $300 a month.[14] The third change would roll back the super-minimum wage that must be paid to guest workers, the Adverse Effect Wage Rate. This wage, $9.72 an hour in California in 2008, would be rolled back by about 10 percent for three years and studied.

Senator Dianne Feinstein (D-CA), citing media reports of farm labor shortages, urged the Senate to approve AgJOBS to avoid higher fruit and vegetable prices.[15] A leading opponent of AgJOBS, Senator Saxby Chambliss (R-GA), countered: "As soon as we give illegal aliens in agriculture legal permanent residence status, they will no longer choose to work the fields, packing sheds, groves and processing facilities."

The deadlock between those who want to legalize farmworkers and give them a path to immigrant status, and those who want guest workers who must leave the United States when their farm jobs end, mirrors the larger debate over what to do about unauthorized foreigners. However, just as the effects of the IRCA's agricultural provisions were unclear, there are many unanswered questions about AgJOBS. What are the likely effects of legalizing up to half of the current seasonal farmworkers, and establishing a complex system to record their farmwork? Will the farm workforce swell in the short term as blue-card farmworkers try to earn immigrant visas as soon as possible, adding to homelessness and privation if the result is many more workers than jobs, or will workers simply buy documentation that they did farmwork from contractors and farmers and move on to nonfarm jobs?

REGULARIZE AND RATIONALIZE

The United States has an agricultural system that is often described as the envy of the world, a prodigious producer of an abundant supply of safe and affordable food and fiber. American agriculture's reputation has been tarnished by the increased attention devoted to subsidies and because of regular outbreaks of food-borne illness, but most Americans continue to have a favorable view of agriculture and farmers.

However, fruit and vegetable farmers increasingly hire unauthorized foreign-born workers who remain near the bottom of the U.S. job ladder. They have not been shy in broadcasting their dependence on unauthorized workers, asserting that Americans will not work in the fields, and that the only way to assure a continued agricultural bounty is easy access to foreign guest workers.

It would be a mistake to open the gates wide to guest workers. Doing so would lock U.S. agriculture into a dependence on low-wage workers that slows productivity growth and risks transferring the rural poor of Mexico and other countries into rural America, into towns not prepared to successfully integrate foreigners with little education. A better policy would be to regularize the farm workforce and rationalize the farm labor market, giving agriculture a legal workforce and ensuring that the employment of guest workers does not lock farmers into low-productivity methods of production that reduce their competitiveness over time. In other words, the policy goal is to have more examples of successful processing tomato mechanization, and fewer of Florida sugarcane growers importing workers from islands that can produce sugar at lower prices.

The key to the regularization of farmworkers and the rationalization of the farm workforce lies in the payroll taxes that were identified in several of the early versions of AgJOBS. Farmers currently avoid paying social security, Medicare, and federal unemployment insurance taxes on the earnings of H-2A guest workers,[16] and AgJOBS does not change these exemptions, making guest workers up to 20 percent cheaper than U.S. workers. This wedge between the higher costs of U.S. workers and the lower costs of H-2A workers is likely to favor the hiring of H-2A workers, especially as recruitment networks evolve. The result may be an even more apartheid-type sector of the U.S. economy, with older white farmers employing young and minority farmworkers.

Farm employers should pay the same taxes on the earnings of H-2A workers that they do on the earnings of U.S. workers. However, since H-2A workers are not generally eligible for benefits under the social security and unemployment insurance programs these payroll taxes finance, the funds collected could be used to accelerate the rationalization of farm jobs now employing farmworkers and refunded to guest workers who returned to their countries or origin.[17]

How much money could be generated for mechanization research and return bonuses by these payroll taxes? Sales of fruits and vegetables were $36 billion in 2006. Not all fruit and vegetable commodities depend on hand workers, but there are also many unauthorized workers employed in the related nursery and floriculture industry. Assume that the sales of the labor-intensive crops most likely to hire immigrant workers are $30 billion, and that labor costs average a third of these sales or $10 billion. If half of these wage costs were paid to legal guest workers, 20 percent payroll taxes would generate $1 billion a year. If this $1 billion were divided equally between mechanization research and guest-worker return bonuses, there would be $500 million for each.

Funding mechanization research and providing guest-worker return bonuses could have desirable effects in both rural America and rural Mexico. In rural America, labor-saving processes as in citrus and raisin harvest mechanization that are already under way could be speeded up, reducing the need for foreign workers over time. In rural Mexico, return bonuses equal to 10 percent of U.S. earnings could provide the spark for developments that allow the children and grandchildren of guest workers to find opportunity at home. The purpose of a payroll-tax-funded policy of mechanization research and return bonuses is to ensure that agriculture and guest workers do not get locked into mutual dependence.

Payroll taxes can accelerate rationalization and ensure that future guest workers have incentives to return and accelerate development in their areas of origin, but what should be done about the million or more unauthorized farmworkers currently employed in U.S. agriculture? AgJOBS would create a path to immigrant visas by requiring continued U.S. farmwork, a strategy that goes against the decades of experience that teach the best way to help farmworkers is to help them to find nonfarm jobs. It is also true that, given the widespread opposition to "amnesty," unauthorized farmworkers have one of the least-compelling cases for legalization, since they could have arrived in the United States much later than others being considered for earned legalization and done farmwork less than a year to qualify.

Farmworkers legalized by AgJOBS are likely to have low earnings whether they stay in farmwork or leave for nonfarm jobs, since most have not completed high school and few speak English. Unlike other legalization proposals, AgJOBS would allow the families of farmworkers to become legal immigrants. This means that if a million rural Mexicans were legalized, the United States may wind up with a quarter of Mexico's 25 million rural poor.

Can the United States solve Mexico's rural poverty problem by transferring many of them to rural America? The United States has overcome skepticism in the past and absorbed waves of immigrants that contemporary observers thought would be difficult to integrate, but transferring 5 to 6 million rural Mexicans to rural America may represent an even larger challenge.

WHITHER AGRICULTURE?

If current trends continue, rural and agricultural America will become ever more firmly locked onto an immigration treadmill, scouring poorer countries for workers willing to fill seasonal U.S. farm jobs at relatively low wages. The major policy impetus to change this labor trajectory is the fact that newcomers to the U.S. farm workforce are unauthorized. The farm status quo is increasing the settlement of unauthorized workers in the United States because stepped-up border controls encourage those who might otherwise be seasonal commuters to form or unite families in the United States.

Farmers and employers in food-related industries argue that foreign workers are essential to their economic viability. Most of these employers would prefer guest workers who rotate in and out of the United States. They find it hard to win support for a large-scale guest-worker program because of the legacy of the Bracero Program, which is associated with the exploitation of poor Mexicans in both Mexico and the United States. As with most guest worker programs, the Bracero Program got larger and lasted longer than anticipated because the guaranteed availability of workers encouraged U.S. agriculture to expand in labor-intensive ways.

The status quo of unauthorized workers increases uncertainty for farmers, workers, and the communities in which both live. The status quo "works," in the sense that it provides the workers needed to get farmwork done, provides jobs and earnings for Mexicans who would otherwise have lower incomes, and provides customers for Main Street stores in rural communities that might otherwise depopulate. However, the status quo keeps agriculture on a low-wage and low-productivity trajectory that is exactly the wrong path for this critical American industry trying to remain competitive in the twenty-first century.

The AgJOBS proposal would legalize many unauthorized workers and their families, but not change a farm labor system that has an enormous appetite for newcomers. Given the failures of the Bracero Program and immigration reforms in 1986, regularization and rationalization offer the best hope to avoid farm labor dilemmas in the future.

Epilogue: The Great Migration

In 2007, the world reached a historic milestone: For the first time, a majority of people lived in cities. Agriculture remains the world's number one occupation, employing 45 percent of the 3.1 billion-strong global workforce. Almost 1.2 billion workers, 35 percent of the global workforce, are employed as farmers, unpaid family workers, and hired workers.

Rural–urban migration is a universal indicator of economic growth and development. The world's 30 high-income countries have less than 5 percent of their workers employed in agriculture, while many of the world's poorer 165 countries have a majority of workers employed in agriculture. Most of the world's farmers and farmworkers will achieve economic mobility by moving from farms to cities, and from farm to nonfarm work.

Most rich countries subsidize their relatively few farmers, while many poor countries tax their many farmers. Farm subsidies in the Organization for Economic Cooperation and Development (OECD) countries are about a billion dollars a day, and institutions such as the World Bank that are trying to reduce global poverty argue that the fastest way to raise the incomes of poor farmers in developing countries is to reduce farm subsidies in the rich countries. It is increasingly recognized that farm subsidies in rich countries hurt farmers in poor countries by increasing farm production and lowering world prices, reducing the incomes of poor farmers and encouraging some to migrate to richer countries.

Breaking this circle of subsidies that create a demand for immigrant farmworkers in rich countries and impoverish rural residents in poor countries means tackling entrenched interests in both. Instead, the 2008 U.S. farm bill would extend farm subsidies and, for the first time, extend them to labor-intensive fruits and vegetables. In developing countries, there is slow and uneven progress in dismantling the monopolies that often provide inputs such as fertilizers and seeds to farmers at high prices and buy their crops at low prices.

Migrant labor is a small but growing part of the larger farm subsidy debate in the rich countries. A failure to agree on reducing them appears to have doomed the Doha round of free trade negotiations in summer 2008, as developing countries complained that industrial countries did not reduce subsidies enough and industrial countries opposed allowing developing countries to raise tariffs during import surges to protect their farmers.

Farmworkers promise to become a larger part of the migration debate, since many of those likely to join the ranks of the world's migrants will come from rural areas in developing countries. About 60 percent of the world's 191 million migrants in 2005, defined by the United Nations as persons outside their country of birth or citizenship for a year or more, are in the high-income countries, and more than half were from developing countries, often rural areas.

Growing and persisting demographic and economic differences between poorer and richer countries, combined with revolutions in communications, transportation, and rights, promise more international migration. Demographic differences between rich and poor countries are bound to increase because almost all population growth is in the poorer countries.[1] Population density varies greatly within both rich and poor countries, but there are more people per square mile in developing than in developed countries.[2] A century ago, millions of migrants left relatively densely populated Europe to find opportunity in the sparsely settled Americas. If history repeats itself, millions of people in developing countries could migrate for opportunity in industrial countries, especially to European countries where shrinking populations promise housing and jobs.

Demographic differences that motivate migration are reinforced by economic differences. The world's gross domestic product (GDP) was $45 trillion in 2005, according to the World Bank, making the value of the goods and services produced by all nations almost $7,000 per person per year. There was significant variation from country to country, from less than $250 per person per year in some African countries to more than $50,000 in Norway.

Young people in developing countries seeking their fortunes do not have to consult World Bank income tables to know that they can earn more in the industrial countries. But it is not widely appreciated that the gap in per capita incomes between the industrial and developing countries, which was 20 to 1 in 2005, has not changed much in the past quarter century despite rapid economic growth in the East Asian "Tigers" in the 1990s and China and India more recently.[3] Per capita income gaps that allow a person to earn as much in an hour abroad as they would in a day at home and hold out hope for upward mobility explain why especially young people are willing to take enormous risks to cross international borders in search of opportunity.

Agriculture plays a special role in the economic differences that promote international migration. Within developing countries, farmers are generally poorer than urban workers, which encourages rural–urban migration and has several implications for international migration. First, farmers in industrial countries prefer workers with experience in agriculture, so industrial countries that allow or tolerate migrants in agriculture encourage migration from the rural areas of developing countries to rural areas of industrial countries. Second, ex-farmers and farmworkers are most likely to accept so-called 3D jobs—dirty, dangerous, and difficult—both at home or abroad; having a supply of such workers available often creates a demand for them, as evidenced by day-labor markets in many urban areas. Third, those leaving agriculture must often make physical, economic, and cultural shifts in their destinations. Since there are migrants from many countries settled in industrial countries, the transition to a new life abroad is no more difficult than the transition to city life at home.

Demographic and economic differences encourage migration, but it takes networks or links between areas to encourage people to move. Migration networks include communication factors that enable people to learn about opportunities abroad, as well as the migration infrastructure that actually transports migrants over national borders and the migrant rights regime that allows them to remain abroad. Migration networks have been shaped and strengthened by three revolutions over the past half century—in communications, transportation, and rights.

The communications revolution helps migrants to learn about opportunities abroad. The best information comes from trusted relatives and friends already established abroad, since they can provide information in an understandable context. Cheaper and accessible communications enable migrants to quickly transmit job information long distances, as well as to provide advice on how to cross borders to take advantage of them. For example, information about vacant U.S. farm jobs may be received in rural Mexico, thousands of miles away, before it spreads to nearby cities with jobless workers.[4] The workers in many industrial country workplaces often come from a particular region of another country, so that local workers may feel out of place, especially if supervision and training have shifted to the workplace language, as with Spanish in U.S. agriculture.

The transportation revolution highlights the decline in the cost of travel. Two centuries ago, British migrants unable to pay one-way passage to the North American colonies often indentured themselves, signing contracts that obliged them to work for three to six years for whoever met the ship and paid the captain for the voyage. Today, the work time required to repay transportation costs is typically shorter, even if migrants pay fees to recruiters and smugglers. While the risks of being exploited by smugglers and traffickers are real, most migrants can repay transportation costs with less than two years' earnings.

The rights revolution affects the ability of migrants to stay abroad. After World War II, most industrial countries strengthened the constitutional and political rights of residents to prevent a recurrence of Fascism and to provide a contrast to Communist countries; most also granted social rights to residents in their evolving welfare states without drawing sharp distinctions between migrants and citizens. Today, policy makers unable to do much about the demographic and economic differences that encourage migration, and unwilling to try to roll back communications and transportation links that promote economic growth, gravitate toward the policy instrument they most directly control—the rights of migrants. For example, concerns about the costs of legal and unauthorized migration prompted the U.S. government in the mid-1990s to reduce the access of migrants to means-tested welfare benefits.

The United States had a great migration off the land in the 1950s and 1960s, when more than a million small farmers and farmworkers a year moved to the cities. Today, there is a great migration off the land in many developing countries. Many of the small farmers and farmworkers in rural Mexico, Central America, and the Caribbean are linked by migration networks forged by decades of guest-worker recruitment and unauthorized but tolerated migration to rural America.

The question is how the U.S. government should think about people leaving the farm in nearby countries. It would not be in the national interest to ratify the immigration treadmill that is developing in rural and agricultural America, especially because there are mechanical alternatives available to produce most of the commodities that rely on rural poverty abroad to generate a labor force. Instead, U.S. policies that promote the rationalization of farm labor markets, strengthen the competitiveness of U.S. agriculture, and avoid the creation of a new rural underclass are much more likely to be viewed by future historians as the wise choice.

Appendix 1. Farm Employment, Immigration, and Poverty

The model used to test for interactions between farm employment, immigration, and poverty in rural California towns consists of a block triangular system of three equations, two of which (farm employment and immigration) constitute a simultaneous subblock that is recursively related to the third (poverty). This model corresponds to a structural partial-equilibrium theoretical model that includes immigrant labor supply, farm labor demand, and poverty outcomes. The specific form of the equation system is

$$(1) \quad FARM_t^i = \alpha_0 + \alpha_1 FOR_t^i + \alpha_2 WPOP_t^i + \alpha_3 FARM_{t-1}^i + \varepsilon_{1t}^i$$

$$(2) \quad FOR_t^i = \beta_0 + \beta_1 FARM_t^i + \beta_2 POP_t^i + \beta_3 WPOP_t^i$$
$$+ \beta_4 FOR_{t-1}^i + \varepsilon_{2t}^i$$

$$(3) \quad POV_t^i = \gamma_0 + \gamma_1 FARM_t^i + \gamma_2 FOR_t^i + \gamma_3 POP_t^i$$
$$+ \gamma_4 WPOP_t^i + \gamma_5 POV_{t-1}^i + \gamma_6 KIDS_{t-1}^i$$
$$+ \gamma_7 OLD_{t-1}^i + \varepsilon_{3t}^i$$

The key dependent variables are the share of people in farm jobs ($FARM_t^i$), the share of foreign-born population (FOR_t^i), and the share of residents in households with below-poverty income (POV_t^i) in town i at time t. The central hypotheses is that (a) farm employment is positively associated with rural poverty in 2000 ($\gamma_1 > 0$); (b) farm employment stimulates migration ($\beta_1 > 0$); and (c) migration, in turn, stimulates the creation of new farm jobs ($\alpha_1 > 0$).

The stochastic error terms ε_k^i, $k = 1, \ldots, 3$ are assumed to be distributed as approximately normal with zero mean and a variance of σ_k^2, uncorrelated across observations. Equations (1) and (2) constitute a simultaneous-equation subblock, which was estimated using three-stage least squares (3SLS). If the errors in this subblock, ε_{1t}^i and ε_{2t}^i, are not correlated with ε_{3t}^i (that is, the disturbance matrix, Σ, is block diagonal), ordinary least squares (OLS) yields parameter estimates for (3) that are optimal and identical to those obtained using full information maximum likelihood. Equation (3) was estimated using OLS. The errors from these regressions exhibited low correlations between the residuals from the 3SLS estimation of the farm employment and immigration equations and those from the OLS-estimated poverty equation, supporting the estimation approach.

Due to lagged right-hand-side variables ($FARM_{t-1}^i$, FOR_{t-1}^i, and POV_{t-1}^i), the model requires data from both the 2000 and 1990 census years, drawing contemporaneous explanatory variables from 2000 and predetermined lagged variables from 1990. Each equation in the simultaneous system is identified, with at least as many excluded exogenous or predetermined variables as included endogenous variables. Because of this, there is no need for instruments from outside the system (see table A.1).

Table A.1 Variables

Variable	Definition
POV_t^i	Share of people in poverty in community
FOR_t^i	Share of foreign-born population in community
$FARMR_t^i$	Share of workforce in farm jobs
POP_t^i	Total population
$WPOP_t^i$	Working-age population
$KIDS_t^i$	Share of population younger than 15 years old
OLD_t^i	Share of population older than 65 years old

Notes

PROLOGUE

1. Fresno County's farm sales of $4.6 billion in 2004 exceeded the $4.1 billion farm sales of New York State.
2. *Raiteros* are drivers with vans who function as a private transport system in rural areas.
3. California had 245,000 bearing acres of raisin grapes in 2004, when there were 85,000 acres of table grapes and 475,000 acres of wine grapes. Depending on the relative prices of raisin and wine grapes, some raisin grapes are harvested mechanically and blended into lower-grade wine or used as a natural sweetener. Average raisin yields were 8.3 tons of green grapes per acre; about 4.5 pounds of green grapes dry into a pound of raisins (www.nass.usda.gov/Statistics_by_State/California/Historical_Data/index.asp).
4. Manuel Cunha Jr. of the Nisei Farmers League asserted that raisin growers were "short" 20 percent of the workers needed for the harvest, and reported 50 calls a day from growers in fall 2005 asking for harvest workers. Dennis Pollock, "Labor Shortage Sours Citrus Harvest," *Fresno Bee,* November 24, 2005.
5. Jensen (2006, 5) emphasizes that most immigrants in rural areas are trying to achieve the American dream by marrying, raising families, and buying homes, but that both the migrants and the communities in which they settle need support to ensure successful integration.

6. The Agricultural Job Opportunity, Benefits and Security Act (S340/H371) would allow up to 1.5 million unauthorized farmworkers to "earn" legal immigrant status by continuing to do farmwork and revise the existing H-2A Program to make it more employer-friendly.

CHAPTER 1: IMMIGRATION TO THE UNITED STATES

1. In fiscal year 2006, there were 1.3 million legal immigrants, 34 million temporary visitors, and 1.2 million apprehensions. Many of the legal immigrants are already in the United States when they get their immigrant visas, and temporary visitor and apprehension data double-count individuals who are admitted or apprehended several times.
2. Kennedy also said: "Our cities will not be flooded with a million immigrants annually."
3. In fiscal year 2005, there were 1.1 million immigrants, including 400,000 or 36 percent from Asia, 346,000 or 31 percent from North America, and 103,000 or 9 percent from South America.
4. FAIR's Web site is: www.fairus.org/site/PageServer?pagename=about_aboutmain.
5. An editorial on July 3, 1986, first made this proposal, which was repeated in an editorial on July 3, 1990.
6. Archbishop Roger Mahoney of Los Angeles is quoted in Capaldi (1997, 17): "The right to immigrate is more fundamental than that of nations to control their borders."
7. Waiting lists are published in the Department of State (DOS) Visa Bulletin, http://travel.state.gov/visa/frvi/bulletin/bulletin_1360.html.
8. The limit is 140,000 a year, but the number of immigration visas can be higher if there are unused visas from earlier years.
9. Employment-based immigration includes five visa categories: (1) priority workers with "extraordinary ability" in the arts or sciences or multinational executives; (2) members of the professions holding advanced degrees; (3) BA professionals and skilled and unskilled workers; (4) special immigrants, including ministers; and (5) investors.
10. Once a foreigner has an immigrant visa, he or she can change jobs, and many leave the employer who sponsored them—that is, foreigners who receive immigrant visas because they are needed to fill U.S. jobs often leave those jobs as soon as they become immigrants.
11. Applicants for diversity immigration visas must: (1) be nationals of countries that sent fewer than 50,000 immigrants to the United States during the past five years in the immediate family or employment preference categories and (2) have a high school education or its equivalent, or within the past five years have had two years of work experience in a job that requires at least two years of training or experience.
12. In 2006, there were 27 countries in the visa-waiver program, meaning that U.S. citizens can visit these countries without visas as well. See http://travel.state.gov/visa/temp/without/without_1990.html.
13. These counts of visitor arrivals do not include Mexicans with border crossing cards that allow shopping visits or Canadian visitors. Note that temporary migrants who enter and leave the United States several times are counted each time.
14. The 2003 National Science Board (NSB) report can be accessed at: www.nsf.gov/nsb/documents/2003/nsb0369/nsb0369.pdf.

15. Quoted in "Gates Urges Change in H-1B Visa Program," *Daily Labor Report,* March 8, 2007, A-8.

16. Pew Hispanic Center, "Modes of Entry for the Unauthorized Migrant Population," Factsheet 19, May 22, 2006. See http://pewhispanic.org/factsheets/factsheet.php ?FactsheetID=19.

17. In the aftermath of the firing of eight U.S. attorneys in December 2006, it was revealed that the same individual generally had to be apprehended at least six times before being prosecuted by the U.S. Attorney's Office. The exception was the Del Rio area of south Texas, where every adult apprehended since 2006 has been prosecuted and jailed, usually 15 days for first offenders, before being returned. "DHS: Border, Interior," *Migration News* 13, no. 2 (April 2007). See http://migration.ucdavis.edu/mn/index.php.

18. In 1953, the year of the Hungarian and East German uprisings that were crushed by the Soviets, more than 10 percent of the public favored increasing immigration (Simon, 1989, 350).

19. Chicago Council on Foreign Relations, 2002. See www.worldviews.org/detailreports/ usreport/html/ch5s5.html.

20. This poll of 800 adults, conducted July 31–August 17, 1997, for the PBS TV show *State of the Union* was reported in Susan Page, "Fear of Immigration Eases," *USA Today,* October 13, 1997, online edition.

21. Fox News poll, November 2001.

22. Patrick J. McDonnell, "Wave of U.S. Immigration Likely to Survive Sept. 11," *Los Angeles Times,* January 10, 2002.

23. Quoted in McDonnell, "Wave of U.S. Immigration."

24. Dan Balz, "Political Splits on Immigration Reflect Voters' Ambivalence," *Washington Post,* January 3, 2006.

25. Pew Research Center, "America's Immigration Quandary," 2006. See http://people -press.org/reports/display.php3?PageID=1045. The survey found that, among the 53 percent who want illegal migrants removed, half would allow them to first work in the United States as legal guest workers. For the 40 percent who think illegal migrants should be allowed to stay, most favor allowing them to become immigrants. Half of the respondents agreed the best way to reduce illegal immigration was to penalize employers who hired illegal migrants; a third favored more border enforcement.

26. Mark Z. Barabak, "Guest-Worker Proposal Has Wide Support," *Los Angeles Times,* April 30, 2006.

27. Quoted in Degler (1970, 50).

28. These Bracero Programs are examined in more detail in Chapter 2.

29. Free-trade agreements negotiated under the president's fast-track negotiating authority must be approved or disapproved by Congress—they cannot be amended. President Bush's fast-track trade negotiating authority expired June 30, 2007.

30. Hufbauer and Schott (1992, 58) projected, based on assumed increases in trade due to NAFTA, that Mexico would add 609,000 jobs and the United States 130,000 jobs.

31. Quoted in President Bush's letter to Congress, May 1, 1991, p. 16.

32. The Mexican government in 1992 also changed land tenure policies in ways that encouraged emigration. Rural Mexico was dominated by *ejido* (communal) farms from

the 1930s through the 1990s. Ejido land could not legally be sold or used as collateral for loans, reducing productivity-increasing investments and increasing rural poverty. The Mexican Constitution was amended in 1992 to allow the sale or rental of ejido land.

33. Mexican Foreign Minister Jorge Castañeda explained in an interview that Mexico wanted "the whole enchilada, or nothing," and that this meant agreements on "regularization, on the border, on permanent visas, and on resources for the [immigrant]-generating communities [in Mexico]." *Business Week,* September 10, 2001. See www .businessweek.com/magazine/content/01_37/b3748044.htm.

CHAPTER 2: AGRICULTURE AND MIGRANTS

1. The Thomas Jefferson quote is from *Notes on Virginia, 1781–82,* and is on the east wall of the South Reading Room of the Library of Congress (www.loc.gov/loc/legacy/bldgs .html).

2. Most plantations had at least 20 slaves and 400 acres of cotton. The price of slaves—$500 to $1,000 for an adult male in the first half of the nineteenth century—fluctuated with the prices of tobacco and cotton. Fogel and Engerman (1974) argued that plantation owners organized slaves into efficient work teams, so that "superior management" and "superior workers" enabled the plantation system to spread west with U.S. expansion.

3. One California farmer said that if farmers were "forced to maintain our labor when it is idle, we would be forced out of business" (quoted in Fuller, 1942, 19864).

4. Japan agreed not to issue passports to its citizens seeking to emigrate to the United States, and the U.S. government promised to end the country's discrimination against the Japanese.

5. Some of the southern and eastern European immigrants who arrived in eastern U.S. cities worked in agriculture. A report of the Dillingham Commission noted that New York farmers were "unanimous in the opinion that if it were not for the Italians it would be impossible to secure the labor necessary to carry on farming in its present scale . . . when [Italians are] employed in gangs under the immediate supervision of an American they are considered better than native farm labor for picking fruit, gathering beans, and for general work on truck farms." Dillingham Commission, "Immigrants in Industries," Part 24, Vol. 2 (1910), 506.

6. Many of those from what is now India and Pakistan were Sikhs from the Punjab region. All South Asian immigrants in the early 1900s were called "Hindoo" or "Hindu," regardless of religious affiliation.

7. Some Department of Labor (DOL) officials were skeptical of the labor shortage arguments. Assistant Secretary of Labor Louis Post said: "the farm labor shortage is two-thirds imaginary and one-third remedial." Quoted on pp. 10–11, RG 83 (Records of the Bureau of Agricultural Economics, Department of Agriculture, 1923–1946), Folder Farm Labor (1941–1946), Box 239: Entry 19, "Reports on Farm Labor Shortages and the Works Projects Administration," prepared by the War Production Agency for the House Committee Investigating National Defense Migration, July 3, 1941.

8. The ninth proviso of Section 3 of the Immigration Act of 1917 seemed to allow the DOL to make exceptions to the literacy test and head tax, but the chair of the House

Committee on Immigration and Naturalization did not think the DOL had the power to unilaterally suspend the bar to the admission of contract workers. The DOL defended its decision by emphasizing that the alternatives were worse, including repealing the Chinese Exclusion Act to obtain farmworkers (Congressional Research Service, 1980, 9).

9. A small number of workers from Canada and the Bahamas were also admitted.

10. This DOL order of April 18, 1918, is quoted in Congressional Research Service, 1980, 10.

11. Scruggs noted that before the Border Patrol was created in 1924, 60 mounted men patrolled the Mexico-U.S. border.

12. The U.S. government established a handful of camps that offered better housing and services. The Weedpatch migrant camp in Arvin (today the Sunset Migrant Center) provided the backdrop for John Steinbeck's *The Grapes of Wrath*. After its publication, farmers accused Steinbeck of having Communist sympathies, he received death threats, and he was investigated by the Federal Bureau of Investigation (FBI).

13. Farmworkers remain among the major groups of private-sector workers without federal collective bargaining rights; other groups of excluded workers include independent contractors, employees of very small businesses, first-line supervisors considered managers, and workers employed in private homes (General Accounting Office, 2002, 2–3).

14. The U.S. Department of Agriculture (USDA) and the DOL InterBureau Coordinating Committee reported that, over the past year (1941), "there was some confusion in the use of the term 'shortage,'" and a tendency in some cases "to identify increases in wages, irrespective of the number of workers available, as a shortage." Quoted in Hahamovitch (1999) from Report of the Interbureau Planning Committee on Farm Labor, "Review of the Farm Labor Situation in 1941," 12/31/41, RG 16, Records of the Office of the Secretary of Agriculture, No. 17 General Correspondence of the Office of the Secretary, 1906–1970, Subject: Employment, File: "1. Labor."

15. The Congressional Research Service (1980, 20) says that U.S. unions were mollified by promises to ensure that the Mexican farmworkers left the United States when their seasonal jobs ended. Mexican Americans were more ambivalent, fearing that importing Mexicans would have an adverse effect on their wages.

16. The Mexican Labor Law of 1931 required foreign employers to pay round-trip transportation for workers taken out of the country, and that Mexicans going abroad to work had contracts approved by the Mexican government.

17. Mexico, which declared war on Germany, Italy, and Japan on June 1, 1942, considered its workers in the United States a contribution to the war effort.

18. Piece rates had to enable the average worker to earn $0.30 or the prevailing wage, whichever was higher (Congressional Research Service, 1980, 23). In 1946, the minimum wage was raised to $0.37 an hour or $33.60 every two weeks.

19. East Coast farmers recruited workers from the British West Indies (BWI) under a separate Memorandum of Understanding made between the War Food Administration and the Bahamas (March 16, 1943), Jamaica (April 2, 1943), and Barbados (May 24, 1944). Some 4,698 Bahama Islanders and 8,828 Jamaicans were admitted in 1943. Florida was the peak World War II employer of BWI nationals, employing 4,688 Bahamians on May 26, 1945.

20. Average hourly earnings of farmworkers in California, as measured by a USDA survey of farm employers, rose 41 percent, from $0.85 in 1950 to $1.20 in 1960. Average hourly earnings of factory workers rose 63 percent, from $1.60 in 1950 to $2.60 in 1960 (both are in nominal dollars).

21. Secretary of Labor Wirtz interpreted the decision to terminate the Bracero Program as signifying congressional intent to reduce or eliminate the presence of temporary foreign workers in U.S. agriculture. The DOL's December 19, 1964, regulations set out the three minimum wages, the requirements that employers provide housing and offer round-trip transportation to H-2 workers, and the 120-day limit, since "the only justification for bringing in labor is to meet the peak conditions of the highly seasonal agricultural industry" (Congressional Research Service, 1980, 65).

22. Farmworkers are the largest group of private-sector workers excluded from the National Labor Relations Act of 1935.

23. Braceros were 80 percent of the peak 46,000 workers who picked the processing tomatoes in the early 1960s.

24. The *California Farmer,* in a July 6, 1963, article (p. 5), asserted that "All agree that the state will never again reach the 100,000 to 175,000 acres planted when there was a guaranteed supplemental labor force in the form of the bracero." A University of California (UC) publication echoed the *California Farmer*: "If seasonal labor should be abruptly curtailed, tomato growers would be left with little choice but to curtail production" (UC Division of Agricultural Sciences, 1963, 50).

25. In 1962, California produced 3.2 million tons of processing tomatoes; in 2007, production was a record 12 million tons. Growers receive about $60 a ton or three cents a pound for their tomatoes.

26. DiGiorgio was an Italian immigrant who became a fruit grower in 1918 in Florida. In 1919, DiGiorgio bought 5,845 acres of land north of Arvin, California, for about $90 an acre, and planted tree fruits by drilling wells hundreds of feet deep. By 1929, DiGiorgio had the largest fruit-packing plant in the nation. Expansion continued, and by 1946, DiGiorgio Fruit had 33 square miles in the San Joaquin Valley, making it the largest grape, plum, and pear grower in the world, and 14 square miles in Florida, making it the largest U.S. producer of citrus fruit.

    In 1943, DiGiorgio employed 2,400 workers in California, two-thirds Okies and Arkies. DiGiorgio refused to recognize a union seeking to represent its workers between 1947 and 1950, but was prohibited from buying cheap surface irrigation water because of its size, and DiGiorgio gradually shed its farming operations to become a distributor of food products.

27. The United Farm Workers (UFW) did not call for an election at Schenley or other grape growers that recognized it as the bargaining agent for farmworkers. Instead, the UFW collected signatures from workers, announced that it represented the workers on a particular farm, and asked the farmer to sign the union's standard contract or begin negotiations; otherwise, the UFW threatened a strike or boycott.

28. Testimony before the U.S. Senate Subcommittee on Immigration and Refugee Policy, "The Knowing Employment of Illegal Immigrants," Serial J-97-61, September 30, 1981, p. 78.

29. *Business Week,* January 30, 1978, reported that stopping University of California labor-saving farm mechanization was the UFW's "No. 1 legislative priority" in 1978.

30. The five targeted chemicals were dinoseb, captan, methyl bromide, parathion, and phosdrin. The UFW alleged they threatened the health of farmworkers and consumers.

31. Von's was the largest grocery chain in southern California. It had a nine-store Tianguis division of stores in Hispanic neighborhoods that were a frequent target of UFW picketers. Von's chief executive officer said that "the UFW's efforts were eminently successful, and volume reverted to free-fall" as a result of the high-tech table grape boycott and picketing. Most Tianguis markets were converted into regular Von's stores. Quoted in "UFW Loses at Coastal," *Rural Migration News* 6, no. 3 (July 1999). See http://migration.ucdavis.edu/rmn/more.php?id=383_0_3_0.

32. Julio César Chávez and Julio César Chávez Jr. are boxers from Sinaloa, a Mexican state that sends many migrants to the United States.

33. Strawberries are picked directly into the clamshell containers displayed in supermarkets. In the mid-1990s, most pickers were paid the minimum wage plus $0.60 for each 12-pint tray picked, or $0.05 a pint.

34. The UFW had a contract with Modesto-based E.&J. Gallo Winery (www.ejgallo.com) between 1967 and 1973, when Gallo switched to the Teamsters to represent its field-workers. The UFW in 1975 focused its efforts on a boycott of Gallo, culminating in a 10,000-person rally in Modesto on March 1, 1975. The Teamsters eventually won an election at Gallo and the boycott faded away.

35. The decertification vote was 125–95. The boycott is explained in greater detail in "UFW: Giumarra, Gallo, CA-U.S. Unions," *Rural Migration News* 12, no. 4 (October 2005). See http://migration.ucdavis.edu/rmn/more.php?id=1060_0_3_0.

36. Farmworker unions seeking a first contract must negotiate with the farm employer for at least 180 days, after which either party can request a mediator to help the parties negotiate an agreement during an additional 30 days. If the mediator's effort fails to produce an agreement, the mediator can recommend an agreement that is binding unless overturned by the Agricultural Labor Relations Board (ALRB) or state courts of appeal. Farmers bitterly opposed mandatory mediation.

37. Marc Lifsher, "UFW Wants Another Way to Organize," *Los Angeles Times,* September 14, 2007.

38. The California legislature approved two UFW-sponsored bills in 2007—SB 180 and SB 650. They were identical except that SB 650 would have ended the card-check procedure in 2013; both were vetoed by the governor.

39. The UFW reported 5,504 members to the DOL at the end of 2006, including 874 retired members. Union LM-2 reports are online at http://union-reports.dol.gov/olmsWeb/docs/index.html.

CHAPTER 3: CALIFORNIA FRUITS AND VEGETABLES

1. These data are from California Agricultural Statistics 2004. See www.nass.usda.gov/ca/bul/agstat/indexcas.htm.

2. The effect of immigration on farm employment was small (though statistically significant). The reason is that nearly all farmworkers are immigrants, but most immigrants work in manufacturing and services, not farm jobs.

3. The model corresponds to a structural partial-equilibrium model of farm labor demand, immigrant labor supply, and poverty outcomes.

4. The farm employment equation also includes as an explanatory variable the share of the workforce in farm jobs during the previous census as a proxy or control for the structure of local labor markets (see appendix 1).

5. For example, the 1990 farm employment share is an explanatory variable in the 2000 farm employment equation.

6. In almost half of the cities, farm employment increased by an average of 34 percent, and decreased in the other half by an average of 31 percent.

7. It should be noted that the share of foreign-born did not significantly affect the poverty rate.

8. In 2001, per capita income in the San Joaquin Valley (SJV) was $21,300, versus $32,600 in California.

9. Counties produce annual reports on their farm sales. The Fresno County report is available at: www.co.fresno.ca.us/4010/default.asp.

10. Fresno County's farm employment as a share of private-sector employment in the county peaks at 20 percent in August, and reaches a low of 13 percent in March.

11. These data are from the Quarterly Census of Employment & Wages (ES202). See http://www.labormarketinfo.edd.ca.gov/cgi/dataanalysis/AreaSelection.asp? table Name= Industry.

12. If Mexican gross national income per capita is adjusted to reflect purchasing power parity to show that, for example, housing is cheaper in Mexico than in the United States, Mexico's per capita gross national income for 1999 rises to $8,100. Mexican-origin Parlier residents are from rural areas of Mexico, where incomes are lower.

13. According to the 2000 census, a third of families and individuals and 41 percent of related children had incomes below the poverty level; in 1999, 15 percent reported public assistance income and 11 percent reported Supplemental Security Income.

14. The median home price in Fresno County was $192,500 in 2004, according to the Realtors' association (www.car.org).

15. Kissam (1998) writes: "Parlier . . . has articulated a housing regulation policy which formally replicates informal social principles prevailing in family/village networks by permitting additional housing units for extended family members but not for unrelated renters (i.e. unaccompanied male migrants). This is loosely enforced . . . the quality of this crowded housing is noticeably better than in many other communities since the informal practice is to pursue and focus abatement efforts on the most egregious cases of sub-standard housing while giving little attention to merely technical violations of the local housing ordinance." See http://migration.ucdavis.edu/cf/more.php?id=121_0_2_0.

16. Center residents in 2004 paid $9.50 a day for two-bedroom units and $10 a day for three-bedroom units, which included the cost of their utilities.

17. Enrollment in Parlier High School, which had 840 students in 2002–2003, was 270 in 9th grade, 250 in 10th grade, 170 in 11th grade, and 150 in 12th grade. Some of those who do not complete high school in Parlier move elsewhere.

18. The Kearney Agricultural Center is the University of California's largest off-campus agricultural research facility (www.uckac.edu).

19. Diana Marcum, "An Annual Cash Crop," *Fresno Bee,* November 2, 2003.

20. The federal Central Valley Project, the largest U.S. irrigation system, supplies water to the 570,000-acre Westlands Water District, which plans to remove at least 100,000 acres from production. The Environmental Working Group, which has created a database on individual farms, estimated that farms around Huron received at least $24 million in water subsidies in 2002, with the largest farming operation in Fresno County, run by the Woolf family, using 29,000 acre-feet of water to irrigate 19,000 acres of crops. Reclamation law allows cheap federal water to go to farms of up to 960 acres (the previous limit was 160 acres). Farms such as the Woolf operation break ownership up into 960-acre units, each owned by a relative or employee but farmed as a unit.

21. In some of the farmworker cities that attracted prisons, less than a quarter of the prison employees are local residents; prison guards must have high school diplomas and pass drug tests.

22. In June 2002, 130,000 children and 91,000 adults were receiving benefits under one or more of these programs. County budget data are online at http://www.sco.ca.gov/ard/local/locrep/counties/0102/0102counties.pdf, p. 52.

23. The average cash grant in 2003 was $635 for 2.2 persons, and recipients were 66 percent Hispanic, 14 percent white, and 11 percent Southeast Asian (Fresno County's population is 40 percent white, 44 percent Hispanic, and 10 percent Southeast Asian). Half of the Fresno County adults receiving cash grants in June 2002 had not finished high school. "California: Welfare, Housing, Napa," *Rural Migration News* 11, no. 4 (September 2004). See http://migration.ucdavis.edu/rmn/more.php?id=908_0_2_0.

24. Quoted in "San Joaquin Valley: Poverty, Housing, Air." *Rural Migration News* 14, no. 1 (January 2007). See http://migration.ucdavis.edu/rmn/more.php?id=1171_0_2_0.

25. The 30-30 Initiative is online at http://www.fresnorji.org.

26. One local farmer said, "We've done more for the employment of unskilled individuals than anyone else. . . . Look at the dropout rates in schools and thank God we're out here" to provide farm jobs. Quoted in George Hostetter, "Broke . . . and Broken," *Fresno Bee,* September 7, 2003. In the same article, the Fresno Farm Bureau asserted that "it's a fair trade-off" to have low-wage workers in exchange for low-priced food.

27. Quoted in George Hostetter, "Welfare Recipients Get Help Getting Out of Town," *Fresno Bee,* September 7, 2003.

28. Cartons with 24 heads of iceberg lettuce are placed in portable tubes, the air is removed, and since water boils at 33 degrees Fahrenheit in a vacuum (rather than the normal boiling point of 212 degrees), the water in the lettuce evaporates quickly. The vacuum tubes reduce the temperature of the lettuce from 80 to 34 degrees in less than 30 minutes, increasing its shelf life for long-distance refrigerated shipping. Vacuum cooling, cardboard cartons, and trucks have replaced the previous system of ice blocks, wooden crates, and railcars that was used to transport lettuce in the 1960s (http://usna.usda.gov/hb66/083lettuce.pdf).

29. About a third of the lettuce grown in Salinas Valley is used by the bagged salad industry.

30. In some cases, grower-shippers have separate growing, harvesting, packing, and marketing operations. For example, Ocean Mist farms (www.oceanmist.com) has about 800 employees growing artichokes and other vegetables. A separate entity, Valley Pride, harvests the crops. The number of growers in the Salinas-based Grower-Shipper Association of Central California rose from 55 in 1978 to 81 in 2003, but only 15 of the original 55 remained in 2003.

31. Two-thirds or 4,450 of the 6,704 births in Monterey County in 1999 were to Latina mothers; 86 percent of the Latinos were of Mexican origin.

32. The percentage of adults in Monterey County with at least a bachelor's degree rose from 21 to 25 percent between 1990 and 2000, while the percentage of adults without a high school diploma rose from 27 to 29 percent.

33. City finances are strained by rapid population growth. In 2004–2005, the city council voted to close the public library system to save money. Private funds eventually allowed the John Steinbeck Library system to remain open, so that Salinas did not become the largest U.S. city without a public library.

34. Salinas was followed by Santa Cruz-Watsonville and Santa Rosa-Petaluma, two other metro areas with many farmworkers. In some of the eastern areas of the city, there are Manhattan-style densities in areas that mostly have single-story homes, reflecting garage conversions and sheds in backyards to house new arrivals from Mexico.

35. Labor contractors are categorized as either farm labor and management services or personnel supply services.

36. Salinas-based Ramsey Highlander developed the machine to harvest lettuce planted in four rows in 80-inch beds (www.ramsayhighlander.com).

37. Manion notes that a six-part test is used to determine whether sharecroppers are truly independent businesses or employees, including whether profit or loss depends on managerial skill, the relative size of the investments made by the two parties, whether the services provided by the sharecropper require special skills, the permanence of the relationship, and the extent of control over the independent sharecropper (most marketers have "field representatives" who visit sharecroppers). In *Real v. Driscoll Strawberry Associates* (603 F.2d 748 9th Cir. 1979), the 9th Circuit Court of Appeals decided that despite a contract that repeatedly called the sharecroppers independent businesses, they were in fact employees of Driscoll. However, in *Donovan v. Brandel* (736 F.2d 1114, 1117 6th Cir. 1984), the 6th Circuit Court of Appeals decided that cucumber sharecroppers were independent businesses.

38. The UFW also demanded "a living wage, clean drinking water and bathrooms, job security, health insurance and an end to sexual harassment and other abuses." UFW website

39. The U.S. Department of Agriculture's Economic Research Service puts the number of California strawberry growers at 684 in 2002 (2005, 4).

40. A ton of grapes makes 150 gallons, or 750 bottles of wine. The average grower price of wine grapes was $547 a ton in 2006, making the value of the grapes in an average bottle of California wine $0.75. The cheapest grapes were in the San Joaquin Valley, which produces half of California's wine grapes. These grapes were worth $300 a ton in 2006, making the grapes in a typical bottle worth $0.40.

41. Most growers plant 900 to 1,200 vines an acre, with vines in 6×8 feet spaces.

42. Most of the state's wine grapes are harvested by machines that straddle the row and use shaking rods to dislodge the grapes from the vine; the berries are caught by conveyor belts that take them to gondolas traveling alongside the harvester. Leaves and debris are blown away from the grapes by a fan and removed by hand. Machines can work efficiently at night, when temperatures are lower, which produces higher-quality wine.

43. In 2005, 4,600 or 7 percent of the average 65,200 employees covered by unemployment insurance were reported by agricultural employers.

44. The workers may be married, but their families are not with them in the centers.

45. Many Napa Valley workers are from Atacheo, a village of 1,500 two hours from Morelia, Michoacan. Napa workers raised $150,000 to build greenhouses, a turkey farm, and a stereo speaker factory in Atacheo, but these investments failed to provide jobs in Atacheo; after a promising start-up, the businesses failed. Edwin Garcia, "Mexican Priest's Once-Promising Plan in Trouble," *San Jose Mercury News*, February 25, 2005.

46. A Napa County ordinance requires a minimum 20 acres to construct temporary farmworker housing and 40 acres to construct year-round farmworker housing. Napa voters in 2002 approved Measure L, which allows the construction of migrant farmworker housing for up to 12 workers on land zoned for agriculture outside the county's five cities.

47. The Salton Sea varies in dimensions and area due to changes in agricultural runoff and rain, but it is generally about 376 square miles.

48. The UFW, which published its demands in the Mexicali newspaper *La Voz* on January 5, 1979, demanded 60 percent wage increases for tractor drivers and irrigators and a 53 percent increase in the piece rate for harvesting lettuce, from $0.57 to $0.87 per 24-head carton.

49. Collective bargaining laws require employers and unions to negotiate in good faith to reach agreement. If there is a deadlock in bargaining, a legitimate impasse, employers are allowed to implement their final offer to keep their businesses going.

50. ALRB Decision. Admiral Packing 7 ALRB 43 (1981). www.alrb.ca.gov/legal_searches/decision_index/vol7.html

51. *Carl Joseph Maggio, Inc. et al., Petitioners v. Agricultural Labor Relations Board, Respondent.* Court of Appeal of California, Fourth Appellate District. 154 Cal. App. 3d 40; April 2, 1984.

52. Sun Harvest was known as Interharvest until changing its name in 1979. John Elmore and Growers Exchange, which also signed Sun Harvest–type agreements with the UFW, also went out of business in the early 1980s.

53. Quail Street Casualty (www.quailstreet.com) is a Bermuda-based insurance company established by the Western Growers Association to provide insurance for losses caused by harvesttime strikes.

54. Miriam Jordan, "Labor Squeeze along the Border," *Wall Street Journal,* March 11, 2005.

55. "California: Freeze, New Cities," *Rural Migration News* 14, no. 2 (April 2007). See http://migration.ucdavis.edu/rmn/more.php?id=1194_0_2_0.

    The Imperial Irrigation District (IID) receives about 3.3 million acre-feet of water a year from the Colorado River, and the San Diego County Water Authority (SDCWA) paid the IID $258 per acre-foot in 2003 and $267 in 2004 for water transferred to San Diego. Some 10,000 acre-feet of water were transferred to the SDCWA in 2003 and 20,000 in 2004.

A panel of three economists assessed the impacts of land fallowing, and concluded that transferring water increased third-party after-tax incomes by $1.1 million in 2003–2004 in the Imperial Valley. This meant that the multiplier effect of spending the money received for the transferred water exceeded the income lost by less farm production due to land fallowing.

CHAPTER 4: FLORIDA SUGAR, ORANGES, AND TOMATOES

1. Allison T. French, supervisor of the U.S. Employment Service in West Palm Beach, Florida, in the early 1940s noted that "Negro labor in Florida will not work for the Sugar Corporation." He admitted that "it was true that Negroes were occasionally beaten for attempting to leave the job when they owed debts at the company's commissary, and others were sometimes required to work as many as 18 hours a day at cane cutting" (quoted in Williams, 1991).
2. These indictments were later dismissed because of improper jury selection.
3. PL 82-414 was vetoed by President Truman on June 25, 1952, because it retained the national origins selection system that gave preference to Western Europeans—70 percent of 270,000 immigrant visas a year were allotted to natives of the United Kingdom, Ireland, and Germany (most went unused). The veto was overridden on June 27, 1952, and the law went into effect December 24, 1952.
4. PL 82-414, Section 212 states the negative, that is, aliens are ineligible for visas unless (14) the secretary of labor has determined and certified to the secretary of state and to the attorney general that (A) sufficient workers in the United States who are able, willing, and qualified are available at the time (of application for a visa and for admission to the United States) and place (to which the alien is destined) to perform such skilled or unskilled labor, or (B) the employment of such aliens will adversely affect the wages and working conditions of the workers in the United States who are similarly employed. See http://tucnak.fsv.cuni.cz/~calda/Documents/1950s/McCarran_52.html.
5. Sugar imports are restricted to keep the price high for U.S. producers. During the 1970s, imports were more than 4 million tons a year; as U.S. production rose, imports were reduced to keep U.S. sugar prices high.
6. About 55 percent of U.S.-produced sugar is from beets and 45 percent from cane; Florida produces about a quarter of U.S. sugar.
7. See Alec Wilkinson, 1992.
8. One Brazilian cutter explained, "Sugar cane teaches you to love anything else that is not sugar cane" (quoted in Simon Romero, "Spoonfuls of Hope, Tons of Pain: In Brazil's Sugar Empire, Workers Struggle with Mechanization," *New York Times,* May 21, 2000). During the 1990s, there was widespread harvest mechanization in Brazil, so that about half of the crop was harvested mechanically in 2000. One reason Brazil is mechanizing the harvest is sharply rising wages for cane cutters—in the South, sugar harvester wages of $122 a month in 2000 were well above the minimum wage of $85 a month.

9. About 80 percent of Florida cane is grown on organic soils, and 20 percent on sandy soils.

10. Mexico has a quota of 276,000 short tons, so total U.S. sugar imports before high tariffs begin were 1.536 million short tons a year in 2004–2005.

11. The Puerto Rican government sold the last two mills of the Puerto Rico Sugar Corporation in 2000, ending cane growing on an island that was once second only to Cuba in Caribbean sugar production.

12. Florida's sugarcane acreage rose from 49,000 in 1960–1961 to 220,000 in 1964–1965, and has been about 400,000 since the mid-1980s (Buzzanell, Lord, and Brown, 1992).

13. The average mill capacity in the early 1990s was 16,400 tons a day, meaning that the industry could grind about 115,000 tons of harvested cane a day. U.S. Sugar is the largest cane miller, with two mills that can grind 22,000 and 16,000 tons of cane a day. In the early 1990s, the cooperative's mill could grind 21,000 tons a day; Flo-Sun subsidiaries Okeelanta and Osceola 21,000 and 12,000 tons a day; Atlantic, 12,000 tons a day; and Talisman, 11,000 tons a day (Buzzanell, Lord, and Brown, 1992).

14. A U.S. Department of Agriculture (USDA) report noted that "in integrated operations the division of returns between field and factory is not economically significant" (Buzzanell, Lord, and Brown, 1992, 18).

15. CP stands for Canal Point, the location of a public-private facility, and CL for Clewiston, the location of a private U.S. Sugar facility. In 2006, CP-89-2143 was planted on 27 percent of Florida cane acreage, CP-80-1743 on 23 percent, CP-88-1762 on 18 percent, and CP-78-1628 on 13 percent.

16. The federal and state governments will share the cost of the cleanup, with sugar companies contributing $230 million. James McKinley, "Sugar Companies Play a Pivotal Role in Effort to Restore Everglades," *New York Times,* April 16, 1999.

17. Most of the sugar mills relied on the Florida Fruit and Vegetable Association to handle worker recruitment, including filing forms with the U.S. Department of Labor (DOL), arranging for the recruitment and transport of workers, and returning migrants to their country of origin when they were terminated and at the end of the harvest.

18. Workers cut two rows of cane, for example, worker A takes rows one and two, and throws his cut cane between rows two and three and his trash between rows one and two; worker B takes rows three and four, throws his cane between rows two and three with worker A, and puts his trash between rows three and four. A continuous loader picks up the cut cane from the pile rows, cuts it into smaller than 8-foot-long pieces, and loads it into cane wagons pulled by tractors—one tractor typically pulls four cane wagons, each of which holds 3 to 5 tons of cane. The wagons take the cane to a transfer station, where it is transferred to trucks or railcars, taken to the mill, and weighed before being ground and processed—by weighing the cane coming from each field, companies know actual yields.

19. A field with 43.56 estimated tons of cane per acre (ET-acre) has one ton of cane in each 1,000 square feet or in 100 cut-row feet of cut row (two rows planted 5 feet apart). If the task rate or row price is $3.75 in such a field, the cutter is being paid $3.75 for cutting 100 feet or $3.75 a ton; if the task rate is $4, the piece rate is $4 a ton, and so forth. The formula to convert the task rate per 100 feet (PR-100) into the price per estimated ton (P/ET) is: P/ET = PR-100//ET-acre/43.56. If the estimated yield per acre is 43.56, the

price per 100 feet, PR-100, equals the price per estimated ton, P/ET. As the yield falls below 43.56, the price per estimated ton exceeds the price per 100 feet, for example, if the yield is 22 tons an acre, the price per estimated ton is twice the price per 100 feet (there are 0.5 tons each 100 feet). If the yield exceeds 44 tons, the price per estimated ton is less than the price per 100 feet, for example, if the yield is 50 tons per acre and the price per 100 feet is \$4, then the P/ET = 4//(50/43.56) = \$3.49.

20. *NAACP, Jefferson County Branch et al., Plaintiffs, v. U.S. Secretary of Labor et al., Defendants, and U.S. Sugar Corporation et al., Defendant-Intervenors,* September 22, 1994, U.S. District Court for the District of Columbia, 865 F. Supp. 903.

21. DOL Regulations at 20 C.F.R. § 655.207(c) state: "In any year in which the applicable adverse effect rate is increased, employers shall adjust their piece rates upward to avoid requiring a worker to increase his or her productivity over the previous year in order to earn an amount equal to what the worker would earn if the worker were paid at the adverse effect wage rate." Some grower experts opposed linking hourly and piece rate increases, arguing that forcing piece rate wages to increase in lockstep with the Adverse Effect Wage Rate might discourage innovation, since the grower could not reap the productivity increases that might result from, for example, lighter ladders or lighter bags for carrying picked apples.

22. U.S. Department of Labor, "Final Report Regarding Methods of Payment in Sugar Cane," November 12, 1993. The DOL wrote that the task rate system utilized by the sugarcane industry is "incapable of the type of mathematical adjustment required" to link the AEWR and piece rate increases.

23. The sugar companies cannot raise the productivity standard from, say, 8 to 12 tons a day during the season, as workers get more proficient and the cane gets heavier. Such a "moving the goalposts" change would require cutters to do more work to earn the same pay and hurt any U.S. workers who joined crews during the harvest. Under the H-2/H-2A programs, employers must hire U.S. workers who show up to work until the harvest is at least 50 percent completed.

24. The precise relationship is: Minimum Hourly Earnings (\$/hour)/Productivity Standard (units/hour) = Task or Piece Rate (\$/unit). The more usual expression is: PS x TR or PR = Task or Piece earnings, which must be at least the minimum hourly earnings or the employer must provide makeup pay. Employers are not required to retain workers who cannot achieve the Minimum Hourly Earnings, and most such workers are fired.

25. Most workers earned \$5,000 to \$7,000 during the five-month harvest.

26. U.S. Sugar had earlier been a staunch defender of the task rate system. In an August 4, 1992 (p. A19) letter to the *Washington Post,* James Terrill of U.S. Sugar wrote: "Cane cutters work an average of six to 6 1/2 hours per day and cut about 1.2 to 1.5 tons per hour. Their typical wage is close to \$7 per hour and is monitored by electronic time-keepers. Housing and medical care are free. Food is subsidized. At home they would earn \$3 per day."

27. U.S. Sugar reported in April 1993 that, under the new piece rate system, the average cutter earned \$48 a day in 1992–1993, up from \$42 in 1991–1992, and average hourly earnings rose to \$7.24 from \$6.54; the fastest cutters earned \$11 per hour when the AEWR was \$5.91.

28. Four Fanjul brothers—Alfonso or "Alfie," José or "Pepe," Alexander, and Andres—control Flo-Sun, Inc., which has sugarcane and mills in Florida and the Dominican Republic. They are major contributors to both Democratic and Republican politicians. Jeffrey Birnbaum, "Cuban-American Contributors Open Checkbooks after Torricelli Exhibits an Anti-Castro Fervor," *Wall Street Journal,* August 3, 1992.

29. However, an analysis of the task rates across the thousands of fields harvested by the mills found that 91 percent of the variation in task rates between fields could be explained by estimated yields.

30. H-2A cane workers were not allowed to become immigrants under the Immigration Reform and Control Act's (IRCA's) Special Agricultural Worker Program. Workers employed in almost every crop grown in the United States were allowed to legalize their status, including those employed in the production of sugar beets, cotton, and Spanish reeds, but sugarcane was deemed nonperishable by the USDA, making most H-2A cane cutters ineligible (some H-2A citrus pickers in Arizona became immigrants via the Seasonal Agricultural Workers Program or SAW, as did a few apple pickers). Al French of the Florida Fruit and Vegetable Association reportedly said that "If these workers [H-2A] became legalized and could go any place, they'd leave." www.jsri.msu.edu/commconn/latnews/apr98.html.

31. "Modern-Day Slavery," *Palm Beach Post,* December 7–9, 2003. See www.palmbeachpost .com/hp/content/moderndayslavery/index.html. Some contractors provide drugs and women to their workers, often operating so-called $21 clubs that charge men $20 for sex and $1 for a condom.

32. Quoted in Diane Laccy Allen, "Migrant Workers Find Jobs Easily in Polk County and across Florida," *The Ledger,* May 22, 2005. See www.theledger.com/apps/pbcs.dll/article ?AID=/20050522/NEWS/505220407/1039.

33. Quoted in Kelly Wolfe, "Immigrant Smugglers Sentenced," *Palm Beach Post,* November 21, 2002.

34. Quoted in "Florida: Oranges, Housing; Texas." *Rural Migration News* (October 2003). Volume 9 Number 4. http://migration.ucdavis.edu/rmn/more.php?id=775_0_3_0

35. Ag-Mart, based in Plant City, Florida, in 2004 used Cuello's wife, Yolanda, a farm labor contractor (FLC) operating as E&B Harvesting & Trucking, to obtain tomato pickers.

36. Individuals are barred from being licensed contractors for five years after criminal convictions. According to the DOL, 510 individuals with criminal convictions were barred from acting as FLCs in 2005.

37. Ronnie Greene, "Fields of Despair," *Miami Herald,* August 31–September 2, 2003.

38. Evans Sr. was convicted of operating a continuing criminal enterprise, conspiracy to distribute crack, trafficking in untaxed cigarettes, violating the Clean Water Act, violating the Migrant and Seasonal Farm Worker Act, and avoiding financial reporting requirements. His wife was sentenced to 15 years and his son to 6.5 years.

39. Florida typically produces more than 200 million 90-pound boxes of oranges a year. In 2006–2007, production was expected to be less than 140 million boxes because of 2004–2005 hurricane damage and citrus canker; growers received $10 a box in 2007. However, production was expected to rebound toward 200 million boxes a year.

40. Some 1,800 goat trucks were registered in Florida in 2004; registration allows them to operate within 150 miles of the registered address. Accidents involving goats, which are

not required to have windshields, have prompted calls to ban them from state roadways.

41. For mechanical harvesting, tree trunks should be less than 10 inches in diameter and trees less than 16 feet high. The University of Florida's Institute of Food and Agricultural Sciences updates the status of mechanical harvesting systems at: http://edis.ifas.ufl.edu/TOPIC_Mechanical_Harvesting.

42. Another mechanical orange harvesting system uses a "pull-and-catch" machine with 900 8-foot metal arms to reach into the tree and pull off oranges with spring-loaded plastic fingers. There is also a machine that moves up and down the rows of orange trees with a rotating device that resembles spinning car wash brushes. Oranges require about 20 pounds of pull to remove from the tree, so abscission or loosening chemicals may have to be sprayed on the oranges to make them easier for machines to shake from the tree.

43. Brazil produced 18 million tons of oranges in 2002–2003, when Florida produced 11 million tons; Brazil exports more than 95 percent of its orange juice concentrate. Brazil's Sao Paulo state had 1.8 million acres of citrus in 2003, compared to 800,000 acres in Florida, when Sao Paulo produced 45 percent of the world's orange juice, and Florida 40 percent.

44. Tomatoes are sold in 25-pound cartons; growers normally produce about 1,400 cartons an acre.

45. The Coalition of Immokalee Workers (CIW) is headed by Mexican immigrant Lucas Benitez, whose help in discovering several cases of forced labor and slavery in southwest Florida resulted in the Robert F. Kennedy Human Rights Award in 2003. In 2006 the CIW had a $500,000 a year budget and 3,000 members, but says that 80 percent of its members during one year are gone the next, reflecting high turnover in the seasonal farm workforce of southwestern Florida.

46. Mike Hughlett, "McDonald's Farmworker Raise Fought by Growers," *Chicago Tribune,* November 6, 2007.

47. The Socially Accountable Farm Employers (SAFE) certification criteria are available at: www.safeagemployer.org/. A third party, Intertek (www.intertek.com), conducts the "audits" of growers who elect to participate.

CHAPTER 5: MEAT AND POULTRY

1. Per capita meat consumption data are available at: http://earthtrends.wri.org/searchable_db/index.php?theme=8&variable_ID=193&action=select_countries.

2. Animal slaughtering and processing (NAICS 3116) employed about a third of the 1.5 million workers in food manufacturing in 2003 and 10 percent of the 5.5 million workers employed in nondurable goods manufacturing (U.S. Statistical Abstract, 2004–2005, Table 982). The industry is making an effort to replace the term butchering with processing and the term slaughtering with harvesting; the terms used in this chapter are those of the U.S. Bureau of Labor Statistics.

3. The data in this paragraph are from the U.S. Statistical Abstract, 2004–2005, Tables 787–840.

4. Nonmetro is a residual category for counties that do not fit the definition of a metro county. Metro counties are urbanized areas with a population of 50,000 or more plus surrounding counties linked by commuting patterns. There are 3,141 U.S. counties, and 2,297 were classified as nonmetro by the Office of Management and Budget as of 2002.

5. About 39 percent of all meat sold at retail in 2000 was prepackaged, or "case-ready," compared with 23 percent in 1997.

6. Hourly earnings for production workers in smaller food manufacturing industries such as oilseed milling, sugar or chocolate manufacturing, and dairy products tend to be higher, in the $15 to $19 an hour range, while hourly earnings in seafood processing are lower than in meatpacking, $10.70 in 2004.

7. The 773 meat-processing establishments with 100 more employees accounted for more than two-thirds of total employment. The meat-processing industry has four major segments: animal slaughtering (NAICS 311611), meat processed from carcasses (311612), rendering and meat by-product processing (311613), and poultry processing (311615).

8. Poultry, NAICS 311615, comprised 311 firms with 536 establishments in 2002.

9. Similarly, flank steak can sell for a higher price than some other cuts of beef because of the popularity of the Mexican dish carne asada.

10. Feedlot cattle typically gain 3–4 pounds a day from eating 18 to 24 pounds of feed. Cattle Briefing Room, U.S. Department of Agriculture, Economic Research Service (www .ers.usda.gov/Briefing/Cattle/Background.htm).

11. The Bureau of Labor Statistics (BLS) data are available at: www.bls.gov/iif.

12. There were 158 strikes involving 40,000 meatpacking workers between 1983 and 1986, a time when average meatpacking wages of $8.24 had slipped 18 percent below the average manufacturing wage of $9.75 (Craypo, 1994, 71).

13. According to Daryl Kelley and Carlos Chavez, "The Carranza family, like many Latino immigrants, found its way into the American middle class by leaving the Golden State." "California Dreaming No More," *Los Angeles Times,* February 16, 2004.

14. Iowa's 1991 law required employers who recruited non-English-speaking workers more than 500 miles from the workplace to report their recruitment efforts to the state and to pay return transportation to the place of recruitment if the worker was not hired or quit within two weeks. Nebraska law imposed similar requirements on employers with at least 10 percent non-English-speaking workers.

15. Jesse Katz, "The Chicken Trail: New Migrant Trails Take Latinos to Remote Towns," *Los Angeles Times,* November 10–12, 1996.

16. Hudson, the nation's seventh-largest poultry producer in the mid-1990s, is based in Rogers, Arkansas, and had 14 facilities in 11 states with more than 10,000 employees in 1996.

17. The manager, who bought the run-down motel for $220,000 in 2004, took every new Hudson worker to the Division of Family Services; the average number of Latinos receiving food stamps in Noel increased from 35 in 1993 to 375 in 1996. In 1997, Hudson built 60 duplex units to rent to newly arrived workers. The number of Hispanic recipients of food stamps in the area increased more than tenfold between 1993 and 1996.

18. Quoted in Jesse Katz, "The Chicken Trail: New Migrant Trails Take Latinos to Remote Towns," *Los Angeles Times,* November 10–12, 1996.

19. Quoted in "Operation Vanguard, IBP," *Rural Migration News* 6, no. 3 (July 1999). See http://migration.ucdavis.edu/rmn/more.php?id=377_0_2_0.

20. For an argument that Operation Vanguard was launched in areas with relatively few migrant advocates and to discourage union organizing in the plants, see David Bacon, "INS Declares War on Labor," *The Nation,* October 25, 1999.

21. The United Food and Commercial Workers Union complained in a letter to the Immigration and Naturalization Service (INS) that Vanguard was perceived "as a thinly disguised attack on Latino workers" and would cause "any documented immigrant workers who are lawfully in the country—as well as unauthorized immigrant workers—to quit their jobs, pack up their families and belongings, leave their communities and flee" Nebraska.

22. "Vanguard and Meat Packing," *Rural Migration News* 7, no. 4 (October 2000). See http://migration.ucdavis.edu/rmn/more.php?id=466_0_2_0.

23. "Tyson Indicted," *Rural Migration News* 9, no. 1 (January 2002). See http://migration.ucdavis.edu/rmn/more.php?id=562_0_4_0.

24. Quoted in "Sanctions: Tyson Acquitted," *Rural Migration News* 10, no. 2 (April 2003). See http://migration.ucdavis.edu/rmn/more.php?id=12_0_4_0.

25. An expert who compared wages at Tyson plants with similar plants concluded that Tyson's wages were lower, but the judge argued that the expert analysis must show that hiring unauthorized workers was the factor that led to lower wages.

26. Immigrations and Customs Enforcement (ICE) estimated that 30 percent of Swift's employees were unauthorized, and charged a Swift personnel manager and a union official with violating immigration laws.

27. The Basic Pilot or E-Verify employee verification system does not flag multiple uses of valid Social Security Numbers, as occurs when unauthorized workers use another person's identity to get hired.

28. Swift is owned by HM Capital Partners LLC, but has publicly traded debt. The company said that costs would rise as it introduced incentives to entice replacement workers.

29. Evan Perez and Corey Dade, "An Immigration Raid Aids Blacks for a Time," *Wall Street Journal,* January 17, 2007.

30. Crider's starting wage was $6 an hour before the raid; afterward, starting wages were raised to $7 to $9 an hour.

31. Peacock cashed some of the workers' checks, leaving them with cash but no documentation of their hours or earnings.

32. Quoted in Evan Perez and Corey Dade, "An Immigration Raid Aids Blacks for a Time," *Wall Street Journal,* January 17, 2007.

33. For example, of the 17.8 million "bad" Social Security Numbers (SSNs) in the 2006 database, 12.7 million are believed to belong to U.S. citizens, according to the Social Security Administration's (SSA's) inspector general.

34. Most meatpacking plants provide health insurance to workers after 60 days of employment, but the required co-payments sometimes encourage workers to seek care at clinics and emergency rooms, especially for their U.S.-born children.

35. The Great Plains are usually defined as all or part of west Texas and eastern New Mexico north to western Minnesota, the Dakotas, and eastern Montana.

36. Mark Gongloff, "Where Are They Now? The Beardstown Ladies," *Wall Street Journal,* May 1, 2006. The club involved 16 women in 1983 whose average age was 70, and their investment successes in the 1980s made national news. Their book, *The Beardstown Ladies' Common-Sense Investment Guide,* was published in 1994 and sold 800,000 copies by 1998. It was later discovered that the women's returns underperformed stock averages, and the book was withdrawn.

37. S. Lynne Walker, "Heartland Finds New Ways to Deal with Newcomers," *Copley News Service,* November 20, 2003.

38. About 96 of the 1,200 workers on the first shift at the Swift Marshalltown plant were arrested on December 12, 2006; total employment at the plant is about 2,100.

39. About 20 percent of Marshalltown residents are Hispanic; some officials say that the city's population and its Hispanic population are underestimated by up to 5,000 people.

40. Shirley Christian, "Latin Immigrants Fuel Dodge City's Meat-Packing Boom," *New York Times,* January 29, 1998.

CHAPTER 6: SEASONAL WORKER MOBILITY

1. One reason this survey was discontinued in the late 1980s was that green-card commuters and other Mexican workers were likely to be out of the United States in December.

2. Excluded from the analysis in this chapter are Social Security Numbers (SSNs) reported by 50 or more employers (there were 602 such SSNs of the total 1,067,948 in 2001, and they had 59,776 wage records or jobs reported by agricultural employers in 2001). Also excluded were wage records or jobs that had less than $1 in earnings and jobs that reported earnings of more than $75,000 in one quarter. These adjustments eliminated 2,750 SSNs in 2001, which represented 62,571 wage records or jobs, and $803 million in earnings, about 0.25, 2.7, and 6.1 percent of the total SSNs, jobs, and earnings, respectively.

3. Workers employed by contractors can move from farm to farm and remain employed by one employer.

4. Each SSN reported by a California employer with a farm Standard Industrial Classification (SIC) code was tagged. The analysis compiled all California jobs for that SSN, and considered the worker to be a farmworker if most of his earnings were from employers with farm SIC codes.

5. Earnings in 1991 and 1996 were converted to 2001 earnings using the Employment Cost Index (ECI) for private industry in the western region, for wages and salaries only. Earnings were adjusted using the ECI rather than the Consumer Price Index (CPI) because the ECI measures changes in the price of labor including wages and salaries, while the CPI measures changes in the price of goods and services. Because the ECI specifically measures changes in wages, the Bureau of Labor Statistics (BLS) strongly recommends using the ECI when converting nominal wages to real wages. See *BLS Handbook of Methods,* April 1997, chap. 8 (http://stats.bls.gov/hom/homch8.pdf).

6. These San Joaquin Valley (SJV) jobs included 277,000 on crop farms (where the farmer hired workers directly), 44,000 in livestock (also direct hire), and 544,000 in agricultural services.

7. The agricultural services sector includes both farm and nonfarm agricultural services, such as veterinary services and lawn and garden services. Farm labor contractors (FLCs) accounted for 70 percent of the employees reported by farm agricultural services.

8. Median earnings are generally less than mean earnings, reflecting the fact that the mean is pulled up by higher-wage supervisors and farm managers.

9. At the state's minimum wage of $6.25 an hour in 2001, a worker earning $1,600 was employed 260 hours.

CHAPTER 7: MIGRANTS: THE INTEGRATION CHALLENGE

1. The Democratic Party platform in 1960 promised "to bring the 2 million men, women, and children who work for wages on the farms of the United States under the protection of existing labor and social legislation; and to assure migrant labor, perhaps the most underprivileged of all, of a comprehensive program to bring them not only decent wages but also an adequate standard of health, housing, social security protection, education, and welfare services." The Republican platform pledged an "improvement of job opportunities and working conditions of migratory workers" (University of California, Santa Barbara, Presidency Project, Party Platforms 1960, http://www.presidency.ucsb.edu/).

2. The U.S. Department of Labor (DOL) uses labor expenditure data for states from the Census of Agriculture, divides these expenditures by average hourly earnings reported in the U.S. Department of Agriculture's (USDA's) Quarterly Farm Labor Survey, and uses the DOL National Agricultural Workers Survey (NAWS) data to translate hours of farmwork by state into various types of workers to allocate its job-training funds to states.

3. The age range was 5–17 until 1988, when it was expanded to 3–21 (Kuenzi, 2002, 3).

4. Until 1994, supplemental education services could be provided to children up to 60 months after the last qualifying move (Kuenzi, 2002, 3).

5. The federal government provided about $11 billion in fiscal year 2005 in Title 1 aid to elementary schools, but only $600 million to high schools.

6. Administrators say that this 1988 expansion of the Migrant Education Program to high-turnover nonfarm food processing industries was motivated by what they perceived as movement of workers between field and processing jobs. However, there are few field jobs near midwestern meatpacking plants.

7. Children who are in a state part of a year count as part of a full-time equivalent (FTE) migrant student.

8. The children of migratory fishers were added in 1974, and the children of dairy workers in 1988 (Kuenzi, 2002, 3). Since 1988, children qualify for Migrant Education if they move with their parents at least 20 miles to engage in a temporary fishing activity in school districts of at least 15,000 square miles, a provision applicable to Alaska.

9. Migrants pay $3 for 12-hour stays in the complex's 60 rooms, which are open between March and December, serving 25,000 farmworkers and their dependents a year (www.arkansas.gov/esd/MFLC/homepage.htm).

10. Eligible children must have a valid Certificate of Eligibility (COE) that explains the child's qualifying move.

11. Tracie Mauriello, "Errors Involving Migrant Workers' Children Could Be Costly for Waterbury," *Republican-American,* August 7, 2005.

12. A retired recruiter said that there was no wrongdoing by the Waterbury recruiters, since they were responding to Hispanic parents who sought extra tutoring for their children. Some parents reportedly knew that saying they moved to the area to work in agriculture would make their children eligible for supplemental services.

13. Jeff Gill, "State to Take Control of Migrant Education," *Gainesville Times,* July 10, 2005.

14. Many of those found ineligible in Portland, Maine, were Somali refugees who moved to Portland from other U.S. cities.

15. Marcus Breton, "Between Two Worlds: Triplets Struggle to Mesh Cultures," *Sacramento Bee,* July 25, 1999.

16. President Clinton echoed the conclusions of many studies when he asserted in his 1993 State of the Union message that "for every dollar we invest [in Head Start] today, we'll save three tomorrow."

17. Migrant Health is now located in Section 329 of the Public Health Service Act (PHSA).

18. In 1975, the federal government funded a separate system of Community Health Centers (CHC) to provide health care in "medically underserved" areas. Most farmworker areas are also medically underserved, making most Migrant Health Programs eligible for CHC funds as well. In practice, intake workers who obtain information from those seeking medical services determine eligibility for free or subsidized health-care services, and checks on income and farmwork can vary from clinic to clinic.

19. The Migrant Health Program defines eligible farmwork as growing crops on farms and processing or packing them on farms, but not work on livestock farms or processing animal products.

20. The state "enumeration profiles" are online at: http://bphc.hrsa.gov/migrant/ Enumeration/EnumerationStudy.htm. State profiles are based on a three-part estimation procedure: (1) take the acres of labor-intensive crops in each county from the 1997 Census of Agriculture; (2) using data from a variety of sources, including farm advisors, multiply acres by the estimated hours of hired work per acre used to produce these crops; and (3) translate total hours of farmwork per crop into days of farmwork by assuming that (a) all hours of work in these commodities were done by migrant and seasonal farmworkers (MSFWs) and (b) workers average 7.7 hours a day.

The two critical variables in this methodology are (1) the hours-per-acre estimate and (2) the estimated length of the peak (harvest) season. If hours per acre increase, so does the number of workers, but longer harvest seasons reduce the number of workers. The published estimates likely produce too many farmworkers and too high a percentage of migrants, largely because of the assumptions.

21. The federal government also directly funds a job-training program for Native Americans, providing $54 million in fiscal year 2005.

22. The more than 50 grantees of the National Farmworker Jobs Program (NFJP), most of which are community-based nonprofits, formed a political action committee (PAC) to persuade Congress that One-Stop centers are unable to effectively serve farmworkers (www.usafarmworker.org).

23. Perhaps because job-training programs serve adults, there has long been an emphasis on measuring their effects on the wages of those receiving services. Agencies that receive job-training funds usually record the earnings of participants as they enter the program, and their continued funding depends in part on participants having higher earnings after completing the training.

24. The U.S. Department of Labor (DOL) in the 1990s used a two-part formula to allocate NFJP funds to states: half of each state's allocation was based on the 1990 census count of eligible farmworkers and half was based on state shares of labor expenses, adjusted for differences in hourly earnings, in the 1982 Census of Agriculture.

25. Individuals must have worked at least 25 days or earned at least $800 performing agricultural work or must have 50 percent of their time employed in or 50 percent of their earnings from qualifying farmwork in the 24 months prior to application.

26. Disadvantaged means having an income below the federal poverty line or having an income that is less than 70 percent of the lower-living standard income level as defined by the DOL's Employment and Training Administration (between $19,000 and $24,000 in 2005 for a family of four persons).

27. A 1989 report prepared for the secretary of labor, "Working Capital," emphasized that there is a " 'general perception' " that contractors tend to recruit the most qualified participants for training programs. Representative Augustus F. Hawkins (D-CA), then chair of the House Committee on Education and Labor, explained that creaming is enrolling "those who seem most job-ready and easiest to place, rather than the hard-core unemployed who may have social, psychological or other problems." Quoted in Martin Tolchin, "Study of U.S. Jobs Program Calls for Focus on the Poor," *New York Times,* May 3, 1989.

28. More information on the U.S. Department of Agriculture's (USDA's) Farm Labor Housing Loan and Grant program is online at: www.rurdev.usda.gov/rhs/mfh/brief _mfh_flh.htm.

29. More than 90 percent of the 14,000 subsidized farmworker housing units were owned by nonprofits, many of which had 50 or more units and received funds under the Section 521 Rental Assistance Program; most were at least 15 years old in 2006.

30. Information on the HUD and other programs is available online at: www.hud.gov/ local/shared/working/groups/frmwrkcoln/fund/sources.cfm?state=nm.

31. The Legal Services Corporation distributed $305 million in grants to 138 programs with 900 offices in 2007 (www.lsc.gov/press/pr_detail_T7_R29.php).

32. Then Senator Phil Gramm (R-TX) asserted that: "Every day in America, the Legal Services Corporation Is Hassling American Agriculture." Quoted in Henry Weinstein, "Powerful Foes of Legal Aid," *Los Angeles Times,* May 30, 2001.

33. Quoted in Henry Weinstein, "Powerful Foes of Legal Aid," *Los Angeles Times,* May 30, 2001.

34. Dan Gerawan testified that California Rural Legal Assistance (CRLA) spent $455,084 to bring the case, and that Gerawan spent $600,000 defending itself. Hearings before the House Committee on the Judiciary, Subcommittee on Commercial and Administrative Law, June 15, 1995.

35. Much of the dispute centered on concrete-block housing that Gerawan built in 1980, remodeled in 1988, and bulldozed in 1991 in response to a DOL refusal to allow Gerawan to close the housing after pruning ended. Gerawan alleges that its worker-tenants intentionally vandalized the housing, as instructed by CRLA lawyers, so that it would be out of compliance with housing laws.

CHAPTER 8: LABOR SHORTAGES, MECHANIZATION, AND FOOD COSTS

1. Nicole Gaouette, "U.S. Lets in More Immigrants for Farms," *Los Angeles Times,* October 7, 2007.
2. Editorial "Immigration Non-Harvest," *Wall Street Journal,* July 20, 2007. The editorial went on to claim that "Migrant workers, often illegal, have picked American crops for decades, crossing the U.S. border during the harvest season and returning home when the work was done. This farm labor system operated almost as its own informal guest-worker program," and is today threatened by stepped-up border enforcement.
3. The National Agricultural Workers Survey data are available online at: www.doleta.gov/agworker/report9/toc.cfm.
4. Quoted in Le Roy Standish, "Too Few Laborers Leave Some Orchards with Rotting Fruit," *Daily Sentinel,* September 1, 2007.
5. Pear grower quoted in Julia Preston, "Pickers Are Few, and Growers Blame Congress," *New York Times,* September 22, 2006. Vegetable grower quoted in "Farm Labor Shortages," *Rural Migration News* 13, no. 2 (April 2006). See http://migration.ucdavis.edu/rmn/more.php?id=1110_0_4_0.
6. Fruit production data are from Fruit and Tree Nuts Situation and Outlook, FTS-2007, October 2007, table A-5, p. 26.
7. These data are from Vegetables and Melons Situation and Outlook Yearbook, VGS-2007, July 2007, table 6, p. 19. www.ers.usda.gov/Briefing/Vegetables/.
8. Miriam Jordan, "Labor Squeeze along the Border," *Wall Street Journal,* March 12, 2005.
9. Quoted in Christine Souza, "Worker Shortage Makes Immigration Reform Urgent," *Ag Alert,* December 7, 2005.
10. Julia Preston, "Pickers Are Few, and Growers Blame Congress," *New York Times,* September 22, 2006.
11. See table 3 at: www.calpear.com/brd_annreporttables.cfm.
12. Quarterly Census of Employment and Wages (ES 202 data) available online at: www.labormarketinfo.edd.ca.gov/cgi/dataanalysis/AreaSelection.asp?tableName=Industry.
13. For example, the California Farm Bureau Federation's weekly *Ag Alert* on September 14, 2005, had a headline "Farm Labor Shortage Approaches Critical Level."
14. Dennis Pollock, "Labor Shortage Sours Citrus Harvest," *Fresno Bee,* November 24, 2005.
15. *California Farmer,* July 6, 1963, pp. 5, 47. There were many other predictions of doom and gloom without braceros. California had about 10,000 acres of strawberries in the early 1960s, and the *California Farmer* on July 20, 1963, had an article headlined "Bracero Loss Will Make Strawberries a Luxury," p. 5. California today has almost 35,000 acres of strawberries.

16. In 1979, then U.S. Department of Agriculture Secretary Bob Bergland eliminated federal funding for mechanization research, saying "I will not put federal money into any project that reduces the need for farm labor."

17. Ending the Bracero Program led to the mechanization of the tart cherry and prune (dried plum) harvests.

18. The U.S. Bureau of Labor Statistics Consumer Expenditure Survey data are online at www.bls.gov/cex. Farm-retail price spreads are available at www.ers.usda.gov/Briefing/ FoodPriceSpreads/spreads/.

19. The average household spent $110 on processed fruits and $82 on processed vegetables in 2004.

20. This means that $357 in retail spending on fresh produce generates approximately $62 for farmers: ($0.16 × $182 = $29 + $0.19 × $175 = $33, and $29 + $33 = $62).

21. The farm labor cost of a $1 retail produce item is 5.7 cents, a third of the farmer's share (17 cents). Raising farm labor costs by 40 percent increases this cost to 8 cents, adding 2.3 cents for consumers.

CHAPTER 9: REFORMING U.S. IMMIGRATION POLICIES

1. The 1790 Naturalization Act permitted white persons of "good moral character" to acquire citizenship after two years' residence. The period was briefly extended to 14 years in 1798, and has been five years since 1800. Immigrants married to U.S. citizens and those who serve in the U.S. military can generally naturalize after three years.

2. To maintain secrecy, members of the order answered inquiries by saying "I know nothing about it," hence the name "Know Nothings."

3. Immigration from China was suspended for a 10-year period until 1892 and was suspended again until 1902; the suspension was made permanent until 1943, when Chinese exclusion was repealed.

4. Quoted in Oscar Handlin, "Memorandum Concerning the Origins of the National Origin Quota System," Hearings before the President's Commission on Immigration and Naturalization, 82nd Congress, 2nd sess. (Washington, DC: U.S. Government Printing Office, 1952), 755. One of the nine members of the Dillingham Commission, Cornell political economy professor Jeremiah Jenks, later wrote a college text entitled *The Immigration Problem* (New York: Hill and Wang, 1912).

   The 41 volumes of Dillingham Commission reports prepared between 1907 and 1911 are online at http://library.stanford.edu/depts/dlp/ebrary/dillingham/body.shtml.

5. House of Representatives, Committee on the Judiciary, House Report 1365, 82nd Congress, 2nd Sess., February 14, 1952, p. 37. Each country was guaranteed at least 100 visas, so that 154,477 visas were available annually. Between 1924 and 1927, immigration was reduced from 1921–1924 levels by limiting immigration to 2 percent of each country's foreign-born persons in the United States in 1890.

6. Refugees appear in immigration data as immigrants one year after they arrive in the United States.

7. Some 750,000 Mexican men and 135,000 Mexican women became SAWs, plus another 200,000 from other countries, for a total of 1.1 million foreigners legalized.

8. More than 700,000 foreigners registered for the Replenishment Agricultural Worker (RAW) Program in 1988–1989, but almost all gave U.S. addresses, dulling the incentive of farmers to press for implementation of the program.

9. See "Prop. 187 Approved in California," *Migration News* 1, no. 4 (December 1994). See http://migration.ucdavis.edu/mn/more.php?id=492_0_2_0.

10. There were limited exceptions to this general exclusion from federal cash benefits for refugees and immigrants who served in the U.S. Armed Services. In the late 1990s, Congress restored federal means-tested benefits to some legal immigrants, including the elderly and children, but unauthorized foreigners remain excluded from almost all federal welfare benefits.

11. The Illegal Immigration Reform and Immigrant Responsibility Act (IIRIRA) also imposed an income test on sponsors of immigrants of at least 125 percent of the poverty line for the sponsor and immigrant together. For example, an immigrant sponsoring his wife and two children in 2006 would have to have an income of at least $25,000, which is 125 percent of the $20,000 poverty line for a family of four.

12. Of the 762 foreigners held in "preventive detention" because they were of "special interest" in connection with the 9/11 terrorism investigation, 611 had one or more deportation hearings that were closed to the public, and 505 were deported; none was charged with terrorism. Eric Lichtblau, "U.S. Report Faults the Roundup of Illegal Immigrants after 9/11," *New York Times,* April 30, 2003.

13. Bush administration officials emphasized that "There is no linkage between participation in this program and a green card . . . one must go home upon conclusion of the program." Quoted in "Bush: Legalization, AgJOBS," *Migration News* 11, no. 1 (January 2004). See http://migration.ucdavis.edu/mn/more.php?id=2967_0_2_0.

14. The House bill also included several controversial items, including making "illegal presence" in the United States a felony, which would have made it hard for unauthorized foreigners to become legal immigrants at some future date. See "Bush and Congress: Action?" *Migration News* 13, no. 1 (January 2006). See http://migration.ucdavis.edu/mn/more.php?id=3155_0_2_0.

15. The Comprehensive Immigration Reform Act (CIRA, S2611) had six titles that dealt, inter alia, with border enforcement in Title 1, interior enforcement in Titles 2 and 3, a new H-2C guest-worker program in Title 4, additional immigration visas to reduce the backlog of foreigners waiting for them in Title 5, and earned legalization in Title 6. "Senate Approves CIRA," *Migration News* 13, no. 3 (July 2006). See http://migration.ucdavis.edu/mn/more.php?id=3199_0_2_0.

16. U.S. employers would have posted their jobs on a new electronic job registry, offering at least the minimum or prevailing wage for that occupation. If U.S. workers did not respond to these ads, the employer could issue job offers to foreigners, who would use them to obtain H-2C visas in their countries of origin. H-2C guest workers could change U.S. employers if they received a job offer from another U.S. employer who had completed the attestation process, a provision aimed at protecting migrants from exploitation.

17. The Kyl amendment, which would have required H-2C workers to return to their countries of origin rather than be eligible for immigrant visas, was defeated 58–35.

18. Y-1 guest workers would have been prohibited from being unemployed more than 60 days at any one time and for more than 120 days during the life of each two-year work visa. Y-1 guest workers could have brought their family members with them to the United States if their earnings were at least 1.5 times the poverty line for their family (about $30,000 for a family of four in 2007) and they had health insurance for their dependents. However, to discourage guest workers from bringing their families, those who brought family members would have been allowed two rather than three U.S. work stints, and family members could have accompanied them for only one of these two stints.

19. Canada launched a point system to select immigrants in 1967, Australia followed in 1989, New Zealand in 1991, and the United Kingdom in 2001.

20. For example, under the point system proposed in CIRA 2007, a 29-year-old Mexican who had worked six years as a U.S. guest worker could achieve 61 points by having five years of U.S. job experience in a high-demand occupation (health-care aide), being young and knowing English, and having a U.S. relative. However, a 45-year-old Indian information technology (IT) worker with a PhD and a U.S. job offer but no U.S. work experience would receive only 49 points, despite his or her knowledge of English.

21. The American Federation of Labor and Congress of Industrial Organizations (AFL-CIO) and most unions opposed CIRA 2007, citing the likely depressing effect of Y-1 guest workers on U.S. wages. However, the Service Employees International Union and Unite Here supported CIRA 2007 despite its guest-worker provisions because it would have legalized many unauthorized residents. See "Senate: Immigration Reform Stalls." *Migration News* 14, no. 3 (July 2007). See http://migration.ucdavis.edu/mn/comments.php?id=3294_0_2_0.

CHAPTER 10: REGULARIZE AND RATIONALIZE FARM LABOR

1. Passel (2005) estimated that 7.2 million of 148 million U.S. workers in March 2005 were unauthorized, that is, 4.9 percent.

2. White House Press Release, June 23, 1995. Clinton's statement continued: "If our crackdown on illegal immigration contributes to labor shortages . . . I will direct the departments of Labor and Agriculture to work cooperatively to improve and enhance existing programs to meet the labor requirements of our vital agricultural industry consistent with our obligations to American workers."

3. Representative Smith's bill, HR 2377, was introduced in the Senate by Gordon Smith (R-OR) as S 1563.

4. Employers wishing to hire H-2C farmworkers would have filed labor condition attestations (LCAs) with their local employment service offices, sent a copy to the Immigration and Naturalization Service (INS) district office, and posted a notice of the attestation in the workplace. Employer LCAs would have had to offer the higher of the prevailing or minimum wage to U.S. and H-2C workers. H-2C workers could have worked up to 10 months in U.S. agriculture.

5. Under the registry proposal, legally authorized farmworkers would have registered with local Employment Service (ES) offices and indicated whether they were willing

to migrate out of the area to fill farm jobs. Employers would have submitted job offers to the ES registry, and ES would have verified that the jobs offered paid prevailing wages before listing them; in other words, the new registry would have assumed responsibility for: (1) verifying the legal status of workers seeking to register by checking the documents and data they provide with immigration and social security agencies; and (2) verifying that employer job offers satisfied program requirements. For example, if an employer requested 100 workers at least 21 days before they were needed, and ES had only 40 workers registered and willing to go to the employer seven days before the need date, the grower would receive a "shortage report" from the registry that would grant permission to bring 60 foreign farmworkers into the United States.

6. AgJOBS was approved as an amendment to the Commerce-Justice-State Department appropriations bill.

7. Gramm's proposal is summarized in: "Guest Workers, Braceros," *Rural Migration News* 8, no. 3 (July 2001). See http://migration.ucdavis.edu/rmn/more.php?id=526_0_4_0.

8. S 340 and HR 371, introduced January 10, 2007, as the Agricultural Job Opportunities, Benefits and Security Act.

9. Applicants can complete 150 days or 863 hours of farmwork to qualify for blue cards. The qualifying farmwork could be documented with pay stubs, tax filings, contracts, and the like, and the legalization program would run for five years. To avoid dealing directly with the Department of Homeland Security (DHS), unauthorized foreigners could file applications with Qualified Designated Entities (QDEs) to transmit to DHS. Farmworker unions and employer associations would be favored as QDEs to receive applications, but a licensed attorney, or an immigration practitioner recognized by the DHS Board of Immigration Appeals could also assist with applications.

10. Blue-card holders seeking immigrant visas would have to perform agricultural work at least 100 workdays a year for five years or at least 150 days a year for three consecutive years, and a workday is at least 5.75 hours. Blue-card holders fired without "just cause" from farm jobs could file requests for credit for farmwork not done because of the firing, and injury or pregnancy could lengthen the period to complete the required farmwork by a year.

11. Blue-card holders could not receive immigrant visas if they had more than three U.S. misdemeanor convictions or a U.S. felony conviction.

12. Under AgJOBs, farm employers would fax or use the Internet to submit applications for H-2A guest workers to the U.S. Department of Labor at least 28 days before workers were needed, and could expect DOL approval of their request within 72 hours.

13. Fair-market rents are available online at: www.huduser.org/datasets/fmr.html.

14. For example, fair-market rents for two-bedroom apartments in 2008 were $805 a month in Fresno County, $1,111 in Monterey County, $1,214 in Napa County, $1,188 in Palm Beach County, and $1,056 in Collier County.

15. Feinstein issued a press release on December 7, 2006, that asserted there was a farm labor shortage because: "There is no readily available pool of excess labor to replace the 500,000 foreign migrant workers we have depended on for years. The work is hard. It is stooped. It is manual. The hours are long. To make a living, the laborer must travel around the region, from site to site, working for more than one employer, to coincide

with the crop harvesting calendar. The problem is, we do not have enough American workers who are willing to do this job."

16. Some states require employers to pay state unemployment insurance (UI) taxes on the earnings of H-2A workers.

17. Administratively, guest workers could be issued special Social Security Numbers to identify their earnings.

EPILOGUE: THE GREAT MIGRATION

1. The average woman in developing countries (excluding China) had 3.3 children in 2007, compared with 1.6 children per woman in developed countries. For a population to replace itself, women must have an average 2.1 children.

2. In 2007, there were 65 persons per square kilometer in low- and middle-income countries, compared to 27 in the high-income countries, according to the World Bank.

3. Per capita incomes averaged $35,000 in the industrial countries in 2005, 21 times the average $1,750 in low- and middle-income countries. At purchasing power parity, which takes into account national differences in the cost of living, the world's gross national income was $56 trillion or $9,400 per capita—$32,500 per capita in the high-income countries and $5,200 in low- and middle-income countries, a 6 to 1 gap.

4. These farmworker recruitment networks are examined in *Rural Migration News*. Various issues. See http://migration.ucdavis.edu/rmn/index.php.

Bibliography

Anrig, Greg, and Tova Andrea Wang, eds. 2007. *Immigration's New Frontiers: Experiences from the Emerging Gateway States*. New York: Century Foundation Press (www.tcf.org).

Bean, Frank, Barry Edmonston, and Jeffrey Passel, eds. 1990. *Undocumented Migration to the United States: IRCA and the Experience of the 1980s*. Washington, DC: Urban Institute Press.

Bean, Frank D., Rodolofo de la Garza, Bryan Roberts, and Sidney Weintraub, eds. 1997. *At the Crossroads: Mexico and U.S. Immigration Policy*. Lanham, MD: Rowan and Littlefield.

Bell, Stephen, and Larry Orr. 2002. "Screening (and Creaming?) Applicants to Job Training Programs: The AFDC Homemaker-Home Health Aide Demonstrations." *Labour Economics* 9, no. 2: 279–301.

Bohm, Anthony, Dorothy Davis, Denis Meares, and David Pearce. 2002. *Forecasts of the Global Demand for International Higher Education and Global Student Mobility*. IDP Education Pty Australia (www.idp.com/marketingandresearch/research/internationaleducationstatistics/article764.asp).

Brandt, Jon, and Ben French. 1981. *An Analysis of Economic Relationships and Projected Adjustments in the U.S. Processing Tomato Industry*. Berkeley: University of California, Giannini Foundation Research Report 331.

Briggs, Vernon M. 2001. *Immigration and American Unionism*. Ithaca, New York: Cornell University Press.

Brown, G. K. 1984. "Fruit and Vegetable Mechanization." In *Migrant Labor in Agriculture: An International Comparison,* ed. P. Martin. Berkeley: University of California, Giannini Foundation, 195–209.

Buzzanell, Peter, Ron Lord, and Nathaniel Brown. 1992. *The Florida Sugar Industry—Its Evolution and Prospects.* USDA Sugar and Sweetener Report, June 11–34.

California Assembly Committee on Agriculture. 1965. "The Bracero Program and Its Aftermath: An Historical Summary." Sacramento, CA, April 1.

California Senate Fact Finding Committee on Labor and Welfare. 1961. "California's Farm Labor Problems: Parts 1 and 2." Sacramento, CA.

Capaldi, Nicholas, ed. 1997. *Immigration: Debating the Issues.* Amherst, NY: Prometheus Books.

Cargill, B. F., and G. E. Rossmiller, eds. 1970. *Fruit and Vegetable Harvest Mechanization: Policy Implications.* East Lansing: Rural Manpower Center, Michigan State University.

Carter, Colin, Darrell Hueth, John Mamer, and Andrew Schmitz. 1981. "Labor Strikes and the Price of Lettuce." *Western Journal of Agricultural Economics* 6, no. 1 (July): 1–14.

Champlin, Dell, and Eric Hake. 2006. "Immigration as Industrial Strategy in American Meatpacking." *Review of Political Economy* 18, no. 1 (January): 49–70.

Christian, Shirley. 1998. "Latin Immigrants Fuel Dodge City's Meat-Packing Boom." *New York Times,* January 29.

Cochrane, Willard. 1993. *Development of American Agriculture: An Historical Analysis.* Minneapolis: University of Minnesota Press.

Commission on Agricultural Workers. 1993. Final Report.

Congressional Research Service. 1980. "Temporary Worker Programs: Background and Issues." Prepared for the Senate Committee on the Judiciary, February.

———. 2006. "Labor Practices in the Meat Packing and Poultry Processing Industry: An Overview." October 27.

Conway, James. 2002. *Napa: The Story of an American Eden.* Boston: Houghton Mifflin.

Cook, Roberta, et al. 1991. *NAFTA: Effects on Agriculture.* Vol. 4, Fruit and Vegetable Issues. Park Ridge, IL: American Farm Bureau Foundation.

Cornelius, Wayne, Philip Martin, and James Hollifield, eds. 1994. *Controlling Immigration: A Global Perspective.* Stanford, CA: Stanford University Press.

Cornelius, Wayne, and David Myhre. 1996. *The Transformation of Rural Mexico: Reforming the Ejido Sector.* La Jolla, CA: Center for U.S.-Mexican Studies.

Cowan, Tadlock. 2005. *California's San Joaquin Valley: A Region in Transition.* Washington, DC: Congressional Research Service, December 12.

Craig, Richard B. 1971. *The Bracero Program: Interest Groups and Foreign Policy.* Austin: University of Texas Press.

Craypo, Charles. 1994. "Meat Packing: Industry Restructuring and Union Decline." In *Contemporary Collective Bargaining in the Private Sector,* ed. Paula Voos. Madison, WI: Industrial Relation Research Association, 63–96.

Cross, Harry, and James Sandos. 1981. *Across the Border: Rural Development in Mexico and Recent Migration to the United States.* Berkeley: Institute of Governmental Studies, University of California.

Daft, Julie. 2004. "Title I Migrant Education Program Trends Summary Report: 1998–2001." Westat Report prepared for the Office of the Under Secretary, U.S. Department of Education (www.ed.gov/rschstat/eval/disadv/migrant/finaloo.doc).

Daniel, Cletus E. 1981. *Bitter Harvest: A History of California Farmworkers, 1870–1941.* Berkeley. University of California Press.

Degler, Carl N. 1970. *Out of Our Past: The Forces That Shaped Modern America.* New York: Harper & Row.

de Janvry, Alain, Elisabeth Sadoulet, and Gustavo Anda. 1994. "NAFTA and Mexico's Corn Producers." Berkeley: University of California ARE Working Paper 275, July.

de Janvry, Alain, Elisabeth Sadoulet, and Gustavo Gordillo. 1996. *Re-orienting Mexico's Agrarian Reform: Household and Community Responses, 1990–94.* La Jolla, CA: Center for U.S.-Mexican Studies.

Drabenstott, Mark, Mark Henry, and Kristin Mitchell. 1999. "Where Have All the Packing Plants Gone? The New Meat Geography in Rural America." *Federal Reserve Bank of Kansas City Economic Review* 84, no. 3: 65–82.

Elac, John. 1961. *The Employment of Mexican Workers in U.S. Agriculture, 1900–1960.* Los Angeles: University of California, May.

Fisher, Lloyd. 1953. *The Harvest Labor Market in California.* Cambridge, MA: Harvard University Press.

Fogel, Robert, and Stanley Engerman. 1974. *Time on the Cross: The Economics of American Negro Slavery.* Boston: Little, Brown.

Fuller, Varden. 1942. "The Supply of Agricultural Labor as a Factor in the Evolution of Farm Organization in California." PhD diss., University of California, Berkeley, 1939. Reprinted in *Violations of Free Speech and the Rights of Labor Education and Labor Committee* [The LaFollette Committee]. Washington, DC: Senate Education and Labor Committee, 19778–19894.

Fuller, Varden. 1967. "A New Era for Farm Labor." *Industrial Relations,* Volume 6, No 2. May

Gabbard, Susan, and Luin Goldring. 1991. *The Occupational Mobility of Current and Former Farm Workers: A Comparative Analysis in Two California Labor Markets.* Employment Development Department,Sacramento, CA: California Agricultural Studies 91–93, July.

Galarza, Ernesto. 1977. *Farm Workers and Agribusiness in California, 1947–1960.* Notre Dame, IN: University of Notre Dame Press.

Gallardo, Lloyd. 1963. "The Green Carder." *Employment Security Review,* January 25–27.

Garcia y Griego, Manuel. 1981. "The Importation of Mexican Contract Laborers to the United States, 1942–1964: Antecedents, Operation, and Legacy." La Jolla, CA: Program in U.S.-Mexican Studies, UCSD, Working Paper 11.

———. 1989. "The Mexican Labor Supply, 1990–2010." In *Mexican Migration to the United States: Origins, Consequences and Policy Options,* ed. Wayne Cornelius and Jorge A. Bustamante. La Jolla, CA: UCSD Center for U.S.-Mexican Studies.

Gelatt, J. and M. Fix. 2006. "Targeted Federal Spending on the Integration of Immigrant Families." Discussion Paper produced for the Independent Task Force on Immigration and America's Future, Department of Education Budget Office, Department of Labor, Employment and Training Administration, February 28.

Gouveia, Lourdes. 2006. "Nebraska's Responses to Immigration." In *Immigration's New Frontiers: Experiences from the Emerging Gateway States*, ed. Greg Anrig Jr. and Tova Wang. New York: Century Foundation Press, 143–198.

Government Accountability Office. 2005. *Immigration Enforcement: Weaknesses Hinder Employment Verification and Worksite Enforcement Efforts*. GAO-05-813, August 31.

Government Accounting Office. 1998. *Community Development: Changes in Nebraska's and Iowa's Counties with Large Meatpacking Workforces*. GAO/RCED-98-62, February 27.

———. 1999. *South Florida Ecosystem: An Overall Strategic Plan and a Decision-Making Process Are Needed to Keep the Effort on Track*. GAO/RCED-99-121, April 22.

———. 2002. *Collective Bargaining Rights: Information on the Number of Workers with and without Bargaining Rights*. GAO-02-835, September.

———. 2000. *Sugar Program: Supporting Sugar Prices Has Increased Users' Costs while Benefiting Producers*. RCED-00-126, June.

Gozdziak, Elzbieta M., and Susan F. Martin, eds. 2005. *Beyond the Gateway: Immigrants in a Changing America*. Lanham, MD: Lexington Books.

Grey, M. A., and A. C. Woodrick. 2005. "Latinos Have Revitalized Our Community: Mexican Migration and Anglo Responses in Marshalltown, Iowa." In *New Destinations: Mexican Immigration in the United States*, ed. V. Zúñiga and R. Hernández-León. New York: Russell Sage Foundation.

Hahamovitch, Cindy. 1999. "Scarcity, Expediency and the Birth of the Agricultural 'Guestworkers' Program." *CIS Backgrounder,* December (www.cis.org/articles/1999/back1299 .htm#3).

Hathaway, Dale, and Brian Perkins. 1968. "Occupational Mobility and Migration from Agriculture." In *Rural Poverty in the United States: A Report to the President's National Advisory Commission on Rural Poverty,* chap. 13, 185–237. Washington, DC: U.S. Government Printing Office.

Hawley, Ellis. 1966. "The Politics of the Mexican Labor Issue." *Agricultural History* 15, no. 3 (July): 157–176.

Hollmann, Frederick W., Tammany J. Mulder, and Jeffrey E. Kallan. 2000. "Methodology and Assumptions for the Population Projections of the United States: 1999 to 2100." U.S. Bureau of the Census, Population Division, Working Paper No. 38, January (http:// www.census.gov/population/documentation/twps0038/tabE.txt).

Housing Assistance Council. 2006. *USDA Section 514/516 Farmworker Housing: Existing Stock and Changing Needs*. Washington, DC: HAC, October (www.ruralhome.org/manager/uploads/FWHousing.pdf).

Hufbauer, Gary, and Jeffrey Schott. 1992. *North American Free Trade: Issues and Recommendations*. Washington, DC: Institute for International Economics.

———. 2005. *NAFTA Revisited: Achievements and Challenges*. Washington, DC: Institute for International Economics.

Issac, Rael Jean. 1996. *Harvest of Injustice: Legal Services vs. the Farmer*. Vienna, VA: National Legal and Policy Center (www.nlpc.org/lsap.asp).

Jamieson, Stuart. 1945. *Labor Unionism in American Agriculture*. Washington, DC: Bureau of Labor Statistics, Bulletin 836.

Jensen, Leif. 2006. *New Immigrant Settlements in Rural America: Problems, Prospects, and Policies.* Durham, NH: Carsey Institute (www.carseyinstitute.unh.edu).

Johnson, Hans P., and Joseph M. Hayes. 2004. *The Central Valley at a Crossroads: Migration and Its Implications.* San Francisco: Public Policy Institute of California, November (www.ppic.org/main/publication.asp?i=461).

Johnson, Nancy. 2001. "Tierra y Libertad: Will Tenure Reform Improve Productivity in Mexico's Ejido Agriculture?" *Economic Development and Cultural Change* 49, no. 2 (January): 291–309.

Johnston, Helen L. 1985. *Health for the Nation's Harvesters: A History of the Migrant Health Program in Its Economic and Social Setting.* Farmington Hills, MI: National Migrant Worker Council.

Johnston, Warren. 2003. "Cross Sections of a Diverse Agriculture: Profiles of California's Agricultural Production Regions and Principal Commodities." In Jerry Siebert, ed., *California Agriculture: Dimensions and Issues.* University of California, Giannini Foundation of Agricultural Economics, 03-1, 29–55.

Jones, Lamar S., and James W. Christian. 1965. "Some Observations on the Agricultural Labor Market." *Industrial and Labor Relations Review* 18, no. 4 (July): 522–534.

Kain, John, and Joseph Persky. 1968. "The North's Stake in Southern Rural Poverty." In *Rural Poverty in the United States: A Report to the President's National Advisory Commission on Rural Poverty,* chap. 17, 288–308. Washington, DC: U.S. Government Printing Office.

Kandel, W., and J. Cromartie. 2004. "New Patterns of Hispanic Settlement in Rural America." Rural Development Research Report No. 99. Washington, DC: U.S. Department of Agriculture.

Kandel, William, and Emilio Parrado. 2005. "Hispanic Population Growth, Age Composition Shifts, and Public Policy Impacts in Nonmetro Counties." In *Population Change and Rural Society,* ed. W. Kandel and D. Brown. Berlin: Springer.

Khan, Ahktar, Philip Martin, and Philip Hardiman. 2003. *California's Farm Labor Market: A Cross-Sectional Analysis of Employment and Earnings in 1991, 1996, and 2001.* Sacramento: Employment Development Department, August (http://www.calmis.ca.gov/SpecialReports/Ag-Emp-1991to2001.pdf).

Kiser, George, and Martha Kiser. 1979. *Mexican Workers in the United States.* Albuquerque: University of New Mexico Press.

Kissam, Ed. 1998. *Parlier's Prospects: Local Government's Role in Integrating Immigrants into Rural California Life.* Mimeo. Available at: http://migration.ucdavis.edu/cf/more.php?id=121_0_2_0.

Kuenzi, Jeffrey. 2002. *The Federal Migrant Education Program as Amended by the No Child Left Behind Act of 2001.* Congressional Research Service, March 11, RL31325.

Lloyd, Jack, Philip L. Martin, and John Mamer. 1988. *The Ventura Citrus Labor Market.* Berkeley: University of California, Division of Agriculture and Natural Resources, Giannini Information Series 88-1.

London, Joan, and Henry Anderson. 1970. *So Shall We Reap: The Story of Cesar Chavez and the Farm Workers Movement.* New York: Crowell.

Mamer, John, and Donald Rosedale. 1980. *The Management of Seasonal Farm Workers under Collective Bargaining.* University of California Cooperative Extension. Leaflet 21147, March.

Manion, Jennifer. 2001. "Cultivating Farmworker Injustice: The Resurgence of Sharecropping." *Ohio State Law Journal* 62: 1665–1684.

Marshall, Ray. 2007. "Getting Immigration Reform Right." Economic Policy Institute Briefing Paper No. 186, March 15 (www.sharedprosperity.org/bp186.html).

Marshall, Ray, and Marc Tucker. 1992. *Thinking for a Living: Education and the Wealth of Nations.* New York: Basic Books.

Martin, Philip. 1990. "The Outlook for Agricultural Labor in the 1990s." *UC Davis Law Review* 23, no. 3: 499–523.

———. 1993. *Trade and Migration: NAFTA and Agriculture.* Washington, DC: Institute for International Economics.

———. 1994. "Good Intentions Gone Awry: IRCA and U.S. Agriculture." *Annals of the Academy of Political and Social Science* 534 (July): 44–57.

———. 2003a. "AgJOBS: New Solution or New Problem?" *International Migration Review* 37, no. 4 (Winter): 127–141.

———. 2003b. *Promise Unfulfilled: Unions, Immigration, and Farm Workers.* Ithaca, NY: Cornell University Press.

Martin, Philip, Wallace Huffman, Robert Emerson, Edward Taylor, and Refugio Rochin, eds. 1995. *Immigration Reform and U.S. Agriculture.* Berkeley, CA: Division of Agriculture and Natural Resources, Publication 3358.

Martin, Philip, and David Martin. 1993. *The Endless Quest: Helping America's Farm Workers.* Boulder, CO: Westview Press.

Martin, Philip, and Bert Mason. 2003. "Mandatory Mediation Changes Rules for Negotiating Farm Labor Contracts." *California Agriculture* 57, no. 1 (January–March): 13–17 (http://danr.ucop.edu/calag/).

Martin, Philip, and Alan Olmstead. 1985. "The Agricultural Mechanization Controversy." *Science* 227, no. 4687 (February 8): 601–606.

Martin, Philip, and J. Edward Taylor. 2003. "Farm Employment, Immigration, and Poverty: A Structural Analysis." *Journal of Agricultural and Resource Economics* 28, no. 2: 349–363.

Martin, William. 1966. "Alien Workers in U.S. Agriculture: Impacts on Production." *Journal of Farm Economics* 48 (December): 1137–1145.

Massey, Douglas S., Jorge Durand, and Nolan J. Malone. 2002. *Beyond Smoke and Mirrors: Mexican Immigration in an Era of Economic Integration.* New York: Russell Sage. www.russellsage.org/

McWilliams, Carey. 1939. *Factories in the Fields.* Boston: Little, Brown.

Melton, Bryan, and Wallace Huffman. 1995. "Beef and Pork Packing Costs and Input Demands: Effect of Unionization and Technology." *American Journal of Agricultural Economics* 77: 471–485.

Metzler, William, and Afife Sayin. 1950. *The Agricultural Labor Force in the San Joaquin Valley, California, 1948.* U.S. Department of Agriculture, Bureau of Agricultural Economics, February.

Mexican Farm Labor Consultants Report. 1959. Reprinted in U.S. Senate, Committee on Labor and Public Welfare, Subcommittee on Migratory Labor, Migratory Labor Hearings, 1960.

Millard, Ann, and Jorge Chapa. 2004. *Apple Pie and Enchiladas: Latino Newcomers in the Rural Midwest.* Austin: University of Texas Press.

Miller, Mark, and Philip Martin. 1982. *Administering Foreign Worker Programs.* Lexington, MA: Lexington Books.

Millman, Joel. 1997. *The Other Americans: How Immigrants Renew Our Country, Our Economy and Our Values.* New York: Viking Books.

Mines, Richard, and Philip L. Martin. 1983. "Foreign Workers in Selected California Crops. *California Agriculture* 37, no. 3–4 (March): 6–8.

———. 1986. *A Profile of California Farmworkers.* Berkeley: University of California, Division of Agriculture and Natural Resources, Giannini Information Series 86-2.

NAWS. Periodic. National Agricultural Workers Survey (www.doleta.gov/agworker/naws .cfm).

Oliveira, Victor, Anne Effland, Jack Runyan, and Shannon Hamm. 1993. *Hired Farm Labor Use on Fruit, Vegetable, and Horticultural Specialty Farms.* Washington, DC: U.S. Department of Agriculture, Economic Research Service, Agricultural Economics Report 676, December.

Ollinger, Michael, Sang V. Nguyen, Donald Blayney, Bill Chambers, and Ken Nelson. 2005. *Structural Change in the Meat, Poultry, Dairy, and Grain Processing Industries.* U.S. Department of Agriculture, Economic Research Service. Economic Research Report No. ERR3, April.

Papademetriou, Demetrios, and Monica Heppel. 1999. "Balancing Acts: Toward a Fair Bargain on Seasonal Agricultural Workers." Washington, DC, Carnegie Endowment Paper 9.

Passel, Jeffrey. 2005. "Unauthorized Migrants: Numbers and Characteristics." Pew Hispanic Center, June (http://pewhispanic.org/reports/report.php?ReportID=46).

President's Commission on Migratory Labor. 1951. *Migratory Labor in American Agriculture.* Washington, DC: U.S. Government Printing Office.

Rasmussen, Wayne D. 1951. A History of the Emergency Farm Labor Supply Program, 1943-47. USDA Agriculture Monograph 13, September 15

———. 1968. "Advances in American Agriculture: The Mechanical Tomato Harvester as a Case Study." *Technology and Culture* 9, no. 4: 531–543.

Reder, Melvin W. 1963. "The Economic Consequences of Increased Immigration." *Review of Economics and Statistics* 45: 221–230.

Roberts, Kenneth D. 1982. "Agrarian Structure and Labor Mobility in Rural Mexico." *Population and Development Review* 8, no. 2 (June): 299–322.

Ruttan, Vernon. 2001. *Technology, Growth and Development: An Induced Innovation Perspective.* New York: Oxford University Press.

Sarig, Yoav, James F. Thompson, and Galen K. Brown. 2000. *Alternatives to Immigrant Labor? The Status of Fruit and Vegetable Harvest Mechanization in the United States.* Washington, DC: Center for Immigration Studies (www.cis.org/articles/2000/back1200.html#2).

Schmidt, Fred. 1964. *After the Bracero.* Los Angeles: University of California, Institute of Industrial Relations, October.

Schmitz, Andrew, and David Seckler. 1970. "Mechanized Agriculture and Social Welfare: The Case of the Tomato Harvester." *American Journal of Agricultural Economics* 52: 569–577.

Schuh, G. Edward. 1968. "Inter-Relations between the Farm Labor Force and Changes in the General Economy." In *Rural Poverty in the United States: A Report to the President's National Advisory Commission on Rural Poverty,* chap. 12, 140–148. Washington, DC: U.S. Government Printing Office.

Scruggs, Otey. 1960. "The First Mexican Farm Labor Program." *Arizona and the West* 2 (Winter): 319–326.

———. 1961. "The United States, Mexico, and the Wetbacks: 1942–1947." *Pacific Historical Review* 30 (May): 251–264.

Select Commission on Immigration and Refugee Policy. 1981. Final Report. Washington, DC: SCIRP.

Simon, Julian. 1989. *The Economic Consequences of Immigration.* New York: Blackwell.

Street, Richard Steven. 2000. "Knife Fight City: The Poorest Town in California." *Peace Review* 12, no. 2 (June): 287–290.

———. 2004. *Beasts of the Field: A Narrative History of California Farmworkers, 1769–1913.* Stanford, CA: Stanford University Press.

Stull, Donald D., and Michael J. Broadway. 2003. *Slaughterhouse Blues: The Meat and Poultry Industry in North America.* Belmont, CA: Wadsworth.

Tanger, Stephanie. 2006. "Enforcing Corporate Responsibility for Violations of Workplace Immigration Laws: The Case of Meatpacking." *Harvard Latino Law Review* 9: 59–89 (www.law.harvard.edu/students/orgs/llr/vol9/tanger.php#Heading171).

Taylor, Don. 1963. "How Mexico Feels about the Bracero Program." *California Farmer,* April 20.

Taylor, Paul. 1929. "Mexican Labor in the United States." In *University of California Publications in Economics,* ed. Carl Phehn, Ira Cross, and Melvin Knight. Berkeley: University of California Press (1929–1933).

———. 1937. "Migratory Farm Labor in the United States." *Monthly Labor Review,* March.

Taylor, Paul, and Tom Vasey. 1936a. "Historical Background of California Farm Labor." *Rural Sociology* 1, no. 3 (September): 281–295.

———. 1936b. "Contemporary Background of California Farm Labor." *Rural Sociology* 1, no. 4 (December): 401–419.

Taylor, Paul S. 1975. "Public Policy and the Shaping of Rural Society." *South Dakota Law Review* 20 (Summer): 475–495.

Teitelbaum, Michael. 2003. "Do We Need More Scientists?" *The Public Interest,* No. 153, Fall, 40–53.

Todaro, Michael. 1969. "A Model of Labor Migration and Urban Unemployment in Less Developed Countries." *American Economic Review* 59: 138–148.

UC Division of Agricultural Sciences. 1963. *Seasonal Labor in California Agriculture.* Berkeley, CA: Mimeo.

U.S. Commission for the Study of International Migration and Cooperative Economic Development. 1990. *Unauthorized Migration: An Economic Development Response.* Washington, DC: U.S. Government Printing Office.

U.S. Commission on Agricultural Workers. 1993. *Report of the Commission on Agricultural Workers.* Washington, DC: U.S. Government Printing Office.

U.S. Council of Economic Advisors. 1986. "The Economic Effects of Immigration: Economic Report of the President." Washington, DC: Council of Economic Advisors, 213–234.

U.S. Department of Agriculture. 2005. *Fruit and Tree Nuts Outlook.* Economic Research Service, FTS-317, July 28.

———. Quarterly. National Agricultural Statistics Service. Farm Labor (http://usda .mannlib.cornell.edu/reports/nassr/other/pfl-bb/).

U.S. Department of Labor. *The Effects of Immigration on the U.S. Economy and Labor Market.* Washington, DC: International Labor Affairs Bureau.

———. 1959. Mexican Farm Labor Program Consultants Report, October.

U. S. House of Representatives. 1963. Committee on Agriculture, Subcommittee on Equipment, Supplies, and Manpower. Mexican Farm Labor Program, March.

———. 1993. "Mexican Agriculture Policies: An Immigration Generator?" Committee on Government Operations, Subcommittee on Employment, Housing, and Aviation, October 28.

U.S. Immigration and Naturalization Service. 1992. Immigration Reform and Control Act. Report on the Legalized Alien Population, Washington, DC.

———. Annual. *Statistical Yearbook of the Immigration and Naturalization Service.* Washington, DC: Immigration and Naturalization Service.

U.S. Senate. 1979. Committee on Labor and Human Resources. Farmworker Collective Bargaining, 96th Congress, 1st Sess.

US Senate Education and Labor Committee. 1942. Violations of Free Speech and the Rights of Labor Education and Labor Committee [The LaFollette Committee]. Washington, DC.

Walker, Lynne. 2003. "Heartland Finds New Ways to Deal with Newcomers." *Copley News Service,* November 20.

Weintraub, Sidney. 1990. *A Marriage of Convenience: Relations between Mexico and the United States.* New York: Oxford University Press.

Weintraub, Sidney, ed. 2004a. *How Long Should We Keep Them Down on the Farm?* Washington, DC: Center for Strategic and International Studies, August, No. 56 (www.csis .org/simonchair/issues200408.pdf).

———. 2004b. *NAFTA's Impact on North America: The First Decade.* Washington, DC: Center for Strategic and International Studies.

Wells, Miriam. 2000. "Politics, Locality, and Economic Restructuring: California's Central Coast Strawberry Industry in the Post–World War II Period." *Economic Geography* 76, no. 1 (January): 28–49.

Wiest, Raymond E. 1973. "Wage-Labor Migration and the Household in a Mexican Town." *Journal of Anthropological Research* 29: 180–209.

Wilkinson, Alec. 1992. *Big Sugar: Seasons in the Cane Fields of Florida.* New York: Knopf.

Williams, Robert. 1991. Testimony before the Commission on Agricultural Workers. West Palm Beach, February 15, 659–660.

Wilson, Woodrow. 1901. *A History of the American People.* Vol. 4. New York: Harper & Brothers.

Wise, Donald. 1970. "Bracero Labor and the California Farm Labor Economy: A Micro Study of Three Crops, 1952–1967." PhD diss., Claremont Graduate School.

World Bank. 1995. *Workers in an Integrating World.* Washington, DC: World Development Report.

Zuñiga, Victor, and Ruben Hernandez León, eds. 2005. *New Destinations: Mexican Immigration in the United States.* New York: Russell Sage.

Index

Note: Tables and graphs are indicated by italicized page numbers.